About the author

Ifi Amadiume is an award-winning poet and a political activist as well as an academic. She has lived in Nigeria and the UK and is currently associate professor at Dartmouth College, Hanover. There, she teaches in both the Department of Religion and the African-American Studies Programme. Professor Amadiume is author of the influential *Male Daughters, Female Husbands* (Zed Books, 1988) which won the Choice Outstanding Academic Book of the Year award in 1989.

Praise for *Male Daughters, Female Husbands: Gender and Sex in an African Society* by Ifi Amadiume:

'Required reading in a cross-cultural women's studies course ... A book well researched, clearly written, with a good bibliography, and efficiently produced – one that can be depended upon to provoke lively discussion.' *Choice Magazine*

'Essential reading for anyone interested in fundamental thinking about the issues of gender and sex in pre-colonial societies.' *Guardian*, Nigeria

'Ifi Amadiume, a Nigerian sociologist, has stepped out of the academic sidelines to tackle head on the issue of racist social anthropology.' *Africa Events*

'This is a text that should be read widely and includes women's studies, social sciences and history. It will surely be an important statement in the catalogue of anti-colonialist historiography.' *West Africa*

'Meticulously researched ... An extremely important contribution.' *Africa*

RE-INVENTING AFRICA
Matriarchy, religion and culture

Ifi Amadiume

Zed Books Ltd
LONDON & NEW YORK

Re-inventing Africa: Matriarchy, religion and culture was first published by Zed Books Ltd, 7 Cynthia Street, London N1 9JF, UK and Room 400, 175 Fifth Avenue, New York, NY 10010, USA in 1997.

Distributed exclusively in the USA by St Martin's Press, Inc., 175 Fifth Avenue, New York, NY 10010, USA.

Copyright © Ifi Amadiume, 1997

Cover designed by Andrew Corbett
Set in Baskerville and Univers by Ewan Smith
Printed and bound in the United Kingdom
by Biddles Ltd, Guildford and King's Lynn

The right of Ifi Amadiume to be identified as the author of this work has been asserted by her in accordance with the Copyright, Designs and Patents Act, 1988.

A catalogue record for this book is available from the British Library

US CIP has been applied for from the Library of Congress

ISBN 1 85649 533 7 cased
ISBN 1 85649 534 5 limp

Contents

v

Acknowledgements

Most of these essays were written in response to invited lectures, keynote addresses, and discussion with intellectuals and friends from 1989–1994. I am grateful to individuals who initiated these invitations and institutions which welcomed me. In the development of my ideas, research certainly played a major role; but equally important are several friends, whose comments, criticisms and passionate interests have been a source of encouragement, enabling me to continue on this quest in spite of great difficulties. Here, I must mention Saba Sakaana, Herbert Ekwe-Ekwe, Chukwunyere Kamalu, Althea Jones-Lecointe, Louis Brenner, Mahmood Mamdani, Ernest Wamba-dia-Wamba, Kojo-Seb Amanor and Thandi Makiwane.

Perhaps the most important source of inspiration for me during the past several years has been the support of students and the youth wherever I have given lectures. Even more inspiring have been the self-help decolonization educational efforts by grassroots Africans in our communities both in Europe and the United States, as they try to construct their own norms and ideals to counter racism and Eurocentrism.

At Zed I thank Louise Murray for saying to me, 'well done!' She read this manuscript and fought to get it, deciding to publish without changing anything. Thanks also to Farouk for his support and encouragement.

My family has been patient and supportive as always. Many thanks to my dad, Chief Ideyi of Nnobi: may you live to record more proverbs and write many more books! Thanks also to my children, Kemdi and Amadi, may you continue to grow strong in character and assertiveness.

This book is dedicated to my grassroots, academic and political friends in London, in appreciation of our work together over many years, and the genuine efforts in the diaspora African communities to construct alternative, anti-racist and counter-imperialist epistemologies of self-representation and self-generated normative and anti-normative ideals.

Preface

These essays, written between 1989 and 1992, are a direct result of two processes which might seem unrelated, yet, in actuality cannot be separated. They are my involvement and experiences in academia and the classroom on the one hand, and social and political involvement with sections of the African community on the other. Irrespective of locality, in a geographical sense, all these spaces have proved to be arenas of contestation of ideas and, therefore, of power.

Power is here defined in the two senses that I have used it in these essays. One is in an imperialist sense, and therefore synonymous with violence. The other is in the sense of autonomy in self-determination. Here, gender-derived meaning seems to be the real issue, that is, the character of the culture and politics of gender. These ideas are consequently considered within the two broad themes in which these papers fall, namely: 1. African-centred responses to European imperialist stranglehold on the production of African studies and the interpretation of African history; 2. political concerns about the neo-colonial state, the role of European-produced African elites and internal imperialism.

These essays were first assembled in 1992, at a time when I was deeply involved with London local communities, especially the Black community, as a community education worker and as a lecturer initiating accredited courses to attract Afro-Caribbean students into higher education. Empathizing with the passions and sensibilities at the grass-roots, I was therefore sympathetic to the Afrocentric perspective, even if critically in my own engagement with it. Some recognition of these interests written into the curriculum proved to be a successful outreach into the Black community in Britain.

The Black communities were energized, and groups and individuals mobilized themselves to set up study groups, and different cultural and educational projects. In all this, the focal point was their curiosity about traditional African cultures and ancient Egyptian cultural and moral values. At the grassroots, Afrocentrism was therefore a moral guiding principle, and I witnessed friends discard the slave masters' names that had been forced upon them as they adopted names of ancient Egyptian goddesses, gods, queens and kings. This perspective also enabled them to engage more positively with Africa, and to shed the hatred and resentment of Africa born as a result of the pain and hurtfulness of enslavement and negative Eurocentric education.

There was a great outburst of creative energy in fashion, hairstyles and jewellery as the ordinary black folks tried to reorganize their lives, seeking wholesomeness and collective community happiness in the face of unrelenting racism. Western culture continues to renew and enrich itself through the high value placed on antique art and artefacts, particularly Egyptian art. Why is there resentment and great concern when diaspora Africans recognize the value of African antiquity?

My personal experience of practical Afrocentrism explains the seeming festschrift for Cheikh Anta Diop in some of the essays, which indeed an Asian female editor of a university press in the US accused me of in 1992. I did not mind that kind of observation at all. What upset me at the time was her inability to read the African data on their own merit and make comments based on them, without superimposing her own Indian experience of the practice of sati (the supposed burning of brides) in order to convey her meaning to me. Educated and cosmopolitan as she was, she still insisted on a translation or communication via her own culture, so that she never moved out of her 'Indianness', even when reading a text about Africa. I had not written about the Indian practice of sati, and there was nothing equivalent to it in my text.

Writing now, in January 1997, I am glad of that experience since I can use it to help to form an opinion on the current debate about Ebonics – the supposed Black English spoken by many African Americans – which some claim to be a dialect of the English language, and others argue is a different language altogether. In California, Oakland Education Board has taken the position that there are African American children coming into the educational system with Ebonics as a first language, and teachers ought to be equipped to recognize this fact, so that they can help in the translation from this dialect into standard English rather than dismissing these young people as stupid. The Oakland case has resulted in heated public debate which, to my surprise, has shown that there are Americans who do not seem to know that many African Americans do not speak standard English at home or in the neigbourhood, no matter what their degree of education. This would be considered an insult as standard English is the language of the school. I am glad to say that this is something they still share with those in Africa. Only a disrespectful and arrogant elite would behave like that. There is, therefore, a class dimension to the Ebonics debate. It would seem we live in many worlds of tradition, despite bourgeois postmodernist ahistorical illusions of discontinuity with the past.

The lesson I learnt from the Indian woman editor is that all other nationalities have an acknowledged language and therefore culture, other than English, through which they can choose to negotiate meaning in a multiethnic and multicultural society. Language use is thus social and political.

Why then should African Americans be a different species of social beings? Why should it be assumed that African Americans would historically not have developed a separate language or a vernacular that speaks their 'creoleness', their otherness, and rich sociocultural histories since the movement out of Africa into the times of enslavement and now civil society? And why should that language not be respected as a space for class expressions of Black autonomy, commentary and resistance – something absolutely different from the learning of English? This difference should be recognized by a teacher of English seeking also to impart the standards of the English language. Such an acknowledgement means that the English teacher would not assume that an Ebonics speaker is attempting to speak English, and would therefore not kill the speaker's self-expression and confidence to communicate. The respect for difference entails that the teacher of English would listen first to the Ebonics speaker and then negotiate a translation, as a teacher would do in an encounter with any other language or ethnicity.

In my opinion, the Afrocentric debate continues in the debate about Ebonics as a discourse on the place of historical memory and cultural continuity in the production of knowledge, as the past informs the present and the present determines the future. This is the thinking that informs the choice of themes running through these essays, including those written after I moved to the USA in 1993. What methodology and what perspective would enable us to recognize and respect the legitimacy of grassroots women, native peoples and village organizations as 'democratic' entities, precisely because of their decentralized political systems and the diffusion of power among various interest groups and their organizations?

The essays are, therefore, interdisciplinary – reflecting the complexity of my cultural, intellectual and geographical mix and experiences. Although the essays reflect several thematic concerns, a major single theme is that of gender and the contestation of the morality of power, whether in my discussion of gendering research methodology in African

Studies (Introduction), the ideologies of gender in social institutions (Chapters 1 and 2), gendered philosophies of power (Chapter 3), women in politics and the question power (Chapters 4 and 7), gendered character of the state (Chapter 5), gendered religions (Chapter 6), race and class contradictions in feminisms Chapters 8 and 9). The whole notion of patriarchal paradigmatic monolithism is dismissed by my thesis of paradigmatic opposition and structural gender contestation, as a result of the presence of matriachy in the fundamentals of the ideas of kinship in ancient and traditional Africa.

In Chapter 6, I use a specific self-named African religion in Nnobi to demonstrate the primacy of gender in the construction and contestation of religious claims, thus showing the visibility of women in religion, both as symbolists and symbols of worship. The fact that there are women's religions and rituals means that one can speak of gendered moralities and ethics of social justice. In which case, would such notions determine the characters of social institutions, cultures and states? Yes indeed, and I have used extensively the work of Cheikh Anta Diop to support this position.

I am not saying that the mere presence of women in power guarantees an equitable social system. Given the masculinizing tendencies of the contemporary state systems, I indeed dismissed such simplistic assumptions in a forthcoming book, *Daughters of the Goddess and Daughters of Imperialism: African Women Struggle for Power and Democracy*. Rather, it is the choice of gendered morality of civility and of state that would determine a just society. Paradigmatic pluralism offers a perspective which takes into consideration the question of contestation and choice. The myths of gods and goddesses embody contesting and complementary systems; as such we have a choice of narratives to think with, to share, to tell lies with (falsification) and to quarrel about.

In reading these essays, I hope that students and activists in the communities will see how they have educated me, and determined my topics of concern and the issues raised. Perhaps this is the best way to support numerous students who have approached me or complained to me about racism in the curriculum and the classroom.

I hope that this book will contribute to debates about the question of methodology in African studies, as it proposes an alternative social history to the unpopular assumptions of anthropology.

Writing Africa: African social history and the sociology of history*

Characteristic of the discourse on colonialism, Kwesi Prah (1991) has claimed that African anthropologists have no definable tradition in anthropology, but are 'appendages of western scholarship'. On the contrary, I examine in this chapter the 2000 years 'history of sociology' proposed by Cheikh Anta Diop in *Precolonial Black Africa* (1987), and his theory of primordial African matriarchy in *The Cultural Unity of Black Africa* (1989), which Diop used to argue an organic and dignified cultural identity for Africa. Diop's project was to show that there is an independent African approach and objective. Much as I support Diop's position, I want to introduce the concept of anti-state decentralized political systems in order to point out some of the contradictions in Diop's methodology, and to suggest a methodology for an African social history and sociology of history.

A problem of language and translation

One of the dangers of having our feet stuck in Western-produced literature is the tendency to use European terms and expressions uncritically when addressing non-European cultures and experiences. The history of European imperialism and racism means that the language which aided that project is loaded with generalized terms which do not necessarily have a general meaning, but serve a particularistic interest. Two examples are the terms 'the world' and 'integration'.

It seems to me that Professor Kwesi Prah (1991) began his proposal on a wrong footing by not discussing the semantics of European terms, and accepting Eric Wolf's idea of a 'shrinking world'. On developments in anthropology, Prah could write, 'The Westerner in his cross-cultural adventures and the integration of the peoples of the globe into a more or less united world economy, imposed a need to understand the non-westerner' (1991: 3). Note the masculinized humanity: the Westerner equals his; the primitive man equals him. It would be interesting to see how these expressions are gendered in African languages. In the Igbo language, for example, the relevant pronoun would be the genderless *ya*. This, as I shall indicate later, has structural implications. What we immediately see is the effect of Europeanization on our thought processes through the English language and its inherent political institutions and gender politics.

Prah aptly introduces the European factor of rationality and self-interest. However, there is an unfortunate use of the expression 'a need to understand the non-westerner'. Yet we know that this was not the case; Prah himself goes on to talk about a Western intention to control non-Western societies through acculturation. Why then claim that Europeans ever intended to understand?

According to V.Y. Mudimbe (1988), the European project in Africa was never a question of seeking understanding in order to control. It was, in fact, a question of transferring knowledge and imposing a specific European construct of Africa and Africans for a colonial imperialist project. It was a rational process, and the subject which acted as a production factory for this purpose was classical anthropology (Adam Kuper, 1988).

The subject of anthropology was, therefore, racist from the start and was not intended to serve an African interest. Rather, it was intended to humiliate and insult Africans by classifying them as primitive savage 'Them/Other' to the civilized European 'We'. Africans are consequently correct in being ashamed of association with this subject. In this we face a dilemma because, unfortunately, a lot of the archival information that Africans need in order to move forward is trapped in this subject. This is obviously the reason for Prah's worry about what he calls the 'rejection syndrome' to anthropology developed by African scholars; by their rejection of the discipline as a whole, Prah claims that Africans will be 'throwing out the baby with the dirty bathwater'. Cheikh Anta Diop did not reject the subject of anthropology completely, but was determined to establish an authentic narrative of African history. I shall argue that the term 'anthropology' is inappropriate and can be substituted with the term 'social history'. First, a critique of Mudimbe's textual anthropology.

Critique of Mudimbe

According to Mudimbe, this European project of imperialism was primarily carried out by Christian missionaries. However, Christian missionaries, explorers and later philosophers drew from an earlier 'geography of monstrosity' constructed by ancient Greeks and Romans, such as Herodotus, who, in the fifth century BC started the ball rolling with his fabrication of a huge space of human monsters living east of Libya. Five hundred years later, Pliny reproduced the same descriptions for North Africa; and Diodorus did the same with Ethiopia – dividing Ethiopians into the Greek educated who were seen as civilized and the Blacks who were equated with savages.

Mudimbe's stand on and analysis of racism is, however, unclear to me. On the one hand, he presents some evidence to show that those writers who claimed that cultural bias in classical Greece and Rome was independent of race were wrong (1988: 69–72). Yet, he does not pursue an analysis of racism. Instead, he reserves this analysis and accusation of racism for Edward Blyden, a nineteenth-century African American missionary in West Africa who is considered a great pan-Africanist by many in the African world! Mudimbe may have shown 'invented Africa' as savage, barbaric, primitive Otherness to European notions of civilized Sameness, but he did not dwell on the racism of Europe. In fact, the word racism does not feature in his criticism of the West; yet in his index, we can see that the word racism features several times in the chapter on Blyden. It is the committed Pan-Africanist, Edward Blyden that Mudimbe was motivated to call a racist! Why is this so? Mudimbe's chapter on Blyden is a good example of the limits of textual criticism and discourse on power and otherness when divorced from a sociological and historical context – a typical problem of American cultural anthropology.

Since European knowledge about Africa was based on a binary opposition – or a simple inversion of Self and Other, of Us and Them, as civilized versus savage monsters – it was fictitious and not factual. Mudimbe's main statement is this: 'The fact of the matter is that, until now, Western interpreters as well as African analysts have been using categories and conceptual systems which depend on a Western epistemological order' (ibid.: x).

But then, Mudimbe himself has also been totally dependent on a Western episteme, since he did not state a contrary or alternative body of knowledge from which he is challenging European-invented Africa. His main gurus are European scholars, namely, Michel Foucault and Claude Lévi-Strauss. From his book, I was neither convinced that he even knows 2,000 years of African history nor that he knows the social structure of any African society, culture and language. Africans have no voice in his book, only European-produced Africans, those who have produced what he calls 'intellectuals' discourses as a critical library'.

Sooner or later, we have to move beyond a critique of racist European anthropologists and their work, and this has resulted in a sizeable *Nzagwalu* literature. (*Nzagwalu* is an Igbo word meaning answering back – when you have suffered an insult, you have to answer back.) There is now a need for consolidating a dialogic literature, as this compels statements, propositions, responses, conversation, and, therefore, a dialogic library. A dialogue necessitates the existence of more than one view. A dialogue exposes the grounds on which we are standing – that is, our partiality or our position/theory on specific issues. This means that we have to make primary fieldwork a priority, in order to begin to open a dialogue which will acknowledge the voices from the wide-ranging bodies of knowledge that have developed within and between cultural groups on the continent of Africa, and in the course of Africa's various historical contacts with other nations and peoples other than Europeans. Indeed, Europeans have had the shortest period of relations with Africans.

It is in the sense of reducing centuries of African history to relations just with Europe and European scholarship that I talk of Prah's and Mudimbe's Eurocentrism. If, as Mudimbe (1988) claims in his introduction, his book 'is only a critical synthesis of the complex question about knowledge and power in and on Africa', it has been a partial Eurocentric one indeed. Thus most of this scholarship has been confined to the debate on the status and identity that Europe has accorded Africa and Africans. This is possibly the literature which Prah is referring to as 'protest anthropology', which he describes as the correction of what African scholarship regarded as crude and sometimes wilful misrepresentation of African humanity (1991: 15). But I understand protest as different from answering back, from *Nzagwalu*. Protest implies powerlessness, while *Nzagwalu* affirms confidence and certainty. I hope to show that Cheikh Anta Diop employed an effective *Nzagwalu* polemic.

History, identity and status

It seems to me that our problem is one of historical depth. Whose interest does the use of a specified historical depth serve? Why is it that European scholars insist that Africans confine themselves to the post-1945 period – the so-called modern or contemporary period – while, in contrast, the British National Curriculum instructs history teachers to regard the post-1960s period as current affairs? My answer to this is simple: because it serves European colonialist and imperialist interests. Imperialism has to construct a self-importance and relevance, and so Europeans have given themselves missionary power as 'civilizers'.

Under such circumstances, Africans can only then assume the status and identity accorded to them by Europeans, and have no resource of classical cultural heritage from which to counter European racism. There will be no heritage or legacy with which to assert maturity and adulthood. Is this why European mainstream academic institutions have not welcomed the teaching of ancient African history? Does this explain why anthropology gives African ethnography a post-1945 status, dependent on the works of British social anthropologists, French spiritual/philosophical and economic anthropologists, and American cultural anthropologists?

Methodology 1: macro history – the history of sociology of Cheikh Anta Diop

Given the determination by European scholars to confine the history of Africa to their own historical construct, we begin to see the main reason why ancient Egypt became central in the works of African American scholars and African scholars led by Cheikh Anta Diop and Theophile Obenga.

What informed Diop's focus on ancient Egypt was the knowledge that any civilization constructs for itself a classical period as an archive which influences both the present and the future. In which case, the authenticity of culture, that is, the civilization which grew out of internal dynamics and through which a people like to distinguish themselves or compare themselves with others, becomes paramount. In a colonial situation, therefore, historical depth tends to be a contested issue, as well as the nature and status of society before conquest and subordination. This has been especially so in the case of Africa, which has experienced racism and colonialism. Which identity, what status should Africa assume? Who should write a people's social history? Is it a people who should first say what they are, before others can then comment on what people say they are? Or is it others who should be telling Africans what they are? I do not know one single case in which Africans wrote the social history of any other nation.

It is in order to tackle these problems that both Diop and Obenga devoted their entire scholarship to the reconstruction of the links – in the sense of root/stem similarities – between ancient Egyptian, Coptic, Nubian and Bantu cultures, philosophy and languages.[1] In order to do this work, Diop had to reclaim Egyptian civilization from eighteenth- and nineteenth-century scholars, who had falsified history and denied the primacy of Egypt as a rich source of European classical knowledge

(James, 1954; Bernal, 1987). It was therefore necessary for Diop to reaffirm that ancient Egyptians were 'jet black' (Diop, 1974). The logic for this affirmation was that since Europeans were racist and had constructed for themselves a racial and cultural supremacy *vis-à-vis* Africa, and ancient Egyptians were Africans, Europeans were consequently talking nonsense since they had been civilized by Egyptian Africans.

Diop's second concern requiring a different methodology was the reconstruction of Self – that is, Africa itself – for a dignified place in world history. Apart from his other political essays on forms of government for independent Africa (Diop, 1978; 1989), the main methodology was argued in Diop's *Precolonial Black Africa* (1987), where he presented his 'African historical sociology', the social factors or the contingency of events that make up history.

Here again, historical depth was essential. Diop went beyond European epistemology and consulted early Arabic sources. In his opening lines, written in 1960, he wrote,

> no researcher has ever succeeded in revivifying the African past, in bringing it back to life in our minds, before our very eyes, so to speak, while remaining strictly within the realm of science. Yet the documents at our disposal allow us to do that practically without any break in continuity for a period of two thousand years, at least insofar as West Africa is concerned ... However, this work is not properly speaking a book of history, but it is an auxiliary tool indispensable to the historian. It indeed affords him a scientific understanding of all the historical facts hitherto unexplained. In that sense, it is a study in African historical sociology. It permits us no longer to be surprised at the stagnation or rather the relative stable equilibrium of precolonial African societies: the analysis of their socio-political structures presented in it allowing us to gauge the stabilizing factors in African society.

Using the testimonies of Arab writers and geographers such as Ibn Khaldun, Idrisi, Ibn Battuta and Al Bakri, and sixteenth-century works by Black writers such as *Tarikh es Sudan* by Abderrahman es-Sadi and *Tarikh el Fettach* by Mahmud Kati, Diop gave an introduction to the study of 'aspects of African national life: the administration, judicial, economic, and military organizations, that of labour, the technical level, the migrations and formations of peoples and nationalities, thus their ethnic genesis, and consequently almost linguistic genesis, etc.'

Diop compared major aspects of African social institutions with the practice in Europe for the same period, illustrating the violence and barbarism of European practices such as slavery, feudalism, state brutality and wars of conquest. For example, the Roman Empire was dismembered in the fourth century AD and Europe remained chaotic until the coming of Charlemagne in 800. Europe at that time had no organization which compared to the African empires. Diop stated:

> With Charlemangne commenced the first effort at centralization; but one can say without exaggeration that throughout the Middle Ages Europe never found a form of political organisation superior to that of the African states. There is agreement on the fact that the African variety of organization is indigenous: it could not have come from the Aryan or Semitic Mediterranean. If one absolutely had to relate it to some earlier forms, the administrative centralization of Pharaonic Egypt, with its *nomes*, might be brought up. Each provincial governor in Black Africa was an image of the king, with his own small court. All the necessary elements were apparently present to give rise to feudalism. So we can ask ourselves why, up to their disappearance on contact with the West, the African empires did not evolve into a political feudalism through the progressive emancipation of these provincial governors. (1987: 99–100)

He went on to give reasons why feudalism did not develop in the indigenous African political systems. Here Diop entered a debate which is still current in the history and anthropology of Africa. It is to do with theories of state formation in Africa, or the processes of state formation in Africa. Was it control of the means of production (the Marxist view), or control of the means of destruction, such as horses, cavalry, firepower (the Formalist view) which led to state formation? Or did the idea of states come from Aryan or Semitic Mediterranean peoples (the Racist view)? This is the racist Hamitic hypothesis which claimed that ideas of divine kingship in Africa are foreign. This thesis was dismissed by Robin Horton (1971: 104, 110).

Diop's historical methodology destroyed this hypothesis. He also used his theory of primordial African matriarchy (Diop, 1989) to dismiss the claim of an Aryan or Semitic influence, since the Aryans and Semites were fundamentally patriarchal. He argued that the African systems were matriarchal with inheritance and succession traced through the female line, either through the sister as in Pharaonic Egypt or the sister's son as in the African kingdoms and all the so-called matrilineal African societies.[2] Diop also showed that queens abound in our history.

Rules about land ownership were, to Diop, the main reason why ancient African kingdoms were not feudal. He argued, 'The king and the little local lord knew that they owned slaves and that they ruled the entire country, the extent of which they knew perfectly well, and whose inhabitants paid them a specified tax. Yet they never felt that they

owned the land. The African peasant's situation was therefore dia-
metrically opposed to that of the serf bound to the soil and belonging,
along with the land he cultivated, to a lord and master' (Diop, 1987:
103).

Diop pointed out that the very character of kingship was uniquely
different, since it was essential that the king had to be seen to retain
his vitality, which was linked to the African moral and holistic philosophical order of balance (Kamalu, 1990). When the king lost this
vitality, he was ritually killed. By contrast, from my own reading of
European history, in Europe the system itself has a momentum of its
own, especially strong in the idea of the divine king, and can therefore
support fools and even mad princes; the bureaucracy rules. We can see
the continuation of this in our imposed European state systems.

Consistent with his theory of radical change as derived from external
factors such as a foreign invasion, Diop claimed that by the eleventh
century, the constitution of the ancient empire of Ghana already
showed Islamic influence since certain offices had to be occupied by a
Muslim. Yet despite the influence of Islam, African political organizations were able to retain their African characteristics as Diop showed
in the cases of Mossi and Cayor: 'The Mossi and Cayorian constitutions
reflect a political organization which must have been in effect since
Ghana, and therefore probably dominated the African states for nearly
two thousand years' (ibid.: 47).

He made the important point that one only needed to look at the
social organization and cultural activities of Senegalese Sufi communities to relive ancient communal life in Africa 2000 years ago. Yet
I have used the social history of a non-Islamic contemporary society,
Nnobi – an Igbo community deep inside rural Africa – to substantiate
some of Diop's ideas of African matriarchy which he based on
examples from ancient African empires (Amadiume, 1987a).

State violence in African history For Diop, in comparison to
much of the violence in European political and social history, Africa
was politically stable under the moral authority of African kings from
the first- to tenth-century Ghana empire, to the empire of Mali, in
spite of its Islamic influence, until radical change occurred with the
secular kings of Songhai. According to Diop, 'Songhai which belongs
to the last phase of the Islamization of sixteenth-century Africa, had
political customs less embedded in tradition. They in every way
resemble those which applied in the Caliphates of Baghdad and the
courts of Arab Orients. The same endless intrigues took place around
the throne' (1987: 50).

Diop saw the main break in the period of stability with the Moroccan invasion. Since this is a very controversial issue, I cite him in full:

> Much has been made of Arab invasions of Africa: they occurred in the North, but in Black Africa they are figments of the imagination. While the Arabs did conquer North Africa by force of arms, they quite peaceably entered Black Africa: the desert always served as a protective shield. From the time of the initial Umayyad setbacks in the eighth century, no Arab army ever crossed the Sahara in an attempt to conquer Africa, except for the Moroccan war of the sixteenth century. During the period of our study, from the third to the seventeenth centuries, not one conquest was ever launched by way of the Nile: that of the Sudan, accompanied with the help of England, came only in the nineteenth century. Nor was there ever any Arab conquest of Mozambique or any other East African territory. The Arabs in these areas, who became great religious leaders, arrived as everywhere else individually and settled in peacefully; they owe their influence and later acceptance to spiritual and religious virtues. The Arab conquests dear to sociologists are necessary to their theories, but did not exist in reality. To this day no reliable historical documents substantiate such theories. (ibid.: 101–2)

In the first half of the eleventh century, the Almoravides besieged Aoudaghast and Ghana in an attempt to impose Islam through violence. When this failed, they resorted to conversion, and this gave rise to the Marabout movement and the holy wars from the eleventh century, and the consequent spread of Islam through indigenous kings.

Unlike the Eurocentric perspective which determines the modern period in Africa by European colonial rule and the presence of European culture and political systems, in Diop's historical methodology the sixteenth century marked the beginning of the modern period. His milestone is the Moroccan war of 1593, with the violent plunder and occupation of Timbuktu, and the massacre of African intellectuals under the Pashas. Diop wrote: 'it is impossible to describe all the dramatic turns of this atrocious war waged by Morocco against Black Africa ... People were even reduced to eating human flesh, as had occurred during the Hundred Years' War in Europe. Plague ravaged the land, as a result of a breakdown of hygiene. Kati and Sadi agree in situating at this time the corruption of morals and, especially, the introduction of sodomy into Black Africa ... It is out of concern for historical truth that we today recall these painful events' (ibid.: 194–5).

The view is that with the decline of Songhai, Africa was consequently weakened through Arab aggression and plunder. Africa was therefore unable to check the onset of European imperialism in Africa in the sixteenth century. The Almoravides' ruthless and violent attack on Ghana in 1076 had also contributed to the decline of that empire and the later ascendancy of Mali.

Critique of Diop's methodology I have two points of difference with Diop. One is his view of centralized political systems as the ideal type of system, and their cultures as classical civilization. The second is his theory of African matriarchy which is based on rules of inheritance and succession.

In all of Diop's works, the evidence which he employs in his refutations and his brilliant and very effective *nzagwalu* polemics are based on the histories of super empires, such as ancient Egypt, Ghana, Mali, Mossi, Songhai, and Cayor, and their famous cities such as Timbuktu, Gao, Ghana, Djenne, Meroe, and so on. In spite of the fact that he was concerned with the writing of macro history, his celebration of the glories of empires based on the wealth and power of cities, kings and queens, meant that Diop failed to develop a critical analysis of two important factors. One is the economic basis of the power of these empires. The second is the structural relationship between these city-based centres of power or accumulation and the surrounding villages and region.

Through a textual criticism of Diop's *Precolonial Black Africa*, let me point out some of the contradictions in Diop's positions as a result of a formalist methodology which concentrates on the so-called formal structure – kings, queens and rulers – and assumes homogeneity, order or consensus. These contradictions directly influenced my analysis of African political systems in Chapter 4. Some of the points made in Chapter 4, especially the comparisons between African state systems and the decentralized political systems, are discussed here; please refer to that chapter for more detail.

Let us look at the ownership and movement of the two principal sources of revenue and measures of wealth in order to show the patterns of economic and power relations between rulers and subjects; between empires; and between regions. According to Diop:

> The principal source of revenue for the sovereigns of Black Africa, from antiquity to modern times, from the Indian Ocean to the Atlantic, i.e., from the Nubia of Herodotus and Diodorus Siculus to the Ghana of Bakri and the Mali of Ibn Battuta and Khaldun and the Songhai of Sadi and Kati, was gold extracted from mines. According to an anecdote supplied us by Herodotus, the abundance of gold in Nubia was such that even the prisoners' chains were forged of this metal. Of course, this sort of tale cannot be taken literally; nevertheless, it symbolizes an economic reality, a society in which

gold seemed more prevalent than all other metals. The established facts conform well enough to this legend: the etymology of Nubia is said to signify 'gold'. Historically, Nubia was the country from which Egypt acquired all her gold. (1987: 105)

We can see the importance of gold in the ancient world, the Old World, and the present modern world. If in the ancient world Egypt acquired all her gold from Nubia, what was the pattern of relations between Nubia and Egypt? Did Egypt contribute to the decline of the Nubian empire? Was there an exploitative factor here? Again in the Old World, we learn of the movement of African gold to Arabia and the Oriental empires.

The figures show a consistent and unbroken history of economic exploitation of Africa's natural resources, through and with the co-operation of African rulers. If we try to quantify the amount of just one resource that was evacuated, for example gold, from the figures that Diop gives, the amount of African gold accumulated in Arabia is mind-boggling. One chunk of gold was said to have weighed fifteen pounds (ibid.: 105). Askia Mohammed, King of Songhai, who completed the Islamization of the monarchy of Songhai, took 300,000 gold pieces to Mecca (ibid.: 67). The emperor of Mali, Mansa Musa, in his celebrated visit to Mecca between 1324 and 1325 distributed thousands of African gold pieces in major Muslim cities, including Egyptian ones, en route to Mecca.

Diop argued that land ownership was the main difference between the African nobility and that of Europe. The European system was feudal since the nobility owned the land; the African one was not since the royals and nobles did not own land. I argue that we cannot use the total factors making for social inequality in Europe to measure economic and political inequality in the African context. We have to look at the different situations contextually, showing what are regarded as measures of wealth and what access the various social categories have to them. How they have this access, why, and to what use the wealth is put, and how this affects power relations between the various social categories.

In the case of gold, for example, even though Diop stressed the point that the African nobility was non-landowning, he admitted that its principal source of revenue was based on taxes, customs duties, slaves (although Diop did not mean slaves in the European sense of a commodity), and the control and accumulation of gold – the main medium of exchange.[3] Due to the abundance of gold, Diop argued that in comparison to the economic situation of the peasants and serfs of feudal Europe, the African subject was not overwhelmed with taxes and tariffs by a sovereign (ibid.: 106).

Diop took the position that feudalism involves ownership of land and peasants were exploited working on that land; African monarchs, he pointed out, did not control land outright. I argue that these African empires were feudal systems; any such monarchical system is feudal since the state is embodied in the kings and queens – the centrepoints of accumulation. The monarchs kept all the chunks and pieces of gold mined in the empires, and left the gold dust to the common people (ibid.: 105). Diop described the royal treasury of Mali thus:

> The treasury of the sovereign thus contained both gold pieces and chunks of gold in the raw state. There were lofts containing taxes in kind such as grains and storerooms for manufactured products: saddles, swords, harnesses, fabrics, etc. A fair share of the treasury of Sonni Ali was deposited with the cadi of Timbuktu, perhaps because the cadis, due to their positions, were traditionally honest men: this treasure did indeed exist, for it was where Askia Mohammed, after his coup and his accession, found the money for his pilgrimage to Mecca. (ibid.: 106).

Having described the luxury in which Nara, daughter of the Manca of Mali, lived in the mid-sixteenth century, comparing it to that of Helen of Troy, Diop wrote:

> Obviously, an illustration of African history is possible: there are more documents than generally stated. They allow us to reconstitute, sometimes even in detail, over a period of almost two thousand years, African political and social life. We know how the members of the different classes in Ghana, Mali, Mossi, Songhai, and Cayor were dressed; what they did with their spare time, their daily routines, and so on. We know what social relationships governed society, and thus the behaviour of an entire society which we can vividly bring back to life before our eyes, even on the stage or in films. The local color would be authentic. (ibid.: 85–6)

So much then for the abundance of wealth at the city centres of these empires. But what do we know of relations with Africans in the surrounding villages? Diop refers to them as 'backward tribes ... in every way comparable to the still-unassimilated barbarians who roamed on the outskirts of the Roman Empire' (ibid.: 130–1). He made reference to the famous ancient trade by barter between the Lem-Lem in Southwest Ghana and Arabs, which went on until the twelfth century. Racist European sociologists and ethnologists had used this particular example to conclude that Africans lacked knowledge of merchandise, reaffirming the supposed primitiveness of Africans. This was a major falsification, which Diop tried to tackle. He wrote:

Africa, in the eyes of the specialists, is depicted as a land which prior to colonization was only at the level of subsistence economy: the individual, virtually crushed by the force of nature, was able to produce only what he absolutely needed to survive. No creation, no activity reflecting a society freed from material constraints might be found there. Exchange relationships were governed by barter. Notions of money, credit, stock market, thrift, or commerce connected with a higher economic organization: they could not have been found at the alleged level of African economy.

Seldom has an opinion been so little founded on fact. This one arose from a preconceived idea of African societies: they had to be specifically primitive, therefore endowed in every respect with systems characteristic of such a condition. (ibid.: 130)

Diop made two mistakes here in the method that he adopted to tackle this insult. By trying to show that Africans had also attained the civilizations of super empires – in fact even before Europeans did – he created a dichotomy between African kingdoms which were equated with the civilized/detribalized/international, and their periphery representing primitive/backward/closed society. Of course, it would be absolute naivety on my part to call Diop a racist on the basis of this uncritical use of European invented terms. It would, however, be to the point to re-echo the call for the decolonization of the African mind and the dangers of White words and Black people. The process of decolonization is a gradual and progressive one, requiring vigilance and continuous effort. Diop wrote *Precolonial Black Africa* in the 1950s. I believe that he would have been his own censor had he rewritten the book in either the 1970s or the 1980s. It is for similar reasons that I feel Mudimbe was wrong to call Blyden a racist.

The second mistake by Diop, produced by this dichotomy, is his lack of analysis of the structures of relations between the empires and the so-called 'tribes' at their periphery or borders. This brings us to the second measure of wealth, that is, slaves. We learn that these Africans who supposedly traded by barter used gold dust. If they were 'tribes living in a virtually closed society' why would they use gold dust and not chunks of gold? Diop has already informed us that the rulers of the empires claimed all the chunks of gold mined in the empire and that the subjects were only allowed to use gold dust. It therefore seems to me untenable to talk of isolated tribes, but to recognize the dependence of the centre on the periphery. Far from behaving in a timid or primitive manner, we can begin to see the Lem-Lem, for example, as a people who were very much aware of their experiences of being raided for slaves by Arabs and city Africans, hence their precautionary measures in avoiding contact with their exploiters and violators.

I have pointed out the implications of Diop's theory of external factors as the cause of radical social change in Africa.[4] One is the assumption of consensus which does not allow for an analysis of social process, contradiction and conflict. For example, he wrote of Ghana, 'Its power and reputation, renowned as far as Baghdad in the East, were no mere legend: it was actually a phenomenon attested to by the fact that for 1250 years a succession of Black emperors occupied the throne of a country as vast as all of Europe, with no enemy from without nor any internal tension able to dismember it' (Diop, 1987: 91).

Yet, an analysis of Diop's own material shows ample evidence of internal contradictions. The empire of Ghana was an authentic African civilization for Diop, since Arabo-Islamic influence on African monarchies and their constitutions became more evident in the empire of Mali and complete in Songhai. Diop wrote of Ghana,

> From the economic point of view, Africa is characterized by abundance. Travelers of the precolonial era encountered no poverty there; according to the *Tarikh el Fettach*, the emperor of Ghana, seated upon a 'platform of red gold', daily treated the people of his capital to ten thousand meals. Such material comfort resulted in an increase in demographic density scarcely imaginable today: in the region of Djenne alone there were 7,077 villages. (ibid.: 141)

With such figures, we begin to see the extensive regions which supported the wealth, commerce, and luxurious lifestyle of the cities. On that most fundamental contradiction in all patriarchal African social systems, slavery, Diop contradicted those who placed the slave trade in Africa in the post-sixteenth century. Describing Ghana, Diop wrote,

> The Empire first opened itself to the world-at-large through commerce; it already enjoyed international repute, which would be inherited and extended by the future empires of Mali and Songhai. But domestic slavery at this time was rife in African society: one could sell his fellow man to another citizen or a foreigner. Which explains why Berber and Arab merchants, grown rich since settling at Aoudaghast, though still vassals of the Black sovereign, could acquire Black slaves on the open market. Some individuals in the city owned as many as a thousand slaves.
>
> This shows the peaceful means by which the white world could possess Black slaves. It was not through conquest, as has often been asserted. These empires, defended when necessary by hundreds of thousands of warriors, and having their centralized political and administrative organization, were much too powerful for a single traveler, thousands of miles from home, to try any sort of violence against them. (ibid.: 91–2)

Violence was thus seen as something inflicted from without and not from within. Diop did not seem concerned about internal contradictions; his quarrel was with European racism, as he tried to show that 'All the white minorities living in Africa might own Black slaves, but slaves and white masters alike were all subjects of a Black Emperor: they were all under the same African political power' (ibid.: 92). When, as Idrisi wrote of the west of Mali, 'The other, more highly developed inhabitants of Ghana went slavehunting in this region, which must have covered part of Lower Guinea and the southern part of present-day Senegal' (quoted in ibid.: 73), we know that this violence was done by Diop's ideal centralized Africa on his so-called 'tribal Africa'.

These polities were not exclusive dichotomies, but systems which were in complex relationship, and even contending contrasting moral and political philosophies. The exploitative and violent character of their relations was to remain unbroken right through the Old World and the trans-Saharan slave trade, throughout the Atlantic slave trade, in which Africa lost a workforce of between one and three hundred million to America alone (ibid.: 142). The same structure of violence and appropriation continues under present day European state systems in Africa between the urban centres and the villages; between the state and the people; between the local government and the communities; between a colonially imposed monolithic male gendered power structure and traditional female generated social and moral values. These systems are in complex relations, and the cycle of violence has remained unbroken.

Methodology 2: micro case studies – the social history applied in *Male Daughters, Female Husbands*[5]

I have implied in my critique of Diop's macro history that he ignored the base, that is, the very foundations of the socio-political systems which he described. He placed emphasis on the kings and queens and not the people; he looked at cities and not the villages; he focused more on centralized systems and not what he called the clan systems, that is, the decentralized systems – in short, African communities.

Yet, every conceivable African political system had communities at its base. What are the social organizations of these communities? What are their moral philosophies? This appears to be the subject given the least importance by African academics. Africans have not yet written their social history. One might then ask on what information local government policies are based. What do African communities know or think of each other?

It was in order to write such a history that would allow a society to speak for itself that I carried out research in Nnobi, an Igbo community in eastern Nigeria. Robin Horton (1971), in his work on types of societies in Africa and the processes of state formation, provided information on main areas of concentration of what he called stateless societies. He showed that geographically they cover a vast area of Africa, ranging across diverse ecological zones and economies, whether pastoral or settled farming. In West Africa alone, not including the huge so-called matrilineal belt of central Africa, we have the Igbo, Ibibio, Ijo, Tiv, Idoma, Biromi, Angass, Yako, Mbembe and Ekoi in Nigeria. Further west, between the Volta and the Niger bend, are the Lodagaa, Lowiili, Bobo, Dogon, Konkomba and the Birifor. Going from Ivory Coast, Liberia and Guinea, we meet the Bete, Kissi, Dan, Gagu and Kru. All along the West African Savannah are the Fulani pastoralists. The Bassa, the Grebo, the Mano, and the Koranko in the south-west area of West Africa are thought to have systems which are between decentralized and state organizations. Writing in 1971, Horton claimed that thirty-five million West Africans were living under 'stateless' social organizations.

The ethnocentrism of European scholars has directly influenced the classification and definition of these societies, seeing them as 'lacking something', such as rulers, states, order, a head. These societies have consequently been described as tribes without rulers, stateless or non-state societies, organized anarchy, and acephalous societies. In Chapter 4, I have adopted a different term altogether, that is, anti-state decentralized political systems.

This definition permits the recognition that these societies can know about centralized states in their region, or even territorially be part of a centralized system, but consciously remain anti-state in their social structure. It permits the recognition that such societies could be working very hard indeed to prevent developing a centralized state system; it avoids the racist assumptions in unilinear developmental evolutionism. The definition also allows for the recognition that communities can break away from centralized state systems and consciously structure state tendencies out of their social structure. It allows us to recognize an anti-state moral philosophy and consciousness. It compels us to reassess European notions of democracy by using African notions of democracy as a recognition and celebration of difference and variety, as opposed to the European obsession with order, uniformity and monolithism.

Indeed Horton's features of decentralized African political systems, such as the relativity of political grouping, the equivalence of lineage segment, and the predominance of leadership over authority, all suggest a conscious inbuilt system of checks and balances in the social structure, in order to contain ascendancy and dictatorship of a social segment.

According to Horton, the Tiv and Central Igbo societies in Nigeria approximate the pure types of the anti-state political systems as an ideal type society to one pole of a classificatory continuum. This continuum ranged from the segmentary lineage systems, through dispersed, territorially defined communities, to the large compact village, and on to kingship-based state organizations. I have already argued against this dichotomization which implies the concept of evolutionism. Horton himself argued that these social processes do not involve a unidirectional scheme of evolution. To him, they are reversible since villages rise and disintegrate into pure segmentary types. Still, these typologies imply a dichotomy since these systems are not presented as in relationship with each other.

For this reason, Nnobi was not studied as an insular society, but as part of neighbouring societies and the historical processes which took place in that particular area and the Nigerian nation as a whole. The study has been detailed elsewhere.[6] I shall not, therefore, reproduce these data here in detail, but will refer to aspects of my thesis which I wish to highlight as particularly essential and relevant to this dialogue on the state of anthropology in Africa; that is the aspects of my findings which directly address Diop's theory of African matriarchy, and the mode of production theory of the French economic ethnography of Claude Meillassoux and Emmanuel Terray.

Nnobi case study Several perspectives were used in a multi-disciplinary approach to the study of Nnobi society. It was important to bridge the gap which separated the Marxist materialist approach and its basic concern with the economy, and formalist functionalist concerns with jural systems. It was therefore necessary to adopt a methodology which recognized the fact that society is multidimensional in its structures, comprising systems with a base – that is, social institutions, the economy – and a superstructure involving a dialectical politics of culture and ideology. A total social history would require the devising of a methodology able to bring into the debate so many aspects of how a society is structured, how it works or does not work, the multiplicity of social drama and social relations such as gender relations, and changes over a given period.

I consequently adopted both a synchronic approach, correlated structural relations at a given time, and a diachronic approach, connected structural changes over a longer historical period. It was therefore obvious to me that I was writing a social history of a given society (micro history), and a sociology of history of a region (macro history). Through literature review, I was able to reclaim useful information from already existing anthropological data, re-analyse relevant data and correct false information. I stored the new information in a different vessel (social history), and threw out the bad and offensive vessel (social anthropology). I did not throw out the baby with the dirty bathwater; I sifted the grain from the chaff and reclaimed what was mine.

The processes of fieldwork and my experiences in the field have already been published.[7] Here, I want to comment briefly on Igbo ideology of gender and its relevance to the debate on the mode of production and the concept of matriarchy. In looking at all aspects of Nnobi social structure, it soon became clear to me that there was a basic ideology of gender as an organizational principle in the economy, social classification and Nnobi culture.

This ideology of gender had its basis in the binary opposition between the *mkpuke*, the female mother-focused matricentric unit and the *obi*, the male-focused ancestral house. The structure of relationship, in the Levi-Straussian sense, between these two paradigmatical gender structures, reflected in the wider social organization and politics of Nnobi, the contest between the moral kinship ideology of motherhood and the jural force of patriarchy. These were expressed concretely, metaphorically or symbolically. They formed interrelating systems representing different values such as compassion/love/peace in the ideology of *umunne*, the spirit of common motherhood, and competitiveness/masculinism/valour/force/violence in the ideology of *umunna*, common fatherhood. Social subjects thus had access to more than one moral system.

In Nnobi social structure, the *mkpuke*, which I regard as the matricentric structure of matriarchy, is the smallest kinship unit and the smallest production unit. It is a good example of where the structure of the production unit determines the consumption unit, for it is a unit which eats what it produces. It produces for self-consumption; it is an autonomous household-based unit. Also this relation of production has an ideological base in a female gendered motherhood ideology of *umunne* or *ibenne*, which has wider political implications.

There is therefore a dialectical relationship between the production unit and relations of production. Those who eat out of one pot are bound in the spirit of common motherhood. This ideological structure is reproduced in the wider political order in which the whole of Nnobi are bound as children of a common mother – the goddess Idemili, the deity worshipped by all Nnobi. Administratively and in political decision making, the human representatives of the goddess are the arch matriarchs, the *Ekwe* titled women, leaders of the marketplaces and the Women's Council, a formal political organization of all women of Nnobi, which excludes men.

The *Ekwe* system formed a political matriarchal system in binary opposition to the patriarchal system. Both systems are in a dialectical relationship. A bridge between these systems is achieved through a third classificatory social system: a non-gendered one in its subject and object pronouns, its non-gendered roles and statuses in the organizational leadership positions. More importantly, it uses a non-gendered universalistic term for a common humanity, *nmadu*, human being, person, as opposed to the European collective, monolithic, male gendered concept of *man*.

Unlike Diop, therefore, I have not defined matriarchy according to rules of succession/inheritance and the reigns of queens. I have located it in the more far-reaching deeper structure of the *mkpuke* and its ideology of *umunne* or *ibenne*. The implications of the *mkpuke* structure seem to me very serious, as it exposes anthropological distortion of African history and its invention of a European type patriarchy in Africa, based on a European paradigmatical theory of patriarchy (Kuper, 1988).

My recent re-reading of West African ethnography shows the presence of the *mkpuke* matricentric structure in all our varied societies. The implication of this finding is that there is a missing matriarchal structure in African studies. The *mkpuke* as a female generated, paradigmatical cultural construct demolishes the generalized theory that man is culture, and woman is nature in the nature/culture debate in anthropology, a theory which sees man as the maker of culture and woman as the voiceless/muted chaotic/unordered object to be classified or ordered. In Nnobi mythology, the goddess Idemili (female woman) is culture, while the deity Aho-bi-na-agu (male man) lives in the wild; he invades from the wild (see Amadiume, 1987b: 106–9 for Ikpu okwa festival).

Marxist domestic mode of production and the missing *mkpuke* structure In Marxist historical materialism, the economic base is seen as the determining factor within the system. For this reason, in order to counter what he saw as exotic fantasies of formalist anthropologists and their concern with myth, ritual and kinship, Claude Meillassoux (1964) introduced the notion of the domestic mode of production in his study of the lineage mode of production of the Guro of Ivory Coast, highlighting the role of the household in the relations of production.

Emmanuel Terray (1972) was, however, critical of Meillassoux's formulations and in his re-analysis of Meillassoux's Guro data argued that, in order to demonstrate fully the processes of a socioeconomic formation, it is necessary to detail the productive units and the processes of production. He writes, 'The analysis of a socioeconomic formation is not complete until these forms and their theoretical status and functions have been described' (ibid.: 103). Unfortunately, the only kinship unit which is given, that is, the matricentric unit, is missed out in his detailing of the productive units.

Both Meillassoux and Terray imposed European concepts of 'natural family' on the Guro data, and were therefore unable to see the matricentric production unit. Thus, they never mention the very basic kinship unit of mother and child, or show its structural status. Terray's varying ranks of kinship groups are thus lineages, segments, and extended families in unilinear groups. He recognizes these as corresponding to varying types of production units.

Although Terray shows the processes as gendered – indicating what men do, what women do, and what both sexes do together – there is no analysis of gender as an ideology. He shows that agricultural activities are complemented by domestic activities, and that these domestic activities are the sole province of women. They are carried out in restricted, that is, family cooperation among the wives. Small groups of wives cultivate a common rice paddy, have their own hearths, and each senior wife is in charge of a granary.

If we look closely at the division of social labour of the Guro, we can see an ideological gender construction. The principal activities of men are hunting and war, while those of women are agriculture and domestic activities. We learn that the greater part of social labour is devoted to agriculture. Yet, it is the masculine activities which are ideologically raised to be superior to agriculture. Meillassoux writes, 'No firstfruits or harvest ceremony, no special cult for agriculture, and only rarely is chicken sacrificed when new land is cleared' (1964: 106).

Men imposed their own ranking system in a wider area of male cooperation, resulting in dominance of one mode of production over the other. Politically, the lineage system dominated, while ideologically, the village system dominated over the lineage system. Terray sees in this a kind of 'cross-dominance' and tries to explain the dominance of one mode of production over another through an analysis of reproduction. Unfortunately, his definition of reproduction derives from a European patriarchal paradigm, since he, just like Meillassoux (1981), sees women as objects of exchange, and marriage as a mechanism of physical and social reproduction of the group.

In this formulation, the starting point for a woman is solely as an object in a patriarchal exchange and transaction. She is therefore already subjected to an ideology, and not seen as autonomous in the status of a pregnant woman. Yet this is a culturally recognized autonomous unit in the African construct of kinship. The recognition of the motherhood paradigm means that we do not take patriarchy as given, or as a paradigm. It is not a paradigm in the African concept since it is a social construct; it is one step above the motherhood paradigm. Hence my distinction of household as the matricentric unit, and family as a wider construct which includes the head of one or more of these household matricentric units.

In Igbo, the status for the role of head of family is genderless. This means that man or woman can be *di*, husband, or *dibuno*, family head. There is consequently the practice of woman-to-woman marriage, which is not only an Igbo practice but widespread in varying African societies.[8] What then is the history of marriage in Africa? We do not know, for the European assumption has been that men have always controlled the movement of women. The facts associated with a matriarchal paradigm would suggest something totally different. However, Eurocentrism has not permitted any thinking or research along these lines.

In spite of a distortion of data, both Terray and Meillassoux have come close to recognizing the matriarchal paradigm, but seemed incapable of analysing it. Terray for example writes, 'control of the producer is, in turn, based on control of women'. Meillassoux for his part calls the child-bearing woman the producer of the producer, accusing men of stealing 'the wild fruits of women'. Terray argues in the case of the power of Guro lineage elders, 'It follows that the elders can only perpetuate their supremacy if they control the circulation of women and bride-prices, and arrange things so that this process reproduces the social structures which sanction this supremacy' (1972: 164).

What we can read in this structure is a material history of patriarchy which is based on appropriation from women, the direct producers, for the benefit of a patriarchal construct as opposed to a matriarchal one. Meillassoux's mode of production theory is that the domestic is the base of every level of society, and society consequently appropriates from it. A gender perspective, on the other hand, pinpoints the actual units that are being appropriated from in the domestic.

My basic argument of matriarchy is that the matri-centric unit is the smallest kinship unit. Its material basis is concrete and empirical, while the material and ideological basis of patriarchy embodies a contradiction. Patriarchy is disputable, since fatherhood is a social construct. The result of this contradiction is the tendency of patriarchal compulsions based on jural force, violent rituals and pseudo-procreation symbolisms and metaphors (Bloch, 1986), as opposed to the moral force of matriarchy.

Although Terray draws a parallel between class relations and kinship relations, he is quick to point out that antagonisms characteristic of class relations are not applicable to kinship relations. He writes, 'I am not saying here that kinship relations are class relations, that kinship relations show the antagonisms characteristic of class relations etc. I am saying that both are the complex result of the interplay of the economic, juridico-political, and ideological phases of the mode of production' (1972: 144).

Yet at the level at which he dealt with kinship construct, that is, the male controlled family as opposed to the female controlled household, there is gender antagonism in a patriarchal construct which is in contradiction with the basic mother-focused unit – the seed or logic or structure of matriarchy. Patriarchy is male gendered, and so is class, hence the coining of such terms as state patriarchy and class ideology of monolithic masculinism. They all involve the exclusion of women from male power constructs, and the controlling of women in order to appropriate from them. The processes of doing this involve a denial of autonomy and the invasion of boundary through violence – symbolic or real, as can be seen enacted in marriage consummation rituals, circumcision rituals, annual festivals, patrilineage rituals and state rituals.

In the social structure of African societies, the household and the family are usually distinct units with distinct terms. In the European system, they are synonymous since European women never achieved a formal autonomous matriarchal system in their social structure. They lacked the types of women's organizations which were historically basic to African societies. I believe that this is why the patriarchal theory and the shocking Oedipus theory were conceivable in European thought systems. Unfortunately for us Africans, Meyer Fortes (1959; 1987) transported these alien concepts to Africa and imposed them on his Tallensi data. Other anthropologists have copied him since.

Anthropological solutions and the question of a national African culture

As a result of the militarization and gradual masculinization of the African continent over the past two thousand years, the ideological structure of patriarchy has been reproduced in all our current forms of social organization, along with associated exploitative modes of production such as family, lineage, feudalism, slavery, capitalism, and totalitarian centralized planning. Their exploitative character and violence has resulted in a perennial tension between centralism/control/power and decentralism/autonomy/anti-power. We can see this tension in Prah's list of current problems of Africa: ethnic conflict, cultural oppression, rights of minorities, African nationalism, and democratic organization. The most fundamental of all, gender conflict, has been left out.

Meillassoux has stressed how capitalism destroys all ties of affection, 'All it can put in the place of these ties is the barbarism of absolute profitability – the last stage of the metamorphosis of human beings into capital, their strength and intelligence into commodities, and the wild fruit of women into investment' (1981: 144). The logic of patriarchy is exploitative because it appropriates; this is its basic structure. Yet it was never total and all embracing in African societies such as traditional Igbo societies, as I showed from Nnobi social history. The idea of considering the structural implications of female-headed corporations and systems never occurred to our Marxist allies.

As European feminists, locked in the production–reproduction debate (see Chapter 8), seek possible ways out of their historically oppressive patriarchal family structure (Engels, 1891), inventing single-parenthood and alternative affective relationships, I argue that in the African case we do not have to invent anything. We already have a history and legacy of a women's culture – a matriarchy based on affective relationships – and this should be given a central place in analysis and social enquiry.

Diop went further, arguing that matriarchy is the basis of our African cultural unity. It is in fact this history, this culture that is manipulated in our nationalist rhetoric when we call for peace, love and unity, as opposed to violence. We refer to the moral compulsions of love and unity based on the spirit of common motherhood when we say our motherland or mother Africa. We are thus constructing a collective identity or consciousness based on a matriarchy in spite of our differences and contradictions.

Conclusion

Central to the works of African decolonization writers, whether of the African identity/Negritude school or Pan-African school, is the issue of self-definition as opposed to a colonial identity, mentality and status. These old arguments have recently been reformulated by Mudimbe in the discourse on the production of knowledge. In this chapter, I have shown a close link between language, thought systems, and socio-political structures. I have argued that it is not enough to be critical of European-invented Africa if we ourselves remain uncritical of the European gender structure of the language which we are using and its effects on our thought process and gender relations.

Regarding specific studies and theories, I have concentrated on the work and theories of Cheikh Anta Diop. As a result of European racism and its closely linked imperialism in its historical relationship with Africa, three issues became central to Diop's scholarship. They were the reclaiming of ancient Egyptian civilization as a Black African construct to serve as a classical reference archive. The second was proposing a historical depth which would incorporate two thousand years of African history and therefore the achievements of ancient African empires, and highlight the link with Egypt and Nubia. The third was the establishment of a fundamental African moral philosophy. This was his theory of matriarchy as a unifying African moral code and culture.

Critical of Diop's bias for empires, I have shown how his methodology resulted in a dichotomy between state systems and the decentralized systems, ignoring a critical analysis of the complex relationship between both systems. Yet Diop's own text showed the economic dependence of the states on the communities, the people. Developing this analysis of economic and power relations, I have argued that this structure of dependence, exploitation, and violence has remained unbroken throughout the past two thousand years of Africa's economic history.

Finally, I showed that even the French economic anthropologists, in spite of their ideological superiority complex, were ethnocentric and lacked a gender perspective in their analysis of class and lineage systems. The most important production unit – the matricentric unit, the basic structure of African matriarchy and common to all African social structures – has been invisible in the theoretical formulations in African Studies. Yet the moral values which this system generated constitute the basis of affective relationships so badly needed as an alternative to the present political culture of violence underlying all the current problems of Africa. I have consequently proposed that we give gender a central place in social enquiry and critical analysis. Since anthropology has a history of racism, we should change it to a combination of social history and sociology of history.

Notes

* First presented at the CODESRIA workshop on 'Anthropology in Africa: Past, Present and Emerging Visions', April 1991, Dakar, Senegal.

    1. See Chris Gray (1989), not so much for his weak master's degree work analysis and assessment of Diop, but for his comprehensive bibliography of works by Diop and Obenga.
    2. See Ifi Amadiume (1987b: 25–38) for a critique of patrilineality and matrilineality as tools of analysis.
    3. See Robin Law's (1978) thought-provoking article on the material basis of the power of precolonial West African states.
    4. Ifi Amadiume, 1989.
    5. Ifi Amadiume, 1987b.
    6. Ibid.
    7. 'The mouth that spoke a falsehood will later speak the truth: going home to the field in Eastern Nigeria', in Diana Bell, Patricia Caplan, Wazir Jahan Abdul Karim (eds), *Gendered Fields: Women, Men and Ethnography*, London: Routledge 1993.
    8. See Laura Bohannan (1949), 'Dahomean marriage: a revaluation', *Africa*, 19(4): 273–87; Hugo Huber (1968–9), 'Woman marriage in some East African societies', *Anthropos*, 63/64 (5/6): 745–52; Dregina Oboler (1980), 'Is female husband a man? Woman/woman marriage among the Nandi of Kenya', *Ethnology*, 19(1); Denise O'Brien (1977), 'Female husbands in Southern Bantu societies', in Alice Schlegel (ed.), *Sexual Stratification: A Cross-Cultural View*, pp. 109–26, Columbia University Press, New York; E. Krige (1974), 'Woman marriage, with special reference to the Lovedu – its significance for the definition of marriage', *Africa*, 44: 11–35; Melville J. Herskovits (1937), 'A note on woman marriage in Dahomey', *Africa*, 10: 335–41.

Bibliography

Amadiume, Ifi, 1987a, *Afrikan Matriarchal Foundations: The Igbo Case*, Karnak House, London.
— 1987b, *Male Daughters, Female Husbands: Gender and Sex in an African Society*, Zed Books, London/New Jersey.
— 1989, 'Cheikh Anta Diop's theory of matriarchal values as the basis for African cultural unity', Introduction to Cheikh Anta Diop (1989).
Bernal, Martin, 1987, *Black Athena: The Afroasiatic Roots of Classical Civilisation, Vol, 1: The Fabrication of Ancient Greece 1785–1985*, Free Association Books, London.
Bloch, Maurice, 1986, *From Blessing to Violence: History and Ideology in the Circumcision Ritual of the Merina of Madagascar*, Cambridge University Press, Cambridge.
Diop, Cheikh Anta, 1974, *The African Origin of Civilization: Myth or Reality*, Lawrence Hill & Co., Westport, USA.
— 1978, *Black Africa: The Economic and Cultural Basis for a Federated State*, Lawrence Hill & Co., Westport, USA.
— 1987, *Precolonial Black Africa*: a comparative study of the political and social systems of Europe and black Africa, from antiquity to the formation of modern states, Lawrence Hill & Co., Westport, USA.
— 1989, *The Cultural Unity of Black Africa: The Domains of Matriarchy and of Patriarchy in Classical Antiquity*, Karnak House, London.

Engels, Frederick, 1891, *The Origin of the Family, Private Property and the State*, Foreign Languages Publishing House, Moscow.

Fortes, Meyer, 1959, *Oedipus and Job in West African Religion*, Cambridge University Press, Cambridge.

— 1987, *Religion, Morality and the Person*, Cambridge University Press, Cambridge.

Gray, Chris, 1989, *Conceptions of History: Cheikh Anta Diop and Theophile Obenga*, Karnak House, London.

Horton, Robin, 1971, 'Stateless societies in the history of West Africa', in J.F.A. Ajayyi and M. Crowder (eds), *History of West Africa*, Vol. 1 (2nd edn), Longman, London.

James, G.G.M., 1954, *Stolen Legacy, the Greeks were not the Authors of Greek Philosophy, but the People of North Africa, Commonly Called the Ethiopians*, Philosophical Library, New York.

Kamalu, Chukwunyere, 1990, *Foundations of African Thought*, Karnak House, London.

Kuper, Adam, 1988, *The Invention of Primitive Society: Transformations of an Illusion*, Routledge, London.

Law, Robin, 1978, 'Slaves, trade, and taxes: the material basis of political power in precolonial West Africa', *Research in Economic Anthropology*, 1: 37–52.

Meillassoux, Claude, 1964, *L'Anthropologie économique des Guro de Côte d'Ivoire*, Mouton, Paris.

— 1981, *Maidens, Meal and Money: Capitalism and the Domestic Economy*, Cambridge University Press, London.

Mudimbe, V.Y., 1988, *The Invention of Africa: Gnosis, Philospohy, and the Order of Knowledge*, Indiana University Press and James Currey, Bloomington and Indianapolis.

Prah, Kwesi, 1991, 'Anthropology in Africa: past, present and emerging visions'. (Proposal for a CODESRIA sponsored workshop to review the state of Anthropology in Africa, Dakar, Senegal.)

Terray, E., 1972, 'Historical materialism and segmentary lineage-based societies', *Marxism and 'Primitive' Societies*, Monthly Review Press, New York.

PART ONE
Re-writing History

1 The matriarchal roots of Africa

In the Introduction, I pointed out the matricentric production unit as the basic material structure of African matriarchy, and claimed that it was common to all traditional African social structures, since it generated affective relationships. My intension in this chapter is to test the hypothesis that there are other gender determined systems with which the patriarchal system is in discourse. Consequently, I intend to conduct a more detailed analysis of three contemporary ethnographic classic texts on contrasting African societies, to illustrate further my thesis of a missing system of matriarchy in European studies of African societies. This chapter is, therefore, an argument against monologism.

Tallensi and Meyer Fortes – *Oedipus and Job in West African Religion* (1959)

European patriarchal monologic paradigm In Fortes's Tallensi data we see the consequences of gender prejudice and ethnocentrism, as a result of the masculinization of language, and the imposition of the structures of Greek and Hebrew mythologies on Africa. The narrative of the data is in the masculine gender as Fortes writes of 'nature of man', 'mankind', 'gods and men', 'man and his … '. Consequently, his reference point is male in man and son, whose relationship is determined by two fundamental principles of European religious thought and custom: the Oedipal principle of the notions of fate and destiny, and the Jobian principle of supernatural justice.

Since Fortes analyses Tallensi kinship on the basis of this European masculine and patriarchal paradigm, he takes the male as his reference point in a European interpretation of the domestic family. Focusing on men and adult sons, Tallensi domestic arrangements become 'a typically patrilineal joint family'. However, this dominant maleness is contradicted by suppressed and fragmented information in the data suggesting a missing matriarchal system. Fortes, for example, writes:

The lineage ancestor cult is by definition a cult of the patrilineal male ancestors. But the ancestress of a lineage or segment is almost as important as the founding ancestor, and the spirits of maternal ancestors and ancestresses play as big a part in a person's life as his personal ancestor spirit. (1959: 27)

Imposing his European paradigm on the Tallensi, Fortes states that jural and ritual authority are vested in the father, and that this consequently gives rise to suppressed hostility and opposition in sons, hence the practice of ritual avoidance between man and first son. He equates this with what he calls 'latent opposition between successive generations'. Even though the practice of ritual avoidance between mother and first daughter also exists, Fortes claims that women had no jural, economic or ritual authority. Mothers had a moral rather than jural power over children. They gave the earliest training in manners and morality. Fathers give commands and punish; mothers persuade and scold. According to Fortes, 'A mother is thought of as a loving food-giver, ready to sacrifice herself for her children, their shield and comforter' (ibid.: 28).

Pursuing his presupposition of the Oedipal principle, Fortes sees the custom of prenatal divination as a simpler version of Oedipal fate, thus transposing on the Tallensi deeper structures of Greek patriarchy. Yet, this is incorrect. As we know, Oedipal fate is specific and concerns the killing of one's father. Fortes writes:

Father's Destiny and son's Destiny are enemies; each wishes to destroy the other so that its protégé may be master of the house and free to give it sacrifices and service. For this reason a married first-born son with children of his own is forbidden to use the same gateway as his father lest they meet face to face, Destiny against Destiny. (1959: 48–9)

Fortes sees this masculine rivalry as Oedipal destiny, and thus forces the concept of violence on the Tallensi data. While it is quite clear from what is described that in place of the word 'destiny', the Tallensi are referring to man to man, that is, adult to adult and not 'Destiny to Destiny'.

The relationship between the two men is to be understood in the context of respect between two adult men who were previously bound to an unequal pattern of relationship. This is obviously why the Tallensi would claim that a father's destiny is superior when a son is still in infancy. In which case, Fortes seems to have misinterpreted the Tallensi concept of 'destiny'. If the Igbo equivalent is *akalaka*, meaning that which has been destined, it also means talent and one's ability in terms of skill and profession. We can thus begin to see what is implied by the

Tallensi claim of the superiority of the father's destiny to that of the infant son. This simply means the difference in knowledge between an infant and an adult. With maturity, the grown up son is not a threat to the father's destiny in the violent sense that Fortes has put it; distance and protocol are maintained to instil respect. But Fortes has seen the relationship only within the European patriarchal ideals of male rivalry and supremacy. I am not saying that there is no rivalry between father and son in African situations; however, their relationship must be understood in the context of the culture in which they live and not through European concepts.

Fortes speaks too confidently for the Tallensi on issues that are so complex. Might it not have been better to provide direct texts of what specific Tallensi men or women said to him, and then provide an analysis of the text? The style of narrative adopted means that Fortes has said a lot that is probably nothing to do with the Tallensi, but much more to do with European and Hebrew philosophy. Having assumed the presence of Oedipal tension and potential violence between father and son, and finding none, Fortes had to explain the void away in terms of supremacy of the male ancestor cult and total submission to their control. Thus Fortes writes:

> Whatever the ancestors do must therefore be, and is, accepted as just, and men have no choice but to submit. The parallel with Job is obvious. But unlike the Biblical hero, Tallensi do not attempt to dispute their ancestor's rights and authority, though they commonly plead with them for benevolence and sometimes protest their own deserts. (1959: 59)

Even though the data suggest that the Tallensi are bound to other moral systems in dialogue and rivalry with the ancestors – as for example the personal spirit or other deities, including Earth ones – Fortes still saw the male ancestors as supreme. He consequently writes:

> Tale cosmology is wholly dominated by the ancestor cult. Even the elaborate totemic institutions, the cult of the Earth and the beliefs about dangerous mystical qualities of evil trees, animals and other natural phenomena are subordinated to it (ibid.: 60–1)

Thus, through patriarchal lineage ideology, Fortes rationalized the construction of the social person, and the passage of the individual person into and through society. The partial and monologic experience of the son became a model for the whole of society.

Since Fortes has left out information on ancestor worship by Tallensi daughters, we cannot make political sense of his material in a social context. The importance of the ancestress of a lineage and maternal ancestresses are mentioned as playing 'as big a part in a person's life as his paternal ancestor spirit', but these two systems are not brought into discourse/conversation. The result is that Fortes has constructed a masculinized system for the Tallensi, and this is not what was operational in reality, where a dual-gendered system formed the basis of social organization.

Tallensi dual-gendered logic/philosophy If we look through a collection of his essays (Fortes, 1987), we see this consistent process of masculinization of data, in spite of evidence of a missing matriarchal system in Tallensi kinship ideology. It is his Oedipal prejudice – or perhaps more correctly paradigm – which determined his analysis of power and ideology in African societies. Given such a paradigm, generational handover of power can only be seen as between men and ritualized in ancestor worship. He seems totally unconcerned about the structural significance of female ancestresses or spirits, even though he admits that 'Tallensi enshrine and sacrifice to their deceased mothers and through them to certain maternal kin. This is related to the function of maternal filiation in lineage segmentation' (1987: 75). We therefore know that there is a 'matrilateral ancestor worship' which affects sibling relations and has significance in determining the status of women, the female gender and the moral system – indeed, the totality of Tallensi society.

Instead of producing a comprehensive analysis of what is obviously a completely new system to Fortes, he imposes European gender prejudices on Africans by claiming that women do not take part in ancestor worship. For explanation, he refers to Fustel de Coulanges and, therefore, European social history, specifically that of Greece and Rome:

> The explanation long ago given by Fustel de Coulanges, to wit that women have no juridical independence, and therefore no religious status in their own right, holds for African patrilineal descent systems. Nor need I elaborate on the fact that accessory lineages of slave or stranger origin never acquire the right of direct access to the shrine of the founding ancestor of their host lineage. (1987: 75–6)

For these reasons, therefore, Fortes reaches the conclusion that Tallensi women can never reach full personhood as they 'remain in a status of jural and ritual minority' (ibid.: 264). The Tallensi ideal of the complete person is therefore portrayed as 'an adult male who has reached old age and lineage eldership', and will become worshipped as an ancestor. Yet, Fortes contradicts himself by talking about parallel attainments: 'Tallensi culture, reflecting the *complementary* relationship of males and females, of paternal and maternal kinship ancestry' (emphasis added). There are, therefore, other systems with which the patriarchal system is in discourse: the system of the females and that of the maternal kin.

If according to Fortes, 'the person emerges through the dialectic interplay of individual and social structure', he has neither shown us the emergence of the female individual nor the structural relevance of the mother-focused relationships. There is for example the relationship of *soog*, which 'links descendants in the female line from a common ancestress usually four or five generations back' (1987: 283–4). Although Fortes plays down the significance of this *soog* kin, we can see that this provides an alternative, matriarchal kinship-based moral ideology and system which is in opposition to the patriarchal system. *Soog* kin appear to be devoid of all the attributes of patriarchy. Since *soog* kin do not live together in one clan locality, the concept is decentralizing. We are told that the relationship does not confer politico-jural or ritual status. It is not based on ruling anyone or controlling any property. The relationship extends beyond the framework of the lineage and clan. It is in complementary opposition to clan relations. Based on the element-ary tie of matrifiliation, 'it creates purely interpersonal bonds of self-contained, mutual trust and amity, free of jural or ritual constraints' (1987: 284).

Fortes stresses the irreducibility of this moral relationship, which is symbolically represented in the belief in the hereditary transmission of the trait of the 'clairvoyant eye', a different perception from shared spiritual insight. This is well expressed by the Tallensi who say of a *soog* kinsman or kinswoman, 'if he sees, so do I, because we have one mother'. It is a mystical empowering gift from matriarchy, and can be used destructively against a perceived enemy in the same way as *soi*, witchcraft, which is believed to be inborn and inherited from the mother. However, the same matriarchy – owing to its abhorrence of violence and bloodshed – prescribes regard for others as a principle of action and love between *soog* kin. Thus, *soog*-by-birth cannot injure one another by witchcraft. Fortes therefore writes of 'unique bonds of matri-siblingship' carried by uterine descent.

On that most fundamental structure of matriarchy in African social structures, Fortes writes:

> It stands for the idea taken for granted as absolutely given and beyond any questioning, that motherhood is the source of elementary relationships of unconstrained mutuality between persons. These are assumed to exist and to be binding absolutely, in their own right, by virtue of unborn dispositions that are ultimately inexplicable and would only be flouted by perverted people.

He goes on to write of:

> a special glow on the face and in the eyes of a person introducing a soog
> kinsman, a special tone of pride and pleasure in describing the significance
> of this relationship that only its prototype, the relations of mother and child,
> and no other relationship, evokes. For this is the only relationship between
> persons that is free of all external social constraints, including those that
> identify persons to persons by their descent and standing. It connects in-
> dividual with individual by a mystical bond which they have to accept as
> given and which transcends and opposes the diversification of person from
> person by other social and cultural criteria. (1987: 285)

Here then is another ideological system which is in binary opposition
to patriarchy, but Fortes does not describe either its social base or the
processes of production and reproduction of this ideology of matriarchy. However, one conclusion is clear, it is wrong to apply the Oedipal
principle in the African context. For in this principle, the line taken is
that 'the struggle is inevitable and the outcome is predetermined; for it
springs from the innermost depths of our human nature' (1987: 245–6).
Fortes says that the defences against this urge are set by custom, and
fantasy provides an outlet. But in the African context, surely, the
presence of the *soog* moral system in the shaping of the social person,
and as a resource with which to deal with the jural prescriptions of
patriarchy, means that it cannot be taken as paradigmatical that sons
in this culture will have the need to kill their fathers in order to possess
their mothers.

Fortes extends the concept of the Oedipal complex in the resolution
of assumed intergenerational tensions to the relationship between
mother and daughter. For this reason, he sees rivalry in the Tallensi
custom which holds that when a daughter starts bearing children,
ideally her mother should stop. Yet this need not be the explanation,
since the mother is expected to be available to help her daughter
through late pregnancy and after giving birth. It does not occur to him
that most of the customs involving the separation of first born children,
as for example fostering, could be due to the inexperience of the
parents. First-time mothers were usually very young and very inex-
perienced. These customs also indicate that it was understood that
motherhood was a taught skill.

According to Fortes, the Oedipus complex is explicit in incest taboo
and motherhood is protected by the incest taboo, while fatherhood is
protected by its sovereign supremacy. This is a European patriarchal
formulation of what it sees as the twin pillars of society. Yet it is not
motherhood itself that is protected by the incest taboo, but the exclusive

right of the father. It is a patriarchal construct which sees woman in her role as wife and mother as an object to be dominated. It denies the autonomy of motherhood and the matricentric unit of production. In reality, what is being dealt with is a conflict between sovereign/auto-nomous motherhood/matriarchy and appropriation by patriarchy. This empirical sociocultural approach seems to me more acceptable than the psychological speculations of Fortes. In his view:

> The Oedipus saga dramatizes the dilemma of how to resolve the parents' conflict between self-preservation and self-sacrifice imposed by Fate – the Greek personification of unconscious urges too monstrous to face – as well as the dilemma of how to reconcile filial dependence and love with the parricidal and incestuous wishes of the offspring. (1987: 244)

The European nuclear family in which Oedipus was an only son is different from the African complex family structure with its unique, gendered, and separate matricentric unit. In many African societies, the son is also classified as husband and his mother addresses him as such. Consequently, he does not need to kill his father to become husband. In the 'matrilineal' household, the father is not part of the residential arrangement; it is the uncle who acts as 'father'. In the case of 'male daughters', or in a situation of woman-to-woman marriage, the 'father' is completely invisible or irrelevant.

Fortes had talked of the supremacy of the jural force of male ancestor worship which is supposed to be oppressive, coercive and arbitrary. This system in which – according to Fortes – women had no power whatsoever and were in fact non-citizens, was the supreme system. Yet he also elaborated on the supreme law of kinship amity which is mother-focused and central to the moral system. We were also informed that the mother's authority is moral and not based on jural force which is the realm of the father. Since the moral system of the mothers is not given a concrete social base, there is confusion when Fortes talks of the material sources for the code of symbolism and ritual in the processes of sociality. The moral codes of matriarchy are co-opted into the patriarchal system, resulting in a distortion of data. Fortes, for example, writes:

> The condition of filial dependence, from infancy to adulthood, is the model of subordination to authority throughout the domain of kinship and descent. Hence the experience of filial dependence, as recognized and interpreted by the culture, provides the material for the code of symbolism and ritual by means of which reverence for authority can be regularly affirmed and en-acted. For it is in this experience that the beliefs and sentiments of respect, reverence, and worship are inculcated. (1987: 81)

He has mixed up sentiments from different moral systems – patriarchal and matriarchal. 'To counterbalance latent opposition and secure
loyalty in spite of it, familiarity and affection are also evoked and
allowed conventional expression' (Ibid.: 81). But we know that both
parents do not excercise authority in the same way, as Fortes himself
informed us that mothers had a moral rather than jural power over
children, giving early training in manners and morality, persuading
and scolding. Fathers, having the jural and ritual power over children,
gave commands and punished. These two contrasting relationships
would generate different gendered moral codes and, consequently,
different experiences of filial dependence and of citizenship – as Paul
Riesman (1977) shows in the Jelgobe data, which I shall also discuss.

Fortes saw ancestor cult as the main ordering force in the social
structure of 'Africans of the Negro stock', the Ga and Nuer being an
exception (1987: 68). According to him, general agreement about ancestor worship includes the observation that it is rooted in domestic,
kinship and descent relations and institutions. Ancestor worship is a
reflection of these relations, which it expresses ritually and symbolically,
extending them to the supernatural sphere.

This is not strictly correct, since it all depends on whether the
institution or relation is patriarchal or matriarchal before we can say
whether it is a correct reflection of social facts or a male fabrication
and, therefore, falsification of them. There are abundant examples of
this in many cases of pseudo-procreation rituals which appropriate
female symbols, but reaffirm male dominance – as we shall see in
Maurice Bloch's Merina data. The fact that ancestor worship has the
corporate lineage as its structural framework shows its patriarchal base.
It usually consists of an exclusive common descent group, and sometimes includes collateral cognates. In the smaller units, it consists of
only a domestic group of an elementary family or an extended family.
It therefore operates above the matricentric unit.

The basic presence of this matricentric unit and its matriarchal
principle in African social structures, I argue, means that even male-
focused ancestor worship, although separate and in binary opposition
to matriarchy, is not monolithically masculine, that is, consisting solely
of male symbols and masculine principles and values. As I indicated in
the Igbo case (see Introduction), there is a binary opposition between
mkpuke as female and *obi* as male. The *oma* is in the kitchen. But in the
obi, mother-focused symbols such as *okwa ibenne* or *umunne* are also
present among male ritual symbols such as *ikenga*. But every year, in
ancestor worship, *ilo nmuo* and its associated *ibu ihu*, the male space *obi*
moves into the female space *mkpuke* to 'dictate' or assert an authority.

If we exclude mother-focused ideas/philosophy, we miss the dialectic of gender, and consequently fail to understand the system of checks and balances in these societies. Ancestor worship cannot be understood outside the religious and philosophical system as a whole. The structure of father is not as autonomous as that of mother.

The central focus, therefore, is the understanding of the matriarchal roots or structures of African societies. If we take into consideration the widely practised custom of mass exodus by women, taking only dependent babies, we can see societies reverting again to matriarchy – consisting of mothers, sons and daughters. In this situation, 'father' status reverts back to that of an outsider. How would society be reconstructed under these circumstances? The range of possibilities is indeed very wide. I pursue further this outsider position of the husband/father and the implied structures of patriarchy and matriarchy in the Jelgobe data, in order to establish similarity of structures in traditional African societies.

The Jelgobe and Paul Riesman (1977)

The material basis of gendered ideology/philosophy The Jelgobe are a Fulani people who live between Mali and Upper Volta. They practice a mixed agriculture of cattle rearing and arable farming, in which they cultivate millet and corn. Paul Riesman tells us that there is a gender division of labour in which men are involved in the production of raw material, while women are involved in processing, building and weaving. While men work outside, women work in the *wuro*, which is seen as a symbol of human society and culture. According to Riesman:

> since the wuro is, in Fulani thought, the symbol of human society and culture, it is logical that feminine work tends toward the creation of culture, that is to say it transforms nature, or bush, into culture, or village. (1977: 64)

The outsiderness of men is also compounded by the fact that they are sometimes involved in transhumance, and even then they will not do women's work such as 'proper cooking', rather they will roast. Similarly, men do not make butter. Although Riesman describes Fulani society as a leisure society, we learn that all able bodied women work, while the productive segment of the male population is aged between fifteen and forty years.

Being a remnant from the Macina religious empire, there are influences from Arabs and Islam, although Riesman claims that Islam has no function in the maintenance of the social system. Caste and race are obviously significant in the social system. The material implements such as hoe, axe, mortar, pestle, the bowl, the milk urn, the milk whisk and so on are made by members of castes who do not intermarry with the Fulani. Their salt comes from outside. Even the pottery comes from outside and is made by wives of blacksmiths. While any Jelgobe woman can spin cotton, only men of servile condition can weave, and the herdsman makes only his own sandals of cowhide. We can therefore deduce that the Jelgobe man is very much dependent on trade for material implements and on the women for shelter, food and clothing, since it is the women who build and own the *wuro*, hut, and process food and weave.

However, it is an image of a masculinized society that we are presented with, although the degree of the masculinization is not as great as that of the Tallensi by Fortes. Riesman's narrative is also in the masculine gender, as for example, 'the Jelgobe, he ... '; 'the traveller, he ... '; 'the informant, he ... '; 'study of man by man'; 'a child, he ... ' etc. As for Jelgobe men themselves, in spite of the heavy dependence on arable farming, they seem to think of themselves as 'herdsmen'. There is consequently the parallels of the construction of woman's relationship with her nature in the sense of mother and child, and man's relationship with his nature in that of man and cow (1977: 257). From these are derived a whole set of gendered symbolisms of binary opposition: female equals woman equals house, *wuro*, on the one hand, and male equals man equals bush, *ladde*, on the other. *Wuro* and *ladde* appear to constitute the basic paradigmatical structures of matriarchy and patriarchy.

It is obvious that Riesman was influenced by Fortes in his psychological analysis of sentiments among the Jelgobe to the extent that he too looks for the Oedipus complex in this society. He thus superimposed his own masculinist concern and anxiety on the Jelgobe by singling out the predicament of a male child, whom he presumed wondered about his father's sexual access to his mother during the night. Incest is seen to be consciously suppressed through the custom of forbidding the utterance of names which have something to do with sexuality.

It is extremely ethnocentric to suppose that the principle of the Oedipus complex is relevant to this society. Riesman himself observes that a child's early childhood is cushioned in the world of women. In this society, people are not alone, least of all children. Unlike the only child that Oedipus was in a European nuclear family in which the mother was the sexual property of the father, Jelgobe children do not have the privacy to experience loneliness and anxiety – they are not alone, by themselves. Jelgobe sons are in a collective movement of children at night and during the day.

The *wuro* is the living unit, and during the day, men never stay at home. Consequently, the man does not possess the woman completely. The man comes into the mother and child domain, the matri-centric unit, in which the children monopolize the mother. Structurally, the father remains as an outsider to the *wuro* structure. An analysis of marriage rituals and symbolism also indicates the outsider status of the husband. The new bride builds the hut. The young husband is forced into the hut, and he takes flight when he is forced into his wife's bed. For the first two years, he goes in there only as a thief; he is said to 'steal' the woman.

We therefore see the role of gender as a basic principle in the social structure, but this has not been taken into consideration in the presentation or analysis of the data. For this reason, gender is not presented as systemic. Rather, the roles of men and women are presented as two irreconcilably opposed principles of social organization (1977: 58). The role of women in the social structure is seen as that of differentiation of segments, while that of men is seen as integration of individuals. According to Riesman:

> It stands out from our description that the men's 'work' consists in strengthening their own unity and thereby that of the entire society, while the women's job is to differentiate the segments within the society and to emphasize the manner in which all these are joined to one another to form a whole. (ibid.: 61)

Riesman sees these differential roles as symbolized in the naming ceremony. Men share out meat which everyone gets. Women share out winnowing-plaques or calabash covers made of straw. This is divided according to the lineage of birth of the women. Those of the highest generational status receive gifts as representatives of the lineage, which means that not everyone gets these particular gifts, but other gifts are also shared out. What is important to Riesman is the supposed symbolic picture of women squabbling, and therefore in disarray, inside the hut of the mother of the newborn child. But what seems important to me is the fact that the women have an organizational structure based on their lineage of birth, and recognized leadership based on age. If meat is shared according to estate, profession and sex, it does not seem to me that the role of men sharing meat represents the integration of individuals as Riesman would have us believe, but the symbolizing of hierarchy and social inequality.

The lack of recognition and analysis of the basic oppositional structures of gender has led to a presentation of incomplete data. Other social institutions, as a result of the mother–child structure, which have relevance in the social structure are missing. We have no data on women's organizational structures, yet we learn that they are builders, weavers, and home makers and that they process food. They have a structure of female representatives of their natal lineages as was mentioned in the naming ceremonies. We are not told how a woman acquires the technology to build a house. Who does she mobilize? Does that compel her to a prescribed behaviour towards a specific category of women in order to ensure their help? These systems of gender discourse which complete the social structure are missing.

Yet, as with the *soog* kin relations of the Tallensi, the moral system generated from the *wuro* seems central to Jelgobe processes of sociality. While man is metaphorically associated with the *ladde*, bush, and is addressed as *jom wuro*, head of the *wuro*, this headship is limited. We should note that the word for headship *jom* is genderless. Woman on the other hand is associated with the *wuro*, hut, which she builds and owns. She is addressed as *jom suudu* (ibid.: 32), meaning head of the house, with headship here implying more extensive headship. *Suudu* in this context means a structural unit.

From this structural unit, the Jelgobe have derived what I see as a whole set of matriarchal meaning and ethics symbolized in the concept of *suudu*, a place of shelter, hut for people, nest for birds and bees, envelope for a letter, a box or case, where anything rests or sleeps. From this symbolism of womb imagery is abstracted customs and rules, and a whole morality binding the wider patrilineage of *suudu baaba*, the father's house.

These gender ideologies form an oppositional category of behaviour and emotions expressed in *pulaaku*, Fulaniness, self control, and *semteende*, shame, modesty. In a relationship of inequality, an inferior feels *semteende*. In this context, the superior or more senior person does not feel the more rigid or heroic *pulaaku*, but feels *yurmeede*, pity, compassion – an emotion regarded as female (ibid.: 200–2). One must not, however, be dominated by it, though it is seen as necessary for the harmony of the group. However, women are not to resist this emotion, especially as mothers.

These matri-centric structures generate alternative moral systems available to social subjects, both male and female, in the course of social relations. The presence of these fundamental matriarchal systems generating love and compassion means that we cannot take the Oedipal principle of violence as a basic paradigm or given in the African context. The balancing matriarchal system acts as a constraint on the patriarchal structure, checking the development of absolute totalitarian patriarchy and a mono-logic system.

Riesman could very well be writing about the *soog* kin relations of the Tallensi or the *umunne* relations of the Igbo when he writes:

The atmosphere of secure human warmth where people feel close and where there is no need to maintain any facade because they feel able to behave altogether 'natural'. Among the Jelgobe this situation arises most usually when one is with one's mother or with her brother ... those in front of whom he does not feel shame ... This ease in the mother–child relationship, even when the child has grown, is largely carried over into the relations between all the children born of the same mother and especially between children of opposite sexes, who can share confidences and talk over their personal problems. It is never forgotten that people have nursed at their mother's breast, and the Fulani conception of the mother–child relationship is quite marked by this fact. (ibid.: 122)

The Merina and Maurice Bloch (1986)

Gender appropriation, patriarchy and violence The Eurocentric concept of cultural or moral society as a solid patriarchal monolith bounded by ritual can be seen reproduced in anthropological concepts and tools of analysis. Anthropological discourse on ritual has thus fabricated monolithic concepts of society in key words like 'solidarity of the group', 'sharing of common substance', 'unity of the group', 'maintenance of order', etc.

Rejecting earlier interpretations of ritual as based on 'hypothetical history', Maurice Bloch (1986) insists that in order to understand the intricate processes of determination which produce such a complex phenomenon as ritual, it has to be seen in real history – that is, a history that has no starting point (ibid.: 7). He therefore saw ritual as a symbolic system being created in history, and joined forces with communication symbolists. To him, this system of communication is not just the decoding and translation of messages, for ritual is between action and statement. Therefore, ritual is a proposition with a historical destiny. Ritual, in spite of its hazy impression of timelessness, would consequently be affected by events. Bloch therefore moved beyond meaning to analysis of how ritual is manifested in history. Let us look at the data provided in his study of the circumcision ritual of the Merina, in order to see if Bloch does what he set out to do. This can be tested by answering two questions: Which history does he choose to see? In which specific history does he choose to contextualize the circumcision ritual?

Merina matri-centric concept Bloch's concern with detailed description and analysis of what he calls the content of ritual, and his conscious effort to indicate the gender of ritual symbols have provided us with a wealth of information for the analysis of the socio-political dynamics of gender systems in Merina social structure. The gendered symbolic oppositions are very clear. In the Merina matricentric concept, biological kinship links children to their mothers and their siblings so that, at birth, humans are only matrilineally related, and there is close bonding between the children of two sisters. Bloch informs us that this matricentric system is in contrast to kinship of descent which is determined by elders. There are consequently two systems here. The matricentric kinship is a construct derived from biological and historical facts, while the kinship of descent is a construct based on a distortion of both biological and historical facts.

In accordance with these two distinct systems – that is, the matricentric kinship and descent kinship – two systems of belief are reproduced or elaborated in ritual, forming a symbolically gender valued opposition. Under female we have: the house, household, dispersal, south, division, women, kinship, and heat. Under male we have: the tomb, the clan, *deme*, unity, north-east, sanctity and order.

There is a third category which is, in my opinion, the most important category for reasons I explain later. This is the Vazimba autochthonous category, considered to be the original owners of the land and natural fertility. As I expected, Vazimba cults are usually dominated by women. Vazimba controls nature spirits, the fertility of all uncultivated things. Wild cattle are the symbols of Vazimba, denoting strength, power and vitality. Vazimba is also associated with water, and seen as powerful, active and unbounded. Therefore streams and lakes are sites of many Vazimba cults.

There are then three categories here: the matricentric system dominated by a motherhood ideology; the descent system dominated by elders and a patriarchal ideology; and an invisible/inverted/externalized matriarchy in the Vazimba category, owners of the land and natural fertility, and therefore owners of the life force from which the power of blessing is derived. Since the power of the elders has been fabricated on their authority to give blessing, Bloch deconstructs the processes of this elaborate fabrication. In blessing, the power of the Vazimba is supposed to be controlled and contained by the ancestral power. This is, therefore, the simple logic/structure behind all the rituals called *tsodrano*, blessing. Circumcision is one of them, and in it we see the dramatization of the violent conquest of the Vazimba. But I prefer to call it patriarchy and matriarchy in contest, since conquest has a kind of totality about it that seems to disregard analysis of structures of opposition.

While categories denote boundaries, actions such as invasion, conquest and appropriation all indicate the breaking of boundaries and, consequently, acts of violation and violence. These are really the issues that Bloch is dealing with in his analysis of the symbolism of Merina circumcision ritual. In gender terms, the house and the tomb seem to represent these gendered boundaries of inclusion and exclusion; the house being female and the tomb being male. Males have to break into the house to take women's sons in order for them to be circumcized. Merina funerary ritual necessitates two burials. The first ritual involving the cleaning and drying of the corpse is in the house of women. For the second burial, women carry the corpse to the tomb, ritually driven forward by men: 'It is as if the journey to the tomb is achieved over and against the world of women and all it represents' (1986: 44). Women are not permitted to stand on the tomb or enter it. Bloch thus supplies another gendered opposition in the tomb being a representation of the *deme* and, therefore, male. House, on the other hand, is a representation of the division of kinship, individual filiation and marriage, birth and women, and death and decay.

Bloch says that in reality Merina women have exceptional economic and political powers which are not reflected in the symbolic role given them in ritual. But this is to be expected since the very purpose of these rituals is to deny these concrete realities. The fear of women's potential in the Vazimba concepts in a patriarchal context necessitates keeping women out of patriarchal rituals. The patriarchal rituals are, in any case, dramatizations of the appropriation of women's roles, and are used to humiliate, humble and control women's cultural potentialities – again that perennial contest between matriarchy and patriarchy. As Bloch puts it:

> It is therefore essential to remember, as is too often forgotten in anthropology, that the roles that people act in rituals do not reflect or define social status. Rather these roles are part of a drama that creates an image and that needs to be created because in many ways it contradicts what everybody knows. (ibid.: 45)

Thus, in the circumcision ritual that claims to be about kinship unity and indivisibility, motherhood is undermined as men appropriate normal female roles and perform them outside the house. For example, they appropriate cooking, doing it collectively outside accompanied by bawdy joking, thus giving the impression of united men cooking. The circumcizer is himself called father of the child, which in reality he is not, and he must not be seen by the child before the event. There is also the appropriation of female gendered elements such as water, and the fertility and potency of wild plants which represent the fertility of nature as lifeforce – the life-giving of living mother. The invading of boundary is symbolized by the requirement that youths should steal certain shoots. According to Bloch, stealing characterizes violence. 'In this instance, however, a new theme is added: that of the need to do violence, by stealing, to this natural, mother-focused, power of repro-duction' (1986: 55).

Merina circumcision ritual constructs an artificial parenthood which is non-biological and non-sexual. Together with the artificial father is the category of young girl virgins who are regarded as mothers of the child. They comfort the child by singing and dancing. The real parents should avoid sex for seven days before the circumcision and until the wound heals.

In this visible male control of the ritual, group divisions are not stressed, but the unity and indivisibility of the whole *deme*, as elders are called by the same name irrespective of gender. This unity of the elders is seen to contrast with the women seen scrambling for bits of the mat on which the water of the blessing had been placed. These scraps are then placed on the walls or under their beds in order to obtain greater fertility. Here then is a clear patriarchal fabrication which claims that the fertility-giving power of the male ancestors is trans-mitted into life-giving potential.

A further undermining of the facts about motherhood is the likening of the child who is about to be circumcized to a falcon, which Bloch calls an anti-motherhood creature which spurns motherhood and the nest. The ritual involving the stealing of bananas by women and the stealing of sugar-cane by men is said to involve repeated mock fighting throughout the night. Bloch sees a parallel between the fate of the child and the sugar-cane and banana stealing, since the child is violently taken out from inside the house to outside the house before his life-giving potential can be released.

Again the breaking and invasion of boundary can be seen in the ritual act of youths of a living father and mother having to act out a violent drama involving the fetching of the water from inside the house. Bloch supplies this consistent symbolic opposition of house as heat, natural birth, matrilineality, warm woman-focused house; and this is assaulted and penetrated violently by the young men coming from the cold outside. They have to break in twice. For the initial entry, the door is smashed down with a pestle, and then there is a re-entry with the powerful water in a mock fight with the women. The breaking of boundary is thus seen to lead to fertility. The youths are likened to a bull and a spear – male and phallic symbols. The gourd which is a female symbol is caught, tied, broken and cut. There is a whole set of heterosexual symbolism here, but Bloch avoids saying so.

The circumcizer sits on a mortar filled with cattle dung. As he performs the cutting, women dance crawling on hands and knees, taking up dirt from the floor and throwing it on their heads. Some women also try to force themselves out of the house but are stopped, for at the moment of circumcision, only men represent the united *deme* and masculinity is equated with the descent group. A senior male relative swallows the cut off prepuce in a piece of banana (1986: 79). Again there is a scramble for pieces of the broken gourd. The circumcized child is finally handed over to his real mother through a window in the house. Merina patriarchal statement in this ritual is that a child leaves the women's house and is received by men as a man. But in order to do this, motherhood is undermined and women are required to subject themselves in the worst self-pollution in Merina belief. The same custom of self-pollution is expected of women mourning the dead during first burial. Bloch's contempt for this falsification is clear, as he writes:

> The whole circumcision ritual is, as we stressed, antibirth by women, yet in the end it acts out a birth by bringing the child out of the female house. In this way the circumcision ceremony not only defines itself as a 'new' birth but it does so with imagery borrowed from what it appears to revile most, the biological process of parturition. Of course, the symbolism of the ritual insists that this second birth is different because it is directly under the control of the ancestors and the elders, yet significantly it cannot get away from the nature of birth in its less 'elaborated' form. (1986: 103)

But this *Othering* of women presents ambiguity in the fact that women who are constructed as wild are also *deme* and part of descent. Therefore, there was no parallel initiation ceremony for women. Women in themselves are complete. As Bloch says, 'Merina women have the potential to reproduce matrilineally by their very nature. Without men they would therefore take over the descent group' (ibid.). There is a problem with this statement. It implies that the presence of men prevents matriarchy. Yet we know that this is incorrect. It is the recognition of the legitimacy of motherhood that is essential to matriarchy. Such legitimacy would recognize matriarchy as an ideological self-construct. Bloch seems to view nature as though it is not itself a construct, and this is why he does not bring in matriarchy as an ideology. Yet that is what this whole effort of Merina elders is about: how to deny or contain matriarchy, while they themselves tap from it or appropriate its symbolism, for it is the oppositional ideology and system for the Merina in the symbolisms of the house and Vazimba.

By not seeing these female structures as patterns of matriarchy, Bloch has helped Merina men to silence women's creativity. In spite of being in sympathy with women, the perspective presented is totally that of men as Bloch goes on and on about all these male fabrications which claim that true fertility can only be achieved through the blessing of ancestors, and that natural existence has to be conquered violently. All these beliefs and practices compel obedience to ancestral custom – which equates with patriarchy – even though Bloch does not use this term at all. The ritual legitimates those in authority, that is, the patriarchs. But according to Bloch, the whole ritual follows a formula and is therefore non-creative,

> The ritual is therefore perceived as totally non-creative; for the participants it is a matter of following a formula. Yet it performs a social function that is clear to the participants and this must have been created in the socio-historical process by people such as the participants who do not see themselves as creating it at all. This is a puzzle that lies at the heart of much social science. (1986: 104)

This is a puzzle for Eurocentric so-called social science and not a puzzle for those whose experiences and histories are being appropriated by European scholarship. For example, as an African woman, I do not accept the conclusions reached by Bloch.

If the ritual we are concerned with is placed socio-historically, as indeed Bloch set out to do, then we must accept as true what the Merina said about having violently taken the land from the Vazimba, and that the Vazimba were Africans with a dominant matriarchal construct. The Merina had to 'conquer' and subvert the culture of the autochthonous Vazimba. Bloch's Eurocentrism has limited him to a two hundred years' depth of history. Yet his two hundred years has not thrown light on the analysis or understanding of the structural relationship between the Merina and Vazimba. We need to go beyond two hundred years and re-open the debate on myth as history in Africa. Why apply structural analysis to symbols and ritual and not to myth and history, since Bloch himself admits that ritual and myth are close in structure, with myth specifying the details of the rituals (1986: 110–11).

In the African context these rituals and myth, time and time again, prove to be dramatizations of real events in history, such as cultural contact, invasion, conquest, migration and other significant social events and social movements. They are histories dramatized in societies of oral history. If we re-examine Merina myth, we can see clearly that it is an account of an Asian invasion of Africa with very strong racist overtones which Bloch chooses not to name, although he supplies all the information needed for one not to miss this racism.

The first statement in the myth supplied by Bloch shows an invasion of a matriarchal people, ruled by queens, by a patriarchal people ruled by that masculinist construct, heroic kings. King Andriamanelo was the founder of the Merina royal line of heroic kings who drove out the Vazimbas, a people ruled by queens. Despite this, the cults of these queens did not disappear, but are still flourishing. The externalization/inversion/silencing/banishment of matriarchy was a real historical experience.

King Andriamanelo is said to have discovered the technique of the smelting and forging of iron, and his people therefore made iron spears – a more deadly weapon of destruction and violence than the clay spears of the Vazimba. However, the Vazimba's obviously anti-violence cultural values are seen as uncultivated, as Bloch reproduces Merina – or is it European – racism, which sees Andriamanelo as 'the complete antithesis of the wild and uncultivated Vazimba' (1986: 106). Also in the myth, the Black people are the slaves. Andriamanelo's mother, however, is Queen Rangita, the most famous Vazimba queen. This would of course make him a mulatto, and involved in two cultures. Rangita is described as small, dark, and the name means curly haired, a woman and a mother. The implication is that although the Vazimba were driven out, their women – at least their queens – were married by the invaders. This was also the strategy used by Arab invaders in North Africa. These are therefore structures of invasions and domestication/subordination by violence. Instead of a dialogue between two different cultural or ideological values, what Bloch sees is, on the one hand, a racist symbolic opposition of the Vazimba as biological maternal, which equals 'world of rude', 'ugly people', 'indigenous', 'female', 'queens'. On the other hand, Merina equals 'beautiful', 'technologically sophisticated', 'conqueror', 'king', 'warlike'.

Bloch's real interest is in the historical changes in the role and control of Merina circumcision in the context of socio-political changes resulting from relations with European systems from the nineteenth century, as a result of colonialism and later independence. What followed is not different from the processes in other colonized African societies. This period saw state intervention in what was a descent group ritual and the linking of Merina circumcision to military expansionism, conquest and state rule, and the use of circumcision as a means of internal regulation. It was now the king who fixed the time of circumcision and used the occasion to collect tax. It also later became an occasion for census of the male population.

Following was the period of liberalization and the permission of the king was no longer needed for circumcision. There surfaced different political groups and interests such as Catholics, Protestants, revolutionary atheists, etc. Following a period of political and economic chaos, religious and cultural chaos reigned, followed by a millenarian movement. Anti-European and anti-Christian voices demanded reinstitution of royal rituals, including circumcision. But royal control of circumcision never returned, instead circumcision became a family affair and more rural, creating an opposition between the traditionalists and the urban elite. With anti-colonial and anti-elite feelings there was a resurgence of circumcision.

Having compared the central structure of power in Merina history with its history of circumcision, Bloch makes the following analysis of this process of 'denial' of motherhood/matriarchy:

> The central point of this structure is the creation of the ordered transcendental by devaluation of the value of human experience and action. The problem of the reintroduction of vitality is a consequence of the first opposition. But it makes the violence of conquest of 'this world' appear as necessary and justified. The particular form of different rituals varies but the basic point is the same: the cultivation of the hatred of life for the sake of authority. (1986: 175) (Cf. Diop's *The Cultural Unity of Black Africa*, 1989.)

If the issue is the imposition of the authority of the male gender over the female, why is it that Bloch never uses the expression patriarchy or masculine imperialism? Bloch sees the same symbols put to similar use in 'the devaluation of feminity and birth, the revelling in putrefaction, ritual wounding of the genitalis, the killing of animals, and so forth' (ibid.).

To Bloch, circumcision was the main ideological apparatus in nineteenth-century Madagascar. And here Bloch superimposes a Marxist understanding of ideology drawn from European social history on the Merina. Marxist theory presents ideology as a state apparatus or an instrument of the state, the state being synonymous with the ruling classes and its means of accumulation or control of capital. It is through the alienation of the worker that appropriation by capital takes place. According to Bloch, in the case of the Merina, the role of capital is taken by ancestors, and the tomb is falsified as the true source of creativity. This ideology therefore depends on the negation of the creativity of ordinary human beings. But, as we have seen, it is not all ordinary human beings that are responsible for this specific creativity, but motherhood/matriarchy. The falsification is being done by the ideologies of masculinism/patriarchy.

Even though he has avoided the word patriarchy, Bloch acknow-
ledges that there is a difference between the ideology of capitalist
systems and non-capitalist systems. In capitalist systems, the ideology
of capitalism devalues the creativity of labour. In non-capitalist systems,
labour and human reproduction are merged. Is Bloch now admitting
that in this system gender is the central issue, since it is only in
motherhood that I see labour and human reproduction as merged?

However, Bloch is not contented with the classical Marxian formulation that sees those exploited as mystified and ideology as falsehood.
He says that politico-economic circumstances do not in themselves
produce ideology, since ideology does not seem to change every time
the social circumstances change. The legitimating function of ideology
remains constant.

Bloch, therefore, seems to be implying that there is a historical
continuity in the function of ideology. This is not correct since we
know that whenever patriarchy appropriates female/matriarchy generated rituals, it has changed them and introduced the element of
violence against those from whom it has appropriated the ritual(s). The
very male construct of heterosexuality and birth which the symbolism
in Merina circumcision ritual, in my opinion, dramatizes is a case in
point. What Bloch has not dealt with is the ability of ideology to
corrupt and co-opt other categories of people in ideologically opposed
categories. The group of the exploited do not remain homogeneous
and constant, since both gender and class are mechanisms of classification and co-optation.

Ideology is not always an oppressive instrument. It can be a non-
oppressive creative model of self-worth; a self-metaphor for self-rule or
organized autonomy. It is therefore important that we distinguish
between ruling class ideology, masculinist, patriarchal ideology, and
matriarchal ideology, and the dynamic role of gender in the processes
that these systems generate. In order to present a fuller picture and
meaning of the symbolisms in Merina circumcision ritual, it would
have been necessary for Bloch to look at women-generated and controlled rituals – in other words, the actual system that the masculinist
or patriarchal construct in the circumcision ritual is in dispute with,
particularly in the African context where these dual-gendered values
seem to be juxtaposed.

Bloch writes, 'Ritual cannot form a true argument, because they
imply no alternative' (1986: 182). This is because Bloch is looking at a
patriarchal ritual whose purpose is to assert masculine supremacy over
women, and since in this case it had to appropriate or steal from
motherhood, it is done in an authoritarian and violent manner, re-

enacting that taking over of the product of the reproducer of the producers. Female ritual symbolisms in maternity and birth rituals are biologically and consequently metaphorically factual. The patriarchal ones are psuedo-claims. They are formalized falsifications or fabrications which seek to dispute the alternative matriarchal system, that other world that it caricatures. Yet it is as a result of our awareness of that other system, or the potentiality of it, that we are able to deconstruct the falsification. For if it is a falsification, the contradictions would be there. Thus, protests and revolutions can bring about ritual creativity and innovation.

On the seeming collusion of participants in their own degradation, Bloch writes:

> The willing participation of women in such an anti-feminine ritual … is illustrative of ritual as a whole. It comes from the fact that the ritual appears to establish the authority of everybody, in so far as it brings blessing to everybody, and by this means transforms everybody, men and women, into decent beings. (1986: 189)

Yet at the same time, it establishes differential degrees of authority, and that is the only relevant political distinction. Those who are able to place themselves in the position of 'elders' changed according to political circumstances, so that the ritual has already created roles which dominant groups have filled and used. This can be compared to our flag independence based on a psuedo-state. State apparatuses and their rituals were inherited ready-made. The propositional force of ritual also lies in its use by opportunists or collaborators. It is not that the abused and oppressed do not know right from wrong, but the fact that there is something to be gained at the expense of others.

In conditions of oppression, everyone is not usually in acquiesence with the oppressive system; it is that the oppressive system of dominance has the ability to divide and rule, corrupt and co-opt. It creates divisions within the oppressed, as for example, more oppressed and less oppressed, and ambitious aspirants. Class and gender work like that; they can create new categories of collaborators. Of course the fabrication constructed can be invalidated by experience. As Bloch says, 'legitimation of violence and domination is only possible for those who already dominate by violence' (ibid.: 191).

It is my consistent argument that the matriarchal structure in the social systems of traditional African societies could only be suppressed if there was rule by patriarchal violence – structural or symbolic. Otherwise, one is able to see both systems juxtaposed in dialogue. Euro-patrifocal methodology imposed on African Studies can only result in suppressed and fragmented information in the data which suggest a missing matriarchal system. Rather than simply treating social competition and conflict as occurring only between generations and between men and women, a gender analysis that makes visible the paradigmatic gender oppositions enables us also to see competition and conflict between structural value systems in which the different generations and women and men all share and participate.

Bibliography

Bloch, Maurice, 1986, *From Blessing to Violence: History and Ideology in the Circumcision Ritual of the Merina of Madagascar*, Cambridge University Press, Cambridge.

Diop, Cheikh Anta 1989 *The Cultural Unity of Black Africa: the Domains of Matriarchy and of Patriarchy in Classical Antiquity*, Karnak House, London.

Fortes, Meyer, 1959, *Oedipus and Job in West African Religion*, Cambridge University Press, Cambridge.

— 1987, *Religion, Morality and the Person*, Cambridge University Press. Chapter 4, 'Ancestor worship in Africa', pp. 66–83; chapter 9, 'The first born', pp. 218–46; and chapter 10, 'The concept of the person', pp. 247–86.

Riesman, Paul, 1977, *Freedom in Fulani Social Life*, University of Chicago Press, Chicago.

2 Race and gender: Cheikh Anta Diop's moral philosophy

When I wrote an earlier version of this chapter under a different title in February 1992 (Amadiume, 1992), the old Soviet Union had been dismantled, its ideology of communism discredited; Iraq had been humiliated and disarmed; and the Eastern Bloc states were disintegrating. Today, three years on, America and European Nato powers have physically moved into Bosnia supposedly for peace-keeping purposes and so-called national reconstruction. This is, of course, the current financial term for guided capitalist transformation through high interest loans and cyclical debt. The situation is no different in the Middle East and Africa, both in politics and academia where European imperialism continues its stranglehold on the production of African Studies and the interpretation of African history. Faced with these realities, the scholarship of Cheikh Anta Diop remains prophetic in his analysis of the philosophies of imperialism as expressed through the ideologies of gender and race.

In 1992, I was more concerned with critiquing the centrist tendency in concepts of nationalism, the state, and popular movements in studies of contemporary Africa. Hence, I was interested in the theoretical implications of Diop's methodology in his study of social movements and the ideology of gender in state formations as demonstrated in *Civilization or Barbarism* (Diop, 1991). This chapter focuses more on his philosophy of culture in the context of contemporary discourses on race and gender. I shall use mainly three texts from Diop's socio-historical studies, namely, *Civilization or Barbarism* (1991), *The Cultural Unity of Black Africa* (1989), and *Precolonial Black Africa* (1987).

Diop on race and gender

Cheikh Anta Diop's main agenda was the definition and reconstruction of African identity. Even though this led him to consider the scientific,

theoretical and philosophical legacy of Black Egypt to Greece; the
historical relationship of Islam, Christianity and Judaism with Egyptian
religious thought, he was an optimistic thinker who saw the possibility
of a new philosophy of reconciliation about which he wrote:

> The African who has understood us is the one who, after the reading of our
> works, would have felt a birth in himself, of another person, impelled by an
> historical conscience, a true creator, a Promethean carrier of a new civiliza-
> tion and perfectly aware of what the whole Earth owes to his ancestral genius
> in all the domains of science, culture, and religion.
>
> Today each group of people, armed with its rediscovered or reinforced
> cultural identity, has arrived at the threshold of the postindustrial era. An
> atavistic, but vigilant, African optimism inclines us to wish that all nations
> would join hands in order to build a planetary civilization instead of sinking
> down to barbarism. (1991: 7)

As we know, instead of a planetary civilization, the new European
cultural identity is a racial one as they repeat a tragic history by
reconvening in Europe 1992.

Diop was not interested in Egypt simply to establish its Black African
roots, character and peopling. He clearly said that stating that the
Egyptians were Blacks is less important than 'making it an operational
scientific concept'. There were two reasons for this. The first is the
deliberate falsification of the history of humanity. The second reason,
which is directly linked with the enslavement of Africans, was the new
Egyptology which 'reinforced the theoretical bases of imperialist
ideology'.

This was the ideology of racism, the ideologues of which Diop
dubbed 'scholarly counterfeitors' to whom anatomical differences corresponded to hierarchical differences in the degree of humanization.
This construct placed White Europeans at the top of the hierarchy
and Black Africans at the bottom. It claims the superiority of Europeans
and European civilization, hence its concept of a universal, specifically
European civilizing value linked to the Greco-Roman classics. Consequently, Diop had to employ his historical comparative method to
correct this European falsification and unfounded arrogance. He traced
the roots of these values in order to analyse and deconstruct them.
Connections with Egypt provided the basis for his five thousand years'
diachronic study of the key socio-political formations and transformations in Egypt/Africa and Europe, and the moral philosophies of
these systems.

In all his works, Diop – in spite of his resistance polemics, frequent
jibes at, and powerful critique of, specific Marxist theoreticians – took

pains to establish a dialectic between the material condition and ideological superstructure, that is, the interrelationships between culture, and social and economic institutions of the civilizations that he investigated. It was his thesis that the systemic racism, the Atlantic Slave Trade, colonialism and imperialism that Africans suffered on such a massive scale at the hands of the Europeans involved a specific European ideology of violence. What is the root or history of this philosophy of violence? Diop (1991) traced it to the nomadic proto Indo-Europeans (the Kurgans), who came from the Eurasiatic Russian Steppes between the Caspian and the Black Seas. It is to them that Diop attributed all the inequities of a violent sociocultural formation: namely, nomadism, patriarchy, the veneration of warrior deities, and the domestication of the horse. Gender valued principles were therefore central to Diop's theorization.

It was these nomads who in 3400 BC invaded and erased the ancient European civilization which Diop (1991) claims originated from the Cro-Magnoids in the south and the last Negroids with direct continuity with the outward migration from Africa. As such, following Diop's thesis of a matriarchal superstructure in early African social formations (Diop, 1989), these systems would retain some of the characteristics and practices which Diop has attributed to African matriarchy.

Contrary to Diop's thesis, Marija Gimbutas (1982) has claimed that there was once an ancient European matriarchy based on a sedentary life and agriculture between 6500 to 3500 BC, allegedly a peaceful society which knew no wars and had a cult of the Mother Goddess and other female deities. Diop has disputed this claim, arguing that this supposed matriarchy remains a hypothesis due to lack of documentation. He also disputed Gimbutas's dating of the third millennium BC for the first Indo-European culture. He, however, agreed with Gimbutas on the characteristics of the first Indo-European Nordic culture as being typical of the North, namely, Germans, Celts, Illyrians, Baltics and the Slavs.

In *The Cultural Unity of Black Africa*, Diop (1989) presented two contrasting superstructural systems and opposing moral values. The matriarchal ones were peaceful societies with relatively no wars, while the patriarchal ones were violent societies, with histories full of invasions and wars. He argued that the transformation from matriarchy to patriarchy did not result from internal dialectics, but from direct invasion. The invaded were principally the Balkans, the most distant European branch, who according to Diop retain Negroid features, reminding one of the Grimaldi type or the Asiatic traits as a result of the Asiatic invasions, of which the Huns and the Hungarians were the last.

Thus Diop again reinforces his theory of African human origin, cultural continuity and discontinuity in the new settlements following later waves of migration. He disputed the polycentric thesis on the grounds that the hypothetical centres were not approximately contemporaneous. Diop's stated position is this:

> all of the so-called centres of the appearance of modern man are more recent than those of Africa and can therefore be explained with Africa as the starting point, by more or less direct filiation through migration and geographical differentiation, as a consequence of paleo-environmental adaptation. (1991: 53)

Johann Bachofen (1861), the nineteenth-century Swiss theorist of matriarchy, had claimed that there had been an internal historical evolution from matriarchy to patriarchy in Europe due to endogenous factors. Diop disputed this theory arguing that the Kurgan Indo-Europeans never knew matriarchy. They had been patriarchal right from the beginning, as a result of their specific ecological and material conditions. They had moved from hunting straight to nomadism, thus generating the sort of belief system or moral philosophy that would justify their consequent violent sociocultural formation.

It was the three Kurgan invasions between 3400 and 2900 BC which marked a break in continuity. Attacking Bachofen, Diop writes:

> it was a patriarchal, nomadic group that surprised a sedentary society and introduced patriarchy and all its corollary practices by force. This shows also that neither matriarchy nor patriarchy hinges on race but stems from the material conditions of life, as we have always maintained. This does not minimize the fact that patriarchy became solidly established in the Indo-European societies at the end of the Iron Age, with the arrival of the Dorians in Greece. This occurred in Rome, Persia, Arian India, Greece, etc.; and it is inconceivable to project a matriarchal past onto the very people who were the vehicles of patriarchy, particularly the Dorians. All evidence suggests that these were people who went from hunting to nomadic life without ever experiencing the sedentary phase. It was only afterwards, with the conquest of the agricultural regions, that they became sedentary. (1991: 20)

Gender and state moral philosophies

To Diop, the moral philosophy of a polity seems as important as its mode of production. This moral philosophy is clearly gendered, hence the contrast which Diop makes between the pacifist ideological superstructure of the so-called Asian Modes of Production (AMP) societies, particularly the Egyptian/African model, and the warlike morality and

militaristic values of the Greco-Roman city state. He traced the origin
of violence in their superstructures which led to the different ventures
in conquest and imperialism.

Focusing on what he called 'the African dynastic monarchy' in which
queens ruled, he showed that the character of state model was different
under this system which lasted in Egypt for nearly three thousand
years, from 3300 to 525 BC. In the West African empires, it ensured
Black self-rule and an unbroken succession of Black rulers for 1250
years, up to the sixteenth century, as demonstrated in *Precolonial Black
Africa* (Diop, 1987).

Under this African state model, the queen mother was important in
Nubia, Egypt and the rest of Black Africa. Holding Egypt as the
authentic model of this system, Diop shows the economic, political
and religious importance of matriarchy (1991: 105). The queen was the
true sovereign, landowner, keeper of the royalty, and guardian of the
purity of the lineage. When, through marriage, she transmitted the
crown to her husband, he acted only as her executive agent. It would
seem that this transmission marked the beginning of the end of matriarchal rule and the emergence of patriarchy under the Pharaohs. This
was specifically in the transition from the Third to the Fourth Dynasty,
hence the superstructural construct of the legend of Osiris – the first,
legendary, king of Egypt – marrying his sister, Isis. From this Fourth
Dynasty, from 2600 BC, (the time of the pyramids), the Pharaoh took
the title Son of God. Thus the sons had overthrown the mothers,
indicating strong gender conflict in the system.

This particular transformation seems to have accelerated the
development of feudalism in the Fifth Dynasty and the consequent
Osirian or 'proletarian' revolution in the Sixth Dynasty, which saw the
sacking of Memphis – the capital and sanctuary of Egyptian royalty –
and other major cities by the destitute masses. They took over both the
powers and possessions of the wealthy and it marked the end of the
ancient empire, in 2100 BC. Diop calls this event the first revolution in
the history of the universe.

However, the revolution failed and the monarchical system was
reinstituted and Egypt seems to have remained, in Diop's opinion, an
authentic AMP state with distinctive characteristics. Diop claims that
in this 'most perfected model, of the African-type state', the civilians
have more power than the state – what he calls 'weight of civilian
power'. The military aristocracy was practically absent. Since war had
only a defensive function, its ideological superstructure stressed moral
and human values, and excluded the values of warfare. Her long lasting
security derived from the fact that Egypt was situated in a valley. This

gave her both natural protection and an abundance of natural resources. Therefore, her geographical location ensured the quasi-permanence of the above mentioned characteristics. Under these non-militaristic conditions, Egypt was able to build a 'Great Civilization' and an empire-like supremacy based on a territorial state. The same structures were reproduced in what Diop called the neo-Sudanese empires, namely the ancient empires of Ghana, Mali and Songhai, which formed the main focus of study in *Precolonial Black Africa*. Diop's point is clear, 'Great Civilizations' can be built on a pacifist moral philosophy.

In my critique of *Precolonial Black Africa* in the Introduction to this volume, I pointed out what I perceived to be weaknesses in Diop's presentation. They included dichotomization and hierarchization of political systems, since centralized political systems seemed to be held as the ideal system and their cultures seen as classical civilizations. The focus on emperors and monarchs also made it appear as if there was no critical analysis of economic exploitation – that is, the power basis of the empires – or of the structural relationship between the empires and the surrounding villages and regions. African kingdoms/empires were considered civilized, detribalized and international, while surrounding villages were considered primitive, backward and closed societies. In this context, it seemed to me there is a need to emphasize the relationship between urban centres and local communities and villages, and the contesting ideologies in sociocultural systems at the regional level. This would mean internal focus on centralizing ideologies and anti-state ideologies of autonomy and non-invasion: patriarchal power structures and matriarchal social and moral systems within and between specific African societies at a micro level, which would complement Diop's general macro historical comparative studies in *Civilization or Barbarism* (1991) and *The Cultural Unity of Black Africa* (1989).

Diop also used this broad sweep of history in *Precolonial Black Africa* (1987), thus linking up two thousand years of state presence in the rest of Africa to his five thousand years' historical depth study of states in Egypt. This framework has its importance in that it provides African Studies with several epistemologies and hypotheses in which to locate intellectual discourse. They are: relations with ancient Egypt; relations with Nubian civilization; relations with the old Sudanese empire, ancient West African empires and kingdoms, and nations which replaced them, the Southern African empires and kingdoms, and the East African kingdoms; trade and commercial relations in the Old World, the Arabo-Islamic experiences; internal regional dynamics between centralist and decentralizing formations; domestic/internal slavery, the trans-Saharan Slave Trade, the Atlantic Slave Trade, and the slave state formations; and social and economic dynamics of nineteenth-century Africa.

However, in terms of general moral values, the contrast which Diop makes between inequalities in the African mode of production as distinct from the European city state model is clear. In the African systems, the emergence of 'a supratribal authority' or 'a national authority' was organic, following institutional social and economic imperatives. As such the general masses would be tolerant of the privileges and even moderate abuses of 'a whole hierarchic body of functionaries'. As Diop states:

> Such inequalities are not imposed overnight by a group of foreign invaders coming from the outside after unification. They are the result of the on-the-spot development of internal contradictions in the system ... We are dealing with a state whose contours exactly match those of the nation. The institutions were not knowingly created to isolate and subjugate a foreign group ... considered to be ethnically different from the conquering group; they are, so to speak, for internal, national consumption, and consequently present a less abrupt aspect. For this reason they are prone to engender a more or less casted social stratification 'accepted' by the people, provided the system foreswears outright abuses. (1991: 130)

Therefore, in the African state model, the state has its validity in acting for the greater good of all citizens and is seen to do so in public, economic, social, and military usefulness. The state can, therefore, be obeyed since it is also seen to transcend 'tribal self-interests'. As Diop says, 'Because the ideological, religious, and social superstructure has been intensely experienced by the group, it does not feel alienated when the state requires work from it' (1991: 135). For Diop, this was how the great pyramids were built. He therefore disagreed with Karl Marx, who saw the mass work mobilizations as 'generalized slavery' as opposed to Greco-Latin private slavery. Diop called it a Eurocentric interpretation to say that these were slaves; these people were not slaves since they were not conscious of having lost their freedom, and, therefore, did not need to play the role of revolutionaries. People of the AMP were less revolutionary because they had less desire for change than those of the Greco-Roman city state. This is the way Diop theorizes an organic growth of institutions and hierarchy, as opposed to colonial rule – direct or indirect. Therefore the issue of consensus, 'accepted' by the people, is important in the analysis and understanding of the history of political and social revolutions.

On characteristics of village production, Diop shows that the conditions for revolution which Marx stated as being possible only in a capitalist system were met in the Egyptian and Chinese AMP societies, which Marx thought stagnant, and that revolution did break out, but did not result in victory. Diop's view is that the study of these failures would be interesting for revolutionary theory.

Diop gave two important reasons why revolutions succeeded in the Greek city state but failed in the AMP and why they did not take place in the African cities. One was the territorial vastness of the African model and its well-developed bureaucratic state machinery. The second was differences in agrarian conditions, specifically access to land, which saw that an individual had at least a usufruct access to land. There was consequently no xenophobia and the associated fear and isolation of the foreigner; and no plebeian class of disinherited, homeless foreigners living on the outskirts of the city.

Radical transformation of moral philosophies

Somewhere between 1800 and 1700 BC (using Martin Bernal's chronological table), Egypt was invaded by the Asiatic Hyksos who introduced the chariot, state violence and imperialism. Having driven out the Hyksos in 1580 BC, Egypt, under the Eighteenth Dynasty (1580–1350 BC) embarked on conquest in self-defence. Thutmose III (1504–1450 BC) came to be known as the greatest conqueror of ancient times as a result of his expansionist policy. One hundred and ten foreign states were conquered and placed under Egyptian rule. As Diop reminds us, 'Fourteen hundred years before Rome, Egypt created the first centralized empire in the world' (1991: 85).

With these conquests, Egypt exhibited the violence of centralist formations and the 'civilizing' missionary zeal of imperialism, even racism, as can be seen from a quote from Diop: 'the royal children of vassal princes were taken as "hostages" and educated in Egyptian style, at the court of the Egyptian emperor, in order to teach them Egyptian manners and tastes and to assimilate them to Pharaonic culture and civilization' (1991: 86). The Pharaoh assumed divine guidance and became recognized as the representative of the gods. Thutmose III invented and used this philosophy of power for empire rule.

The degree of state violence in Egyptian imperialism can be seen in these key words collected from *Civilization or Barbarism* (1991: 85–102), where Diop describes the conquests and achievements of the Egyptian Eighteenth Dynasty. It is a vocabulary of patriarchy, violence, humiliation and enslavement of vanquished peoples: 'conquered', 'integrated', 'empire', 'collected', 'gold', 'tributes', 'paid', 'vassals', 'authority', 'divided', 'placed under', 'governors', 'taxes', 'defeated', 'generals', 'territorial guards', 'army', 'centralized empire', 'inspection tours', 'conquered territory', 'taken hostage', 'teach manners and tastes', 'assimilate', 'absolute power', 'be obedient and faithful', 'execute orders', 'Pharaoh as a god', 'bow at feet', 'compulsory', 'slaves', 'conflicts', 'arrest', 'invade', 'beheaded', 'a felon', 'in chains', 'divine will of Amon-Ra', 'obey', 'power over all the nations', 'rebel hordes', 'your subjects', 'domination', 'sovereignty', 'pledge allegiance', 'administration', 'haughty', 'warriors', 'chariots', 'commander', 'troops', 'divine blood', 'garrisons', 'treasury', 'Pharaoh's harem', 'horses', 'colony', 'son', 'father', 'conquests', 'spoils', 'subjugate', 'defeat', 'submission', 'fled', 'victory', 'yoke', 'offer daughter', 'crush', 'armaments', 'weapons', 'terror', 'young bull', 'tremble', 'lord of terror', 'roar', 'furious lion', 'corpses', 'captivity', 'annexed'. And on relations with Nubia, in Thutmose III's *Hymn of Triumph* there appears the phrase 'the barbarians of Nubia' (1991: 93). Diop gives the word *Nahas* (barbarian) and *Nahasiou* (barbarians) as 'the term by which the Egyptians designated the Nubians and other Blacks of Africa' (1991: 181).

Diop is consistent in attributing radical change, and state violence and patriarchy in Africa to external factors, as demonstrated in *Precolonial Black Africa*. In the case of ancient West African empires, the milestone of change was the Moroccan War of 1593 and the sacking of the ancient intellectual centre of Timbuktu by the Arabs.

In Diop's formalist approach to the study of precolonial African states, he stressed consensus and stability. In my critique of Diop's approach to violence in my introductory chapter, I emphasized the need to include a structural approach, looking at violence also as an internal contradiction in the mode of production generating a specific ideology of violence in order to justify specific economic appropriation and social control (see also Amadiume, 1995; Chapter 5 in this volume). There was also structural violence in the predatory existence of large-scale centralized states and large areas of uncentralized peoples, living between the forest and the savannah, which resulted in dynamic social movements. No doubt the history of militarism, and the gradual processes of militarization and masculinization of the African continent had direct effects on radical changes in moral philosophies and social movements in Africa. Reference here is specifically to the introduction of military technology and the ownership of the means of war and destruction, such as a particular breed of horses and firearms which supported state power, from a specific period in our history when these items were paid for by the capture and sale of human beings commoditized as slaves. The war horse, tamed by the Hittites, had entered

Africa via the Nile Valley and revolutionized warfare in Africa. This adds weight to the evidence pointing towards an Indo-European legacy of violence to the world; that is, patriarchy as an ideology of violence and the war horse used to effect conquest and rule – in other words violence and imperialism.

In Diop's analysis of race and social classes, the attack is directed at 'All the authors who deal with violence' (Marx and Engels?), whom Diop accused of avoiding an analysis of racism: 'this primary level, where bestial violence is practiced on a collective basis, where a whole group of people organise not to subdue another group, but to annihilate it' (1991: 125). He took his research to continental European history for examples of situations where 'social class, in an economic sense, ... fits the outlines of the ethnic group of the conquered race'. His example comes from the twelfth to the eighth century BC, during the European Dark Ages, when the Spatiates of Dorian origin conquered and en-slaved the Helots.

It is the individualistic, slave-based economy of the city state, constructed by these Dorians, that Diop calls 'the authentically Indo-European model of state'. Diop's specific aim was to trace Indo-European structures of violence that fuelled systemic slavery and imperial conquests. He therefore proceeded to analyse deep structures of state patriarchy, that is, the processes of masculinization and militarization of a specific society. Diop was consequently graphic in his description of how the Spartan monolithic masculine state was constructed. Here Diop, the authentic African, is hard-hitting in his *nzagwalu* polemics (*nzagwalu* is an Igbo strategy of answering back an insult, which I liken to Diop's resistance polemics; see Introduction):

> In Sparta, all male adults were career soldiers until the age of sixty. They spent their lives in military camps, separated from their wives and children. Family life did not exist, and the existence of the couple was of marginal importance, the proverbial perversion of morals, the extraversion of mas-culine habits raised to the level of an institution in all of Greece, especially in Athens (over which the modern West always throws a veil of modesty), had their origin in the particular style of life, which, long after settlement, still carried the stigmata of the prior period of nomadism. Decency forbids the detailed discussion of the moral decay of Greek society, even and especially at the level of its greatest men: Aristotle, Plato, the family of Pisistratus, the tyrant of Athens, etc. The moral license of Spartan women was legendary. Until he was thirty, the male Spartan slept in barracks and could see his wife only furtively. (1991: 155–6)

The colonization, dehumanization and enslavement of the 'Other' always involves a two-way process, which progressively leads to the decline of the society – involving militarization, loss of freedom, and perpetual fear of revolt (1991: 155). The Spartan state constructed a psuedo-procreative role for itself, thus appropriating the role of women. The state claimed all newborn males, who had to be physically perfect otherwise they were killed. Their training centred on the Spartan ideals of endurance, courage and blind obedience. The child, like all colonial soldiers, was taught to steal to feed himself. He had to catch a Helot by surprise at night and kill him. Since colonialism always leads to regression and decline, between the eighth and the fourth century BC, following violent social struggles, Greece disintegrated.

To Diop, the parallel with the roots of Germanic history was clear, and directly related to the historical movement from nomadism to sedentary life. Theft and murder, the killing of an enemy, were all moral ideals and tests which a young German had to pass before he could enter the circle of adults.

Diop attributed to these Indo-European state systems certain characteristics of the contemporary states, such as state repression, racism and xenophobia. The classical individualistic European city state had been incapable of territorial centralization or even defending itself. It was the conquests of 'the semi-barbarian' Philip II of Macedonia in 338 BC which led to a transformation from the individualistic city state to the Egyptian model in preparation to invade Persia. It was also this regime which reversed previous reforms by introducing new decrees which have strong echoes of the reactionary anti-revolutionary contemporary state's obsession with the maintenance of law and order and banning of the processes through which the masses had overthrown their rulers – that is, the role and status reversal processes such as banishment of rulers, confiscation of the property of the wealthy, redistribution of land, abolition of debts, liberation of slaves, etc.

Diop maintains that this counter-revolutionary reaction which was led by the monarch was carried into modern times. Also all subsequent empire-seekers seem to have copied the Egyptian state model, from Alexander the Great, and others after him, to the new Greek kings of the Hellenistic epoch. Diop wrote:

> It was therefore the AMP state that was perpetuated by integrating some elements of the bygone city of antiquity. The cult of the sovereign was instituted, which took on divine character, as in Egypt … the Indo-European religion of the city, too individualistic and Xenophobic, died; it was vanquished by the new oriental cults and, in particular, by the cult of Isis, which introduced universalism, the notions of the immortality of the soul and of individual salvation in the Northern Mediterranean. (1991: 163)

> [T]he present difficulties encountered by world revolutions are to a great extent linked to the AMP character of the modern states, on the double plane of the size and complexity of the wheels and structures of organised intervention (United States, Europe, etc.). (1991: 163–4)

Just as the counter-revolutionary xenophobia of the European city state was carried into modern times, so also was intra-European racism – which reduced social classes to ethnicity – carried into modern Europe, surviving the French Revolution and Nazism. Diop writes, 'progressively, since the sixteenth century, this intra-European racism has moved outward, serving sometimes as support and justification for colonial expansion'. As we know, European enslavement and colonization of Africans was tied to the notion of a 'civilizing mission' rationalized by a construct of Africans as inferior or inhuman.

Diop clearly stated that absolute separation of ethnic groups in a situation of conquest 'will always be resolved, in ancient and modern history, by genocide' (1991: 132). Almost prophetic, he wrote, 'most of the present states of the modern world belong to the model of the state founded on genocide' (1991: 133). Hence we are witnessing the systematic elimination of native populations by the contemporary state system founded and built on violence, and the transformation of class conflicts to ethnic conflicts both in Africa and Europe.

Issues raised by Diopian moral philosophy

We have seen how important gender-valued principles were to Diop's theories. The moral philosophy of a polity is as important as its mode of production. This moral philosophy is gendered, giving rise to Diop's contrast between a pacifist ideological superstructure and a warlike morality and militaristic values which generate violence, conquest and imperialism. Therefore, characteristic values and the moral philosophy of a state are very important to Diop. This is to be understood in the context of European racism and imperialism in Africa, the maintenance of its hegemony through violence and the reproduction of this violence. Since Europe constructed a 'civilizing mission' based on imperialism and violence, what are these 'superior values'? Having shown the invalidity of this claim, he showed that there were other possibilities for internationalization, based on less violent and more humane philosophies, under which equally 'high culture' or civilizations had flourished in history – as exhibited in the ancient AMP models, of which the Egyptian/African state model was the most perfected. This encapsulates Diop's point about comparative historical and scientific methods.

Like the Marxists, Diop is critical of social inequality, but is not on a civilizing ideological mission to impose an untested proposed alternative to capitalism, derived from European social history, on Africans. He insisted on contextualization, and I think this is mainly due to his 'law of phenotype', that is, the law of Darwinian bestial violence (1991: 124), which puts firmly on the agenda the historical primacy of racism. This is his main critique of Marxist historical materialism. As we know, class solidarity does not appear to have checked racism.

The historical evidence of racism made Diop a very angry man. This anger gave him strength, confidence and clarity; it is the driving force behind his *Nzagwalu*/resistance polemics. With the recent blocking of armed struggle in Africa, those in literature and social movements need to study this unique African mode of orature and strategy of struggle, that is, the devastating power of 'the mouth' or the hard-hitting accuracy of the 'pen'.

Diop and African Studies

There are specific issues central to African Studies, which are raised by Cheikh Anta Diop's works: Diop's methodological framework and the issues of historical depth, epistemology, African status, African identity, comparative perspectives on culture and political systems, and the central issue of gender and moral philosophy.

As Walter Rodney (1972) said, 'To be colonized is to be removed from history'. Diop put it more forcefully: 'The erasing, the destruction of the historical conscience also has been since time began part of the techniques of colonization, enslavement, and debasement of peoples' (1991: 212). Diop's broad frameworks containing several epistemologies enable us to relocate discourses contextually rather than making the humiliating racist assumption that meaning and self-awareness in Africa only began with European contact, or exist only in reference to European standards.

Coupled with this removal of Africans from their own self-history is a problem with the continuous presentation of Africans as a people with no philosophical history. There is usually a marginalization of the question of epistemology as the history of ideas, and intellectual debate in all fields of learning are introduced with reference to European thought, without concern or respect for Africans as a people who should be understood within their own self-constructed status and identity and as creators of their nations. By so doing, Africanist scholars tend to ignore the primary rule of academic excellence requiring that we lay out the historical intellectual background to specific events.

This is the relevance of Diop's comparative historical methodology. Diop, an African scholar, the best of them all, for he does not magnify out of proportion the petty tyrants we call dictators in Africa today by giving them as much space in books as our political scientists and Marxist scholars have done, in what looks now like a dead-end scholarship, producing an endless, repetitive catalogue of male dictators and their violent regimes. Instead, Diop traced the historical roots of this state based on violence in his historical analysis of types of states and social movements, and different moral philosophies and thus cultural differences and historical continuity. He thereby provided a methodological framework within which can be theorized a lot of work currently circulating as history or anthropology or political science texts, but which are, in reality, simply comments on current affairs.

Diop's historical study of those states based on violence enables us to see the structures of violence in the contemporary political set up. With this awareness, it is easy to see and explain the current forces of imperialism, namely, capitalism, postmodernism, modernization theory, dependency theory, new International Economic Order, Structural Adjustment, the agency role of managers of neo-colonial African states as 'custodians of law and order'. These are all evidence of the triumph of European violence in Africa. This is the triumph of the state founded on genocide which Diop categorized.

In the context of struggles against this contemporary state founded on violence, all alliances have been betrayed and agreed programmes discarded once our men and some male-women have 'captured' state power. This is because the patriarchal state inherited from the Indo-Europeans masculinizes; as Diop argued, it is a violent reproductive machine for imperialism.

As Diop showed, even ancient Egypt had the experience of a peasant revolt. Thus Africans did not begin to resist oppression after World War Two, but well before the usual dating of nationalist struggles in Africanist scholarship, which takes the so-called independence period as the 'dawn of nations' or 'attainment of maturity' for Africans. Giving Africans a post-1945 history and status of national struggle means that we never quite know these Africans as unconquered and uncolonized. It is a Eurocentric perspective. Both the moral and political perspectives continue to raise their valid heads, since in the context of subordination both are inseparable – hence Diop's contrast: 'civilization or barbarism?'

It is the main periods or points of historical rupture that should be of interest. In which case, it would be necessary to give a fuller picture and analysis of the 'moral community' or 'moral nation' (Diop's cultural identity in macro history and micro history), the whole body of philosophical knowledge over time, and the effects of change and continuity. The successful invalidation of and challenge to the supremacist claims of this neo-colonial state come from Diop's wider comparative history and epistemology. This is what leaves room for historical renewal located in the main debate between economic materialism and the status of culture/ideology/moral philosophy.

Mobilizing Diop in the classroom

In order to assess what Cheikh Anta Diop has meant to me both in my scholarly work and the classroom, I want to recall one particular incident that I promised myself to one day acknowledge publicly. In 1990 while teaching (substituting for an absent lecturer and, therefore, an outsider) the ethnography of West Africa course at my ex-university, School of Oriental and African Studies, once again I learnt that African students had had a public confrontation/debate with their all-White European lecturers over the curriculum content of African Studies. The students were questioning what was being taught, how it was being taught, and who was teaching it – in other words, what? how? and who?

I later got some feedback both from the students and one of the lecturers who had had the courage to attend. Many lecturers had not bothered to attend. The lecturer had felt triumphant. According to him, the students did not seem to have an argument, since all they had done was to question why African history was being taught from an anthropological perspective, and why was it that White Europeans felt that they could teach Africans African history. Now, according to this lecturer, the students did not seem to have an answer when asked what they meant by history being taught from an anthropological perspective. The student was, of course, raising the issue of historical depth and comparative method and the lecturer knew that, as much as he did not wish to admit it. These are some of the experiences which African students describe so well. They are situations which leave the disempowered so humiliated and wounded as a result of uses and abuses of privilege and power.

A young African female student had reported this same meeting differently. She had been asking to meet me, through several people, but without being definite about it. Finally, we met and it was a very young woman in her early twenties who sat before me. She was very slim, with long fingers which she locked firmly together while talking to me. In this slight person, I saw so much strength, beauty and courage. Looking straight into my eyes, she told me how they had lost the argument in their meeting with their lecturers. According to this young woman, the African students had had several informal and formal sessions and meetings in which they had shared their experiences of Eurocentrism and racism in the curriculum. They had been very sure how they felt about these issues in their various courses. They had also been quite articulate in analysing these issues during their meetings. But, when it came to saying 'all these things' to their lecturers, they realized that they did not quite know how to express themselves in an academic manner that would command the respect of their lecturers. So they lost and the lecturers won.

As I was watching this young woman, I was crying silently inside. There was no difference between us. I had been in exactly the same position. She said to me that she hoped that I would resource students to enable them to articulate these problems better. In response, I showed her some of the literature which I had added to the course, particularly because of the African students. She told me she knew I would do it. Approval by that young woman was a morale booster for me.

I have gone to some length in recounting this incident in order to show that scholarship and the classroom are spaces of political struggle, just as much as anywhere else is. I have consequently argued that it is in a colonial or neo-colonial context – that is, in the given reality of Euro-Western imperialism – that the continuous decolonization movements (mental and concrete) are to be understood. It is also in this context that I have pointed out the importance of the work of Cheikh Anta Diop, which I have used extensively. His macro history and what he termed 'history of sociology' provided a 2000 years' depth comparative socio-historical study in *Precolonial Black Africa* (1987). This method or framework enabled him to see differently alternative bodies of knowledge other than European constructed epistemologies. With his 5000 years' historical depth study of comparative state systems in world history in *Civilization or Barbarism* (1991), Indo-European socio-cultural formations could at last be subjected to comparative critical analysis from an 'objective' African perspective. It is in this sense that I see Diop as both a deconstructionist and a renewer, opening up new grounds for creativity and social research.

In *Precolonial Black Africa*, Diop listed the specific social institutions constituting the socio-political structures, which can be investigated in his proposed 'history of sociology'. They include: (a) aspects of national life; (b) the administration; (c) the judical organization; (d) the economic organization; (e) the military organization; (f) labour; (g) the techno-logical level; (h) migrations and formations of peoples and nationalities, and their ethnic and linguistic genesis.

Diop obviously understood scientific comparative method to mean something different to the way European scholars have understood and used it. To him, scientific methodology means comparison of like with like, of practices in African social institutions with practices in Europe for the same period. Thanks to the historical comparative methodology of Cheikh Anta Diop, questions have been posed here in a way that 'the centre' and its mainstream academics cannot fail to respond to if it is to retain even one iota of its claims to democratic liberalism.

I pay tribute to this great Pan-African thinker, scholar and revolutionary whose work gave scholarship meaning and purpose for me, at a point of near despair and hopelessness. I am glad that I have had the opportunity to introduce students to Diop. This has given me the unique privilege of witnessing the most amazing transformations in the commitment, confidence and intellectual curiosity of 'Black'/African students once they have grasped the scope, perspective and methodology of Diop's scholarship, even if we do not always agree with him.

I am also glad to say that these positive changes are not limited to 'Black' students, that White students have also expressed a new awareness and sometimes anger that these texts have been denied them by mainstream academia. To these White students, it is unbelievable that Africans do not seem to be making the most of these invaluable resources as a framework, a guideline and a reference, using these ideas and narratives to think with and quarrel about.

Based on Diop's proposed framework for a 'history of sociology', I developed an accredited access course in Britain, entitled 'sociology of African history'. It was extremely popular with African diaspora students/youths, and it can also be taught at undergraduate level. At the time, some wondered why I called it 'sociology of African history' and not social history. I argue that social history should absorb what is currently considered as anthropology, that is, the social of the micro history of particular communities, groups, nations, etc. – ethnography or ethnology being primary field work, whose destination is in social history. Sociology of history, therefore, involves more general thematic concerns in the social of macro history.

Distinguishing these two levels of history Diop wrote in *Civilization or Barbarism*:

> But then, what would we call an African history? We need to distinguish two levels: The immediate one, of local histories, so dear, deeply lived, in which the African peoples, segmented by diverse exterior forces the principal one of which is colonization, are shriveled up, find themselves trapped, and are vegetating today.

A second level, more general, further off in time and space and including the totality of our peoples, comprises the general history of Black Africa, insofar as research permits restoring it today from purely scientific approach: each history is thus pinpointed and correctly situated in relation to general historical coordinates ...

The review of the historical and linguistic factors as constituent elements of cultural personality brings to light the necessity for a total recasting of the African program of education in the fields discussed above, and for a radical centring of these on Egypto-Nubian antiquity, in the same way that the Western educational system has its foundation in Greco-Latin antiquity: there is no way more certain, more radical, more scientific, more sane and salutary to reinforce the African cultural personality and, consequently, the cultural identity of Africans. (1991: 214, 215-16)

This then was Cheikh Anta Diop's own idea of Afrocentrism. It is African centred and not the direct opposite of Eurocentrism which is directly linked to the European project of imperialism. Diop is talking about self-definition and self-determination in creative difference.

Need I say that issues raised here are also equally a challenge to our African and other Black male colleagues in the Afrocentricity school in the United States and the Curriculum Movement as a whole. So far, unlike Diop to whom gender ideology was a central issue, these other brothers of ours have failed to address the fundamental issue of gender politics, and are therefore unable to discuss an alternative, non-masculinist philosophy and political system to the centrist European imperialism that they seek to overturn. For this reason, their arguments have so far remained within the monologism of masculinist patriarchy and its inherent oppression and violence, as they continue to stress imperial achievements that rival or outshine those of the Europeans. Cheikh Anta Diop's gender-determined moral philosophy equips us to counter and move beyond Eurocentric patriarchy and racism.

Bibliography

Amadiume, Ifi, 1992, 'Gender and social movements: the relevance of Cheikh Anta Diop's *Civilization or Barbarism*'. (Paper presented at CODESRIA 7th General Assembly on the theme: Democratization Processes in Africa, in February 1992, Dakar, Senegal.)

— 1995, 'Gender, Political Systems and Social Movements: A West African Experience', in Mahmood Mamdani and E. Wamba-dia-Wamba (eds) *African Studies in Social Movements and Democracy*, CODESRIA Publications, Dakar, Senegal.

Bachofen, Johann, 1861, *Das Mutterrecht*, Benno Schwabe Co. Verlag, Basel.

Bernal, Martin, 1987, *Black Athena: The Afroasiatic Roots of Classical Civilisation, Vol 1: The Fabrication of Ancient Greece 1785-1985*, Free Association Books, London.

Diop, Cheikh Anta, 1987, *Precolonial Black Africa: a Comparative Study of the Political and*

Social Systems of Europe and Black Africa, from Antiquity to the Formation of Modern States, Lawrence Hill & Co., Westport, Connecticut.

Diop, Cheikh Anta, 1989, *The Cultural Unity of Black Africa: The Domains of Matriarchy and of Patriarchy in Classical Antiquity*, Karnak House, London.

— 1991, *Civilization or Barbarism: an Authentic Anthropology*, Lawrence Hill Books, New York.

Gimbutas, Marija, 1982, *Gods and Goddesses of Old Europe 7000–3500 BC: Myths, Legends and Cult Images*, University of California Press, Berkeley.

Rodney, Walter, 1972, *How Europe Underdeveloped Africa*, Howard University, Washington.

3 Theorizing matriarchy in Africa: kinship ideologies and systems in Africa and Europe*

My major problematic in this chapter is the theorization of the vexing concept of matriarchy, not as a totalitarian system – that is, the total rule governing a society – but as a structural system in juxtaposition with another system in a social structure. Using contemporary data, I intend to throw into doubt certain established Eurocentric certainties about the origins and social character of kinship.

It has become increasingly clear that there is a major point of difference between Eurocentric scholarship and an Afrocentric perspective, particularly as represented by the work of the African scholar Cheikh Anta Diop, on the so-called scientific reconstruction of both human origins and the origins of social forms, especially the institutions of kinship, kinship ideologies and the state (Cheikh Anta Diop, 1991).[1] It is these key differences in the understanding of matriarchy that I am attempting to highlight in this chapter and I shall, hopefully, establish the possibilities for a creative theoretical formulation of gender and empowerment in African social histories.

Henry Maine's Patriarchal Theory: the persistent European model

Adam Kuper (1988) has provided a useful assessment of nineteenth-century European male theorists of kinship and descent. What seems clear to me from his review is that, in spite of the general claims to a comparative historical perspective, these theories were derived from specifically Indo-European histories but applied well beyond the European experience. Other peoples and their cultures were seen through European eyes, with the result that the so-called scientific reconstructions were full of subjective bias, prejudice and falsifications, as demonstrated by Cheikh Anta Diop (1991).

The nineteenth-century debate on kinship became simplistic when seen as a dichotomized choice between matriarchy and patriarchy as the determinant of the total social structure, and as a general progressive evolution from one system to the other. Yet it was not the structural relationship of institutions in a society that was studied, but the jural codes – that is, the instrument devised for ruling and not the character of that which is to be ruled or controlled. Thus, from his legal background, Henry Maine (1861) theorized a totalitarian patriarchy: a primordial patriarchal despotism for the human race. His one general gender history is known as the Patriarchal Theory, which forms the basic patriarchal paradigm in European philosophical and political thought. His so-called comparative jurisprudence was strictly limited to the Roman patriarchal agnatic corporate group system. Here, the central focus of power was the father, and the factual importance of motherhood kinship structure and history was denied.

On the origins of wider society itself, Maine's theory stated a movement from status to contract with the idea of citizenship and individualism. From this strictly European experience, Maine concluded that individualism and social contract were the highest form of civilization and superior to kinship-based status systems. Since African systems were seen as status systems and lacking the concept of state, they were placed on the lowest rung of the ladder of development and civilization. The implication of this position is that the oppressive rule of absolute patriarchy is the highest form of civilization. Diop (1991) has argued that this basic patriarchal ideology was reproduced at the state level in the European model, but that the actual concept of state came to the Europeans from Egyptian Africa as a result of direct colonialism.

Having thus developed a theory of a primordial patriarchy, and a progressive development from family societies, to gens (house), to houses, to 'tribes', and then to societies of territory and state, Maine (1871) found supportive evidence from the German village community and that of an Indian Hindu village. Both had had direct Aryan influences. Maine's data were therefore based on Indo-European social history, and his theory became known as the German model.

Cheikh Anta Diop and the matriarchy theorists

Diop would have no quarrel with the Patriarchal Theory of Henry Maine as long as it is limited to Indo-European social history. His disagreement was with generalized evolutionist theorists of kinship, marriage and mother-right/matriarchy, such as J.M. McLennan (1865;

1876), L.H. Morgan (1871) and J. Bachofen (1861). They postulated a progression from barbarism and savagery in primitive sexual promiscuity, to matrilineal descent, to matriarchy and mother-right, and, finally, to masculine imperialism in patriarchy, monogamy and the nuclear family. All these so-called scientific reconstructions were based on ethnographies of nineteenth-century Australian Aborigines, eighteenth-century Iroquois Indians, ancient Greeks, Imperial Romans, ancient Germans, and ancient Hebrews.

Diop does not follow the theory of a general evolution, but is specific about where and when patriarchy came into being as the ideological superstructure of a specific socio-economic formation (Diop, 1991). He traced the origin of patriarchy to the nomadic proto Indo-Europeans (the Kurgans), who came from the Eurasiatic Russian Steppes between the Caspian and the Black Seas. Diop attributed to them all the inequities of a violent sociocultural formation, namely nomadism, patriarchy, the veneration of warrior deities, and the domestication of the horse – the instrument of conquest and mass destruction. It was these nomads who, in 3400 BC, invaded and wiped out the ancient European civilization which Diop claims originated from the Cro-Magnoids in the south and the last Negroids from Africa. Acording to Diop:

> patriarchy became solidly established in the Indo-European societies at the end of the Iron Age, with the arrival of the Dorians in Greece. This occurred in Rome, Persia, Aryan India, Greece, etc.; and it is inconceivable to project a matriarchal past onto the very people who were the vehicles of patriarchy, particularly the Dorians. All evidence suggests that these were people who went from hunting to nomadic life without ever experiencing the sedentary phase. It was only afterwards, with the conquest of the agricultural regions, that they became sedentary. (1991: 20)

Diop (1989) postulated four cradles or histories of kinship and gender: Africa as the agricultural matriarchal south, Europe as the nomadic patriarchal north, the Mediterranean basin as the middle belt where matriarchy preceded patriarchy, and Western Asia as the zone of confluence.

In all the so-called scientific comparative reconstructions by nineteenth-century theorists, African data were left out. It is significant that it was African data that effectively overturned theories of a general evolution of kinship. The concept of matriarchy as female rule has been the main reason why the idea was ruled out as non-existent in history. Diop mashalled an array of empresses and queens from as far back as the fifteenth century BC and through into recent history, from

Ethiopia, Egypt and the rest of Africa – to challenge this Eurocentric conclusion. He argued that in precolonial Africa there was no transition from matriarchy to patriarchy, since the social structure was essentially matriarchal in the sense of female rule, female transmission of property and descent, and man being the mobile element in marriage or sexual union. Fundamental changes in the African social structure began with Arabo-Islamic invasions (Diop, 1987), and became more far-reaching under European imperialism (Diop, 1989).

Contemporary African data and the matriarchy debate

It would be easy to dismiss all these 'reconstructions' as based on long dead and static ethnographies and therefore irrelevant to contemporary issues. Yet the problem of history and continuity cannot be so easily ignored, as Emmanuel Terray (1972) argued in his essay on Morgan's *Ancient Society* (1877) and its importance for contemporary anthropology. The relevance of historical materialism is the fact that one can look at continuity, reversibility, transitory systems, aggregates, borrowing from systems, actual processes of negotiation and new formations; but, more importantly, one can locate instances of cultural imperialism following foreign invasions. In a colonial conquest, radical change derives essentially from forces external to a social structure. Colonial rules are violent impositions, and are maintained by violence (see Chapter 5 in this book and Amadiume, 1992).

On the question of kinship structures in contemporary social formations, Diop points out dynamic social processes which overturn any strict theories of a single progression or pattern of change. He maintains that it is the material condition and not race which determines the structure of kinship and its patterns of change or evolution. Far from seeing a complete transformation from matriarchy to patriarchy as an event completed in ancient times, Diop maintains that these processes are still taking place today:

> This transitional phase, the passage from matriarchy to patriarchy, is rich in information for sociology. We see at work the very historical and material conditions that have given rise to both the matrilineal and patrilineal systems and the avuncular relationship.
>
> Kinship, filiation, inheritance, all derive essentially from the privileged social situation of the spouse who remains in his or her clan and therefore hosts the other. (1991: 116)

Citing Evans-Pritchard and Robert Lowie, Diop refers to their data on the Nuer, the Ouehi of Ivory Coast, Hupa Indians, Pueblo Indians, the Hidatsa, Owambo of South Africa and the Khassi of Assam. In all these cases, filiation was matrilineal and the child bore the name of the mother's clan. Husbands went to wives. However, the child's name changed according to where the child went. If the wife moved to the husband's clan, the child took its father's clan name. Diop did not therefore take woman exchange as given, as is stipulated by the alliance theory – that is, woman as an object to be exchanged by Lévi-Strauss's men (Levi-Strauss, 1969).

I believe that this objectification of woman is the main failing of McLennan (1865); although, according to Kuper (1988), he effectively overturned Maine's theory of primordial patriarchy by focusing on the actual means of reproduction – the mother. However, I believe that he unfortunately postulated the thesis of exogamy and wife-capture. He therefore saw women as objects to be moved, owned or shared, a central thesis of the alliance theory which saw woman as an ex-changeable and stealable object, while men generated hostility and managed warfare. This line of thinking consequently led to the theory of a universal incest prohibition to mark the triumph of 'culture' over 'nature' and, by association, the exchanged woman.

From his study of wide-ranging 'primitive people' and Indian polyandry and infanticide, Mclennan had made the important point that the first kinship system had to be traced through the one constant and certain person – the mother, since at first, biological fatherhood was unrecognized. After this, there was wife-sharing by a set of brothers. With the practice of polyandry, society was getting close to the recognition of fatherhood. Then finally with levirate, fatherhood became recognized, since this implied ownership. There then followed the development of economic property and rules of inheritance and, therefore, agnation. Following this formulation, family came at the end and not at the beginning as postulated in the Patriarchal Theory from the German model.

It seems to me that the main problem in these theories of kinship is the construction of woman as an object to be moved or owned. If kinship is determined through the one constant and certain person – the mother – and if we remove the concept of movement and owner-ship and focus on the African concept of collectivism and usufruct access to land, we are back to the basic matriarchal tripartite structure or what I might call the matriarchal triangle consisting of mother, daughter and son. These kinship terms should be seen as classifications in a grouped collective sense and not in the European individualistic sense.

By focusing on this structure and the wide-ranging possibilities of shift of power, we can at least theorize about structural change, and compare the social dynamics of coexistence of different but interracting cohesive systems. This cuts out the limitations of theories based on assumptions and the racism of unilinear evolutionism or simultaneous universal transformations.

Writing on the transformation in African dynastic matriarchy in ancient Egypt between the Third and Fourth Dynasties, Diop (1991: 105) argued that there was plenty of evidence of ancient or indigenous feminine forms showing designation of uterine descent through daughters. Egyptian *sat* equals daughter, and *sent* equals sister. Whether a woman is called daughter or sister, it seems to me, would depend on the gender focus. If the mother is the focus, she is daughter. If the son is the focus, the same mother's daughter becomes sister. With transition to patriarchy/matriliny, as in the Wolof example, *sat* equals grandson, descent, which is a derivation from *sant*, the proper name of a clan which perpetuates the family line and is derived from the family line of the mother. With a patriarchal shift of focus, the reference is to the sister of the uncle in a matrilineal system. In this way, there was transmission of rights and perpetuation of the clan through sisters, who in actual fact are a mother's daughters.

The matriarchal structure of kinship, or the matriarchal triangle of power, was reproduced in African queendoms as the tripartite power-sharing system. The names of the queens were uttered jointly with those of the kings on the throne to be occupied. Diop refers to Ibn Battuta's testimony on fourteenth-century Mali that men were not named after their fathers; that genealogy was traced through the maternal uncle; and that sons of the sister inherited to the exclusion of his own children (ibid.: 107).

The origin of culture based on Lévi-Strauss's (1969) theory of incest taboo depends entirely on belief in the exchange of women. In the old matriarchy proper and its tripartite mother-focused system, if incest was allowed, as in ancient Egypt (Reed, 1974), Burundi, etc., the children would come from daughters/sisters who remained at home. If incest was not allowed, children would still come from daughters/sisters remaining at home in the so-called matrilineal system, or as a result of the widely practiced woman-to-woman marriage, or male daughter institutions. With the old system of marriage where men provided agricultural labour for sexual access to a woman's daughters, children would still come from daughters/sisters who remained with their mothers. These practices, particularly the institution of woman-to-woman marriage, mean that neither exchange nor ownership need take place. The matricentric structure does not need to be dismantled for the purpose of reproduction.

The whole thesis of incest taboo as marking the beginning of civilization, following the assumption that clanic organization is founded on incest taboo and that clanic organization marks the progression from animality/nature to order/civilization, in actual fact only explains the beginning of patriarchal exchange and ownership. It does not explain the beginning of social regulation on sexual relations, for there is an assumption that the matricentric unit is not itself already a cultural construct – that is, that the mother or the woman cannot make culture and rules. She does not have a distinct social unit or material base for that mode of production. Yet in the African data, the matricentric unit is an autonomous production unit; it is also an ideological unit.

Diop says that the pure state of matriarchy was only at the truly elementary stage of the first emergence of the matriarchal clan, and was characterized by avuncular inheritance. Is he calling matriliny matriarchy? Or is he saying that matriliny is a characteristic of matriarchy? He makes the important point, however, that mistakes made in analysis of matriarchy result from studying clans in Africa which have already undergone very complex evolution.

The notion of the pure primitive stage in Africa used by anthropologists is a fallacy and has led to a racist 'othering', maintaining a constant savage and primitive Africa to a civilized, high-cultured Europe (Mudimbe, 1988). As Diop (1987) argued and demonstrated in his reconstruction of precolonial Black Africa, with his 2000 years' historical depth study of ancient African socio-political systems, African societies had been densely populated and extensively centralized under empires and monarchies in well-developed urban cities and with thriving international commerce. Diop called it the period of detribalization which lasted up to the sixteenth century.

Under the territorial state of the African dynastic state model, seemingly autonomous villages were in actual fact subjects of the city-based monarch (Diop, 1991). African societies had again retribalized to different degrees during the period of the Atlantic Slave Trade from the sixteenth century, following the Trans-Saharan Slave Trade and the weakening of authentic ancient African empires by Arabo-Islamic conquests and imperialism (Diop, 1987). Regression and decline then intensified under European colonization and the imposition of the European state system. As Diop writes, as a result of all these forces of change, '[t]here was then a co-existence of tribal and monarchical elements as well as varied systems of filiation that misleads the observer who is not perspicacious' (Diop 1991: 119).

It is these varied coexisting systems that interest me, particularly how under our very eyes gender valued colonial influences are leading to specific types of radical change in the structures of kinship. These types of transformation did not take place either in the centralization in the ancient monarchies or under Islamic colonialism, as Diop acknowledged that even in the African monarchies 'the matriarchal system was subjacent' (ibid.). Instead of 'subjacent', I have called it juxtaposition of systems (Amadiume, 1987).

In contrast to African socio-political systems, even under colonial pressures of change, in Indo-European societies there was an absence of a *matrius* opposite a *patrius* in the juridical role (Diop, 1991: 121). This to me explains the source of the Patriarchal Theory. Diop is very concerned to show that these historical structural differences in social structures between Europe and Africa had nothing to do with race, but with changes in the material condition.

Similar arguments concerning the varied character of African systems of filiation were made by Wendy James (1978) in her critique of Engels's theory of a historical loss of woman power as a result of property and ownership. Whereas Diop's thesis stressed the difference in ideological construct, that of Frederick Engels (1891) was based on a materialistic construct. However, in a moral sense, both arrived at the same conclusions. Diop characterized the Aryan Greek and Roman cultures of Europe as idealizing the patriarchal family, war, violence, crime and conquests. Guilt, original sin, pessimism and individualism pervaded their moral ethics. Their women were home bound and denied a public role and power, being totally under the control and ownership of fathers and husbands to whom they were chattels (Diop, 1989).

Based on ethnographic and historical reconstruction, Engels made the following contrast: non-class and pre-class societies were based on an egalitarian tribal order in which sexual (gender) egalitarianism reigned. Everything was communally owned and people fulfilled their subsistence needs. Families in the European sense did not exist, rather there were large communistic households which were centred on women and where decisions were reached consensually. Women's kinship bonds formed the basis of women's solidarity.

This egalitarian, woman-centred and caring society was overturned by men (we do not know precisely when, how and why) with the introduction of the notion of ownership, which saw woman as property and a thing to be owned. This, to Engels, was the beginning of class societies and associated characteristics of ownership, inequality, the male-centred family as an economic unit, the dependent wife and decline in the social status of woman, and the appropriation and exploitation of surplus production for exchange. Engels's indictment of European patriarchy and capitalism was articulated in strong moral language, in expressions such as 'the slave of his lust and a mere instrument for the reproduction of children' (about the servitude of the European woman to man); 'icy water of egotistical calculation'; and 'callousness' (about the logic of capitalism).

These transformations led to changed gender relations with state intervention in the family, as industrial production was presented as the valued public and power domain. On the other hand, labour in the family was considered domestic and a valueless private domain. Hence, as argued by a tendency in European feminist scholarship, the universal subordination of woman is directly related to her domestic role (Rosaldo and Lamphere, eds, 1974). This was yet again a generalization from a specifically European experience.

Like Diop, James countered that the historical experience of African women was different, since they had relative structural power in all institutions of social organization, but failed to theorize this reality of empowerment. She looked at descent from anthropological data, pointing out that Africa is the major home of matriliny, which she defines as 'the systematic tracing of descent through women'. This matriliny remains dominant in some regions, while in some cases it belongs to recent history, hence James' expression 'the persistence and resilience of matriliny among many of the populations of the continent' (1978: 141).

One of the disagreements which James had with Engels's formulation was the representation of matriliny and female rule as the same thing. This suggests that James is saying that matriliny (the tracing of descent through women) is not matriarchy, that is, 'female rule'. To her, the supposed historical passage from matriarchy to patriarchy 'belongs to the realm of myth and fantasy rather than history' (ibid.: 143), and the evidence used for matriarchy echoes the Amazon myth of the ancient Greeks. So, we are quite clear that James understands matriarchy as 'female rule'. Having dismissed matriarchy, James concerned herself with patrilineal and matrilineal descent systems, assessing which of them is more stable politically and which gives way to the other.

James dismissed Engels's assumption of the mutual exclusiveness of modes of lineal descent and a universal unilinear evolution, stating four reasons:

1. There is no clear link between gender and a specific line of descent, that is to say, power and authority of a specific gender are not

linked to a type of descent system. As James put it, 'In fact it would not even be agreed by modern anthropologists that such a correlation can be found' (1978: 143).

2. There are dual descent systems and non-unilineal modes of reckoning inheritance and succession.
3. The persistence of matriliny in sophisticated political organizations.
4. Continuing relevance of matriliny as a metaphor (biological connection between generations), and matriliny as a moral system.

By dismissing the link between gender and a particular type of descent, specifically the possibilities of authority and power for women in matriliny (Schneider and Gough, 1961; Fox, 1967; Schlegel, 1972), I believe that European anthropologists were misled by their own ethnocentrism into insisting on a general theory of male dominance in all types of descent systems. However, it is on the structural analysis of the metaphorical symbolism of matriliny (biological connection between generations or motherhood) and the matriarchal ideological construct generated from this symbolism that Eurocentric scholarship has failed African Studies.

The importance of Diop's comparative historical perspective is in his understanding of matriarchy/matriliny as a shift of focus from man at the centre and in control to the primacy of the role of the mother/sister in economic, social, political and religious institutions (Diop, 1989). In the anthropological framework, these are the institutions which make up a society or a social system. The European writers did not seem to have had a parallel historical experience of mother-focused systems to draw from. Their patriarchal paradigm was taken from the fixed point of the father. This affected their understanding and interpretation of African data. They kept looking for man as father or man as the axis around which all rotated, or man as the owner and the controller of everyone and everything. James called it the 'patrifocal syndrome'.

The invisible, transitory or distant role of man as father in African kinship was extremely difficult for the European mind to accept, as can be seen from James's quotes from famous anthropologists such as Lévi-Strauss (1969), Evans-Pritchard (1965), and I.M. Lewis (1976). These European men were perplexed by the imagined 'conflict between male domination and citizenship traced through women', as Lewis put it. Since they assumed male dominance, citizenship traced through women was a strange phenomenon. The general position was that the seizure of political control by women would transform matriliny to matriarchy, and artificial insemination would make things very different.

Consequently, there was a failure to see the culturally constructed invisibility of the father role as approximate to artificial insemination.

Unlike the Europeans, Diop as an African had no difficulty in talking about a 'matriarchal regime'. James in contrast rejected the application of matriarchy, suggesting an alternative view of matriliny which focuses on ideas of citizenship and identity, authority, status and ties of loyalty, instead of focusing on structures of power, and therefore contradictions and conflicts. Following Evans-Pritchard, she concluded that on the status of women, one is dealing with 'a moral question'.

In genealogical representation of a so-called patrilineal society, women are left out, but in a matrilineal diagram, individuals are defined through female links. Consequently, James writes:

> Society is more than a diagram, and where the matrilineal principle is enshrined, for whatever practical or symbolic purpose, the nodal position by women must be more than a diagrammatic matter. There must surely be evaluative connotations, even a theory of the central focus provided by women in the definition of social relations stemming from the matrilineal principle. The granting of a key position to women in the logical, formal ordering of wider relations surely invites us to look further, not necessarily for 'female rule' in a crude power sense, but for equally strong affirmations of the central qualities, even the primacy, of women's position. (1978: 149)

James goes on to provide examples of the centrally creative role of women in production and reproduction in African societies: founding a family, building a household, and the respected and honoured role of motherhood. This motherhood is 'represented as a central social category, from which other relationships take their bearing – particularly connections with the next generation' (ibid.: 150). Yet James does not describe the organizational unit for the sociocultural construction of these roles, because she is avoiding an analysis of power and conflict – that is, politics. The result is an inhibited analysis of matriarchy; a refusal to see what is staring one in the face!

This is evident in the interpretation which she gives to the case studies cited. On Rattray's 1920s Ashanti data, James points out the prevalence of matriliny, the primacy of the mother as a central fact on which Ashanti ideas focus, the physiology of reproduction as the metaphorical symbol. Consequently, James settled for the term 'matrifocality' as 'an indigenous view of the moral primacy of biological motherhood in the definition of social relations' (ibid.: 150). In Ashanti society, matrifocality was expressed in socio-economic terms and a jural framework of matrilineal descent groups.

This so-called matriliny is therefore both concrete and ideological.

It is through their mother and not through their mother's brother that men trace status, rank and rights. The matrilineal group holds and transmits property. Had James included a study of the political organization, she would have seen the reproduction of the matricentric unit, the tripartite matriarchal triangle at the superstructural level in the centralized political systems, as pointed out by Annie Lebeuf (1963). This would again bring back the much dreaded term 'matriarchy'.

In her second case study, the Uduk of the Sudan-Ethiopian border, James again points out the relevance of matrifocality in the reckoning of status and the social structure: 'in personal and moral terms the mother is the key figure in the kinship world of the Uduk' (1978: 153). Behind the seemingly patrilineal organization there is a matrifocal logic. Having listed several so-called patrilineal societies in Africa in which it is possible to perceive underlying matrifocal ideas, James concludes, 'patrilineages are artificial constructs built up from the fragments of many natural matrilines' (ibid.: 156).

I believe that this is a very important statement which needed to be developed for an analysis of the socio-economic basis of the ideological construct of matrifocality. Matrifocality is a cultural construct even if the metaphor used derives from the female reproductive role. It throws into question the derogatory dismissal of these ideas by European feminists as essentialist and limiting to women's choices. It seems to me that the important thing here is the ideological message generating the notions of a collectivism of love, nurturance and protection derived from womb symbolism. As James says of most African societies, whether patrilineal or matrilineal, 'there is a deeper and historically more enduring level at which the nature and capacity of women are given primacy in the definition of the human condition itself' (ibid.: 160).

James acknowledged that the European experience and fundamental theory of the family are patrifocal. This has led to biased comparisons and caused difficulties in the present analysis of matriliny, just as it affected the nineteenth-century debate on matriarchy. Significantly, James saw bridewealth and the exchange of woman as the key factor responsible for patriarchal formation. If there is not bridewealth, the system shifts back to matriliny. Contrary to James, I am arguing that with matriliny, there is already a shift of focus or power in the matriarchal triangle from mother to son, who in matriliny is seen as the all-important uncle. Yet he is a son, a brother, a husband, an absentee/invisible father, as well as an uncle.

The matricentric unit and the ideology of matriarchy in four African ethnographies

In the critique of Claude Meillassoux (1964) and Emmanuel Terray's (1972) analysis of the lineage mode of production of the Guro of Ivory Coast, I argued that both men imposed a Eurocentric concept of 'natural family' on the Guro data (see Introduction, this volume). In detailing the productive units and the processes of production in order to analyse the socio-economic formations in Guro domestic mode of production, the very basic kinship unit – the matricentric production unit – was left out. Its structural importance was therefore not taken into account.

It is a common error which stems from a definition of reproduction derived from a European patriarchal paradigm which sees woman as an object of exchange. Marriage is consequently presented as a mechanism of physical and social reproduction of the group. Woman in this formulation starts off as an object in a patriarchal exchange and transaction. She is not seen in her autonomous status as mother. Yet the motherhood paradigm is culturally recognized as an autonomous unit, as we have already seen in African constructs of kinship in a few ethnographies.

I have argued that the recognition of the motherhood paradigm prevents the error of taking patriarchy as given, or as a paradigm. Both matriarchy and patriarchy are cultural constructs, but patriarchy is one step above the motherhood paradigm. This is the basis of my distinction of the household as the matricentric unit, and family as a wider construct involving the head of one or more household matricentric units. As I have already argued, the matricentric unit does not need to be dismantled for the purpose of reproduction. Also with the practice of woman-to-woman marriage the family need not be headed by a male.

In order further to press my point about the structural presence of a basic matriarchal system in the social structures of traditional African societies, I examine the following evidence from four ethnographic texts on contrasting African societies.

Nnobi case study (Amadiume, 1987) In the Igbo rural village of Nnobi in contemporary Nigeria, the paradigmatical gender structures of kinship in the indigenous society[2] are in binary opposition. They are expressed or represented concretely, metaphorically or symbolically in the *Obi* (ancestral or family house) which is male, and the *Mkpuke* (the matricentric unit or mother and child compound) which is female. The following is a sketch of the dynamic systems:

Obi – male

Headship = *diokpala* (first son)
di (dibuno) = husband

- the person has a male status in cultural classification of gender
- in biological sex-gender the person can be man or woman.

The unit composition

Headship over:
- one or more *Mkpuke* units (matri-centric units or households)
- therefore family

Economy

- dependent on *Mkpuke* productive units for labour, raw food and cooked food.

Ideology

- patriarchal in ideology of *umunna* (common fatherhood)
- jural force
- competitiveness
- masculinism, valour
- force, violence.

Mkpuke – female

Headship = Mother-wife-mother

- the person is culturally classified as female, even when playing the role of *di* = husband

The unit composition

- matricentric = mother and siblings
- therefore household

Economy

- the smallest production unit
- autonomous
- has its own farm or garden.

Ideology

- matriarchal in ideology of *umunne* (common motherhood)
- moral force
- collectivism
- ideals of compassion, love, and peace.

In Nnobi matriarchy as an ideological superstructure, there is a dialectic between the matricentric production unit and the relations of production. Therefore, those who ate out of one pot were bound in the spirit of common motherhood. This basic ideological superstructure was reproduced at wider levels of social organization in the political order. In the all-encompassing matriarchy, all Nnobi were bound as children of a common mother, the goddess Idemili, the deity worshipped by all Nnobi.

The matriarchal ideology thus provided the logic of overall administration. There were four named days in a week, each of these was also a market day and was named after the goddess in honour of whom the market was held. In these names – Oye, Afo, Nkwo, Eke – the Igbo achieved a logical configuration of a space/place, a time/day and a goddess. Most of the festivals which provided the yearly calendar in the seasonal rhythm of village life were in celebration of life-cycle events and productivity associated with the goddesses.

In the Igbo dual-sex political system (Okonjo, 1976; Amadiume, 1987), the titled women were central to consensual decision making and controlled the marketplaces. In Nnobi, it was *Ekwe* titled women, the earthly representatives of the goddess Idemili, who controlled the village Women's Council, holding overall veto rights in village assemblies. The *Ekwe* system can therefore be seen as a political matriarchal system, which was, however, in dialectical or structural relationship with the *umunna* based patriarchal system, both in dialogue with each other. The middle ground for manoeuvre is a third classificatory system: the non-gendered collective humanity, *Nmadu*, person, which is again based on non-discriminatory matriarchal collectivism, as a unifying moral code and culture generating affective relationships as opposed to the political culture of patriarchy, imperialism and violence.

In Meyer Fortes's data on the Tallensi (1959; 1987), contradictions in the kinship system can be glimpsed, despite suppressed and fragmented information, which suggest that there is a missing system in dialogue with the male-centred patriarchal system. But as a result of the enthnocentric bias of the European ethnographer, the partial and monologic experience of the son became a model for the whole society. Yet a dual-gendered system was in operation. One can consequently accuse Fortes of masculinization of data – a very European syndrome.

The structural significance of female ancestresses and spirits was not analysed from the *soog* kin ideological system, which appears to provide an alternative matriarchal kinship based moral ideological system. The *soog* kin concept, we are told, extended beyond the framework of the lineage and clan. It was in complementary opposition to clan relations and was based on trust and amity. There was, therefore, another ideological system in opposition to patriarchy, but its socio-economic base and the processes of its reproduction were not described.

Similarly Paul Riesman's Jelgobe data (1977) provide a whole set of gendered symbolism in binary opposition in *wuro* (house) equals female equals woman, and *ladde* (bush) equals male equals man. *Wuro* and *ladde* appear to constitute the basic paradigmatical structures of matriarchy and patriarchy, with the father remaining as an outsider to the *wuro* structure. The woman builds and owns the hut, and as such was addressed as head of the house, *Jam suudu*. From this structural unit is derived a whole set of matriarchal meaning and ethics symbolized in the concept of *suudu* – a place of shelter, hut for people, nest for birds and bees, envelope for a letter, a box or case where anything rests or sleeps. Customs, rules and morality binding the wider patrilineage of *Suudu baaba*, the father's house, were derived from this womb symbolism.

In Maurice Bloch's Merina data (1986), we again see two gendered systems of kinship. The matricentric kinship was considered the biological kinship linking children to their mothers and their siblings. At birth, therefore, humans were only matrilineally related. There was a close bond between children of two sisters. The other kinship system is that of descent which was determined by elders. In accordance with these two distinct systems, two systems of belief were reproduced or elaborated in ritual, forming a symbolically gender-valued opposition. Under the heading of female we have woman, the house, household, dispersal, south, division, kinship, and heat; under that of male we have, man, the tomb, the clan, unity, north-east, sanctity and order.

A third category was the Vazimba autochthonous category considered to be the original owners of the land and natural fertility. Vazimba cults were usually dominated by women. There were, therefore, three ideological systems: the matricentric system dominated by a motherhood ideology; the descent system dominated by elders and a patriarchal ideology; and an invisible/inverted/externalized matriarchy in the Vazimba category. In these four ethnographic texts there is a juxtaposition of systems. The matricentric structures generated alternative moral systems available to social subjects, male or female, in the course of social relations. The presence of these fundamental matriarchal systems generating love and compassion means that we cannot take the Oedipal principle of violence as a basic paradigm or given in the African context, as Meyer Fortes unfortunately introduced it into African Studies. The balancing matriarchal system acted as a constraint on the patriarchal structure, checking the development of totalitarian patriarchy and monolithism which are typical of the Indo-European legacy. Out of the European legacy emerged the concept of cultural or moral society as a solid monolith glued together by ritual. That ritual meant patriarchal ideology equals society, equals power, equals state.

Much has been written in denounciation of studies focusing on origins. Yet for colonized people, historical depth and continuity on which a non-colonial status and identity depends is an imperative as strongly demonstrated by Diop (1987; 1991). The advantage in looking at kinship from the perspective of historical origins is in the sense of meaning, in order to locate the origin of a social concept or phenomenon. Others have argued that kinship is best analysed as a phenomenon being created in history, in which case, kinship would therefore be subject to change. Again the problem in this approach, from the point of view of colonized people, is the question of which history is seen and in which history an event is to be contextualized? In any case, there is the fundamental question of what was the original character of that which is undergoing change.

Notes

*This chapter was first presented as a paper at the interdisciplinary conference on Matrilineality and Patrilineality in Comparative and Historical Perspective, University of Minnesota, 30 April–3 May 1992; and at the workshop, Women and Work: Historical Trends, 7–10 September 1992, Centre for Basic Research, Kampala, Uganda.

1. See Ifi Amadiume, 1992. In this paper, I looked at the comparative scientific methodology used by Diop in his study of the ideology of gender in state formations in his 5000 years' historical perspective on socio-political formations and transformations in Egypt/Africa and Europe. I showed specifically how Diop saw the moral philosophy of different types of states as gendered. Hence, he made a contrast between the pacifist ideological superstructure of the so-called Asian Mode of Production (AMP) societies, particularly the matriarchal Egyptian/African model, and the warlike morality and militaristic values of the patriarchal Greco-Roman city state.

2. Data here are presented as static only for the purpose of analysis. The processes and effects of systemic masculinization by British colonization and the imperialism of the neo-colonial Europeanized state on this society has been dealt with elsewhere. See Amadiume, 1987 and Chapter 5 in this book.

Bibliography

Amadiume, Ifi, 1987, *Male Daughters, Female Husbands: Gender and Sex in an African Society*, Zed Books, London/New Jersey.

— 1992, 'Gender and social movements: the relevance of Cheikh Anta Diop's *Civilization or Barbarism*. (Paper presented at CODESRIA 7th General Assembly on the theme Democratization Processes in Africa: Problems and Prospects.)

Bachofen, J., 1861, *Das Mutterrecht*, Benno Schwabe Co. Verlag, Basel.

Bloch, Maurice, 1986, *From Blessing to Violence: History and Ideology in the Circumcision Ritual of the Merina of Madagascar*, Cambridge University Press, Cambridge.

Diop, Cheikh, Anta, 1987, *Precolonial Black Africa: a Comparative Study of the Political and Social Systems of Europe and Black Africa, from Antiquity to the Formation of Modern States*, Lawrence Hill & Co., Westport, USA.

— 1989, *The Cultural Unity of Black Africa: The Domains of Matriarchy and Patriarchy in Classical Antiquity*, Karnak House, London.

— 1991, *Civilization or Barbarism: An Authentic Anthropology*, Lawrence Hill Books, Brooklyn, New York.

Engels, Fredrick, 1891, *Origin of the Family, Private Property and the State* (4th edn), Lawrence and Wishart, London.

Evans-Pritchard, E.E., 1965, 'The position of women in primitive society', in *The Position of Women in Primitive Society and Other Essays in Social Anthropology*, Faber, London.

Fortes, Meyer, 1959, *Oedipus and Job in West African Religion*, Cambridge University Press, Cambridge.

— 1987, *Religion, Morality and the Person*, Cambridge University Press, Cambridge.

Fox, Robin, 1967, *Kinship and Marriage*, Penguin, London.

James, Wendy, 1978, 'Matrifocus on African women', in Shirley Ardener (ed.), *Defining Females: The Nature of Women in Society*, Croom Helm, London.

Kuper, Adam, 1988, *The Invention of Primitive Society: Transformation of an Illusion*, Routledge, London.

Lebeuf, Annie, 1963, 'The role of women in the political organization of African societies', in Denise Paulme (ed.), *Women of Tropical Africa*, University of California Press, Berkeley.

Lewis, I.M., 1976, *Social Anthropology in Perspective*, Penguin, London.

Lévi-Strauss, C., 1969, *The Elementary Structures of Kinship*, Eyre and Spottiswoode, London.

Maine, Henry, 1861, *Ancient Law*, John Murray, London.

— 1871, *Village Communities in the East and West*, John Murray, London.

McLennan, J.M., 1865, *Primitive Marriage*, Black, Edinburgh.

— 1876, *Studies in Ancient History*, Quaritch, London.

Meillassoux, Claude, 1964, *L'Anthropologie économique des Guro de Côte D'Ivoire*, Mouton, Paris.

Morgan, L.H., 1871, *Systems of Consanguinity and Affinity of The Human Family*, Smithsonian Institute, Washington.

— 1877, *Ancient Society*, Macmillan, London.

Mudimbe, V.Y., 1988, *The Invention of Africa: Gnosis, Philosophy, and the Order of Knowledge*, Indiana University Press and James Currey, Bloomington and Indianapolis.

Okonjo, K., 1976, 'The dual-sex political system in operation: Igbo women and community politics in midwestern Nigeria', in N.J. Hafkin and E.G. Bay, (eds), *Women in Africa: Studies in Social and Economic Change*, Stanford University Press, Stanford, CA.

Rattray, R.S., 1923, *Ashanti*, Clarendon Press, Oxford.

— 1927, *Religion and Art in Ashanti*, Clarendon Press, Oxford.

— 1929, *Ashanti Law and Constitution*, Clarendon Press, Oxford.

Reed, Evelyn, 1974, *Woman's Evolution from Matriarchal Clan to Patriarchal Family*, Pathfinder Press, New York.

Riesman, Paul, 1977, *Freedom in Fulani Social Life*, The University of Chicago Press, Chicago.

Rosaldo, M.Z. and Lamphere, L. (eds), 1974, *Woman, Culture, and Society*, Stanford University Press, Stanford, CA.

Schlegel, Alice, 1972, *Male Dominance and Female Autonomy: Domestic Authority in Matrilineal Societies*, HRAF Press, New Haven.

Schneider, D., and Gough, K., 1961, *Matrilineal Kinship*, University of California Press, Berkeley.

Terray, E., 1972, 'Historical materialism and segmentary lineage-based societies', in *Marxism and 'Primitive' Societies*, Monthly Review Press, New York.

4 Women's achievements in African political systems: transforming culture for 500 years*

Today, in African Studies, it appears that African scholars are delving further into history, using much greater historical depth to challenge, reject or re-interpret what has mainly been a Eurocentric construct of African history. This apparent stock-taking exercise is taking place in the various disciplines, including literature. Therefore, in this generalized chapter, which is based on preliminary research aimed at stimulating debate and pointing out new areas for research, I attempt to introduce a critical class and gender perspective into the analysis of African political systems and some of the studies of Ancient Egypt.

How are we to understand the level of violence, dictatorship and violation of human rights on our continent today, if we do not face up to the roles that different classes of Africans themselves played in the history of slavery for example? How are we to understand the ascendancy of patriarchy and abuse of women on that continent today, if we do not re-examine the issue of gender relations historically? Taking a much wider regional perspective, therefore, I show the dynamic relationship between the different state systems, and the effects of external intervention, especially the militarization of the African continent by both the slave trade and by Arab and European colonialism.

My thesis is that there were two opposing tendencies – centralism under feudal state systems, and decentralized anti-state political systems, with matriarchy as an opposing, alternative or ameliorating parallel social and moral system. In these systems, the role of ruling class women was quite different. Which legacy should African women be proud of – the feudal queen mothers or the market queen mothers?

It is therefore something of a paradox that a great majority of African scholars, both on the continent and in the diaspora, have come to hold as ideal and thus glorify types of political systems similar to those which were instrumental in some of the greatest abuses of human rights in the entire history of the world. These are centralized political systems, whether feudal political economies based on chiefship, monarchy or present day nation states. This apparent self-contradiction must be understood in the context of the African experience of Western imperialism and violence over the past five hundred years; as broken and dispossessed people, we would seek self-esteem and to reclaim our rightful legacies.

It is only logical that anywhere something has been broken or destroyed, the need arises to rebuild or reconstruct. But who is to do this rebuilding given the different interests and attitudes to African scholarship? For example, where European scholars might see Africa as an endless sea in which you can catch an infinite variety of fish, on the contrary, the highly respected African-American scholar, Ivan Van Sertima, likened Africa to a shattered diamond, and said, 'we are now putting the pieces together'.[1]

This piecing together has, however, been almost a male monopoly, with all resources pushed into researching the achievements of ancient Egyptians. Scholars like Yosef Ben-Jochannan, Charles Finch and Ivan Van Sertima have, for example, been interested in ancient Egyptian influence on Greco-Roman architecture, philosophy and science. They have pointed out the importance of certain historical achievements as a source of pride for Africans, such as the antiquity of temple building in Egypt; the spiral of the church in Rome being a copy of the church in Alexandria; the invention of mummies; the invention of navigation; and how twelve hundred years before Rome and Greece, an African was able to effect a change in the course of the Nile. Africans were also moving Nubian marble a distance of 250 miles by boat; they were hewing tunnels through rock. The Greek father of history, Herodotus, learnt history in Egypt. All the Greek scientists and philosophers studied in Egypt. If they did not, they found it necessary to claim that they did in order to have some credibility. In Tanzania, Africa was smelting steel at 1850 degrees centigrade in a single process, using less fuel than later comparable Western methods, when this technological innovation was yet unknown in the Western world. Egyptians were also able to conduct a pregnancy test five thousand years ago by observing the effect of urine on cereals. Observers also described a Caesarean section, conducted in hinterland Africa in the nineteenth century, during which the woman was stupified with banana wine.

These scholars have made revelations which show that certain falsehoods, which were and are still taught by Europeans about Africa's so-called primitiveness and backwardness, can only now be understood as a calculated conspiracy to distort and debase for a specific purpose – to justify European racism, and its related imperialism and colonial expansion into Africa.

Van Sertima has summarized some of the findings from this research in his foreword to *Blacks in Science,* in which he writes:

> Five centuries of these falsehoods have been exploded in just five years. These years have seen the discovery of African steel-smelting in Tanzania 1,500–2,000 years ago, an astronomical observatory in Kenya 300 years before Christ, the cultivation of cereals and other crops by Africans in the Nile Valley 7,000 years before any other civilization, the domestication of cattle in Kenya 15,000 years ago, the domestic use of fire by Africans 1,400,000 years ago (one million years before its first known use in China), the use of tetracyclene by an ancient African population fourteen centuries ago, an African glider-plane 2,300 years old, a probe by microwave beams of an American radar satellite beneath the sands of the Sahara, revealing cultures 200,000 years old and the traces of ancient rivers running from this centre. Some of these buried stream valleys seem to be 'ancient connections to the Upper Nile tributaries,' towards which blacks migrated, later peopling Nubia and Egypt. (1983: 5)

However, in spite of these morale boosting revelations, the over-emphasis and focus on ancient Egyptians, as opposed to hinterland Africa, have often been criticized. This focus on Egypt has meant that the limited available resources have also been diverted from the rest of Africa where African culture is still very 'authentic' in the rural communities. Van Sertima (1984) has stated that the focus on Ethiopia and Egypt rests on the existence of more voluminous documents in the Nile Valley, while information on other parts of Africa is much sketchier. To him, these areas are important because the influences of the queens and goddesses of Ethiopia and Egypt have been traced in Western cultures and civilization.[2]

Would it then be wrong to say that this attitude smacks of similar bias in Western scholarship which measures civilization in terms of literacy. As a result of this prejudice, Africa was 'written out' of ancient and classical history. If we are not to repeat the errors of the past, we must adopt a more regional, historical and sociological approach to these studies. We must, for example, address questions such as: What was happening in the social systems in the rest of Africa? What was the relationship between the various social systems in the rest of Africa, Ethiopia and Egypt? Who was supplying whom, with what, in material terms?

As African scholars, we must commit ourselves to rewrite history with a different emphasis and orientation. This is already in progress, with African scholars devising new methodologies and historiography in African Studies, such as oral accounts, other non-documentary evidence, and a different and more relevant yardstick of culture and civilization. We have realized that if only we can keep our eyes and ears open and let our people speak for themselves, all those characteristics that are truly African can be given voice, and thus be seen in their own right today, in this living world.

My own contribution has been in sharing with others what I consider the greatest achievement of African women and their singular contribution to human civilization: African matriarchy. Both Cheikh Anta Diop and Van Sertima were concerned with the issue of African matriarchy. Unfortunately, this concern has been limited to Egypt. They have speculated on changes which early African matriarchal patterns underwent as the Africans moved northwards into Egypt.

My argument is a contrasting one; considering the degree of political centralization reached by the ancient Egyptians, and the economic and social differentiations seen in the palace culture and life style of their royals, it is obvious that patriarchal masculine culture had already gained some measure of dominance over African matriarchy in Egypt. This is why I highlighted the fact that these African queens seem to have been operating male systems, which would have been exploitative of and oppressive to other categories and classes of women. Some of the queens were in any case wearing male symbols of power, such as a beard or male war garments (Amadiume, 1987a).

Runoko Rashidi (1984) has cited from ancient records how King Apries erected a pair of five-ton, seventeen-foot obelisks which were dedicated to Neith and Tum. There was also a huge court which was the entry to the temple of the goddess. From this entry, the worshippers would pass into an avenue which was flanked by obelisks, statues and sphinxes, and then into the great hall. To Neith, King Apries also dedicated an Elephantine Island, a chamber made of a single block which was cut from a solid rock. We learn that to transport this to Sais required the labour of two thousand boatmen and took three years of unremitting labour. Rashidi describes this venture as 'the sunset of dynastic Egypt, one of her last bright moments'.

In spite of the prominent sculptures of queens and goddesses,[3] the mere presence of such overwhelmingly masculine symbols as the massive pyramids, temples, stone chambers and tombs in their material culture must compel us to ask certain questions: What amount of labour was required to construct and build, or transport these things? How was the revenue for building them derived? What were the relations of production, and how were the workers paid? Given the historical link between colossus sculptures and the celebration of masculinity, patriarchy, dictatorial power and imperialism, such beyond life-size monuments are suspect.

My question is this: at what cost – material, social and human – was this gigantic civilization built? As I argued in Chapter 2, African matriarchy and its decentralizing characteristics (including its inherent system of checks and balances) had already been subverted by central-ism and a feudal political economy. If we recognize this destruction of a more moral system, then it is obvious that ancient Egyptian civilization already embodied in its own social structure its own disintegration and destruction. Royals feed off everyone else; similarly states feed off the people and other weaker polities.

The Egypt generally written about also became an imperial power which indulged in conquest and the use of slaves, although it has been argued that she never became a colonial power.[4] Young Nubian girls can generally be seen serving Egyptian princesses.[5] Again, some have said that Nubian women and royal Egyptian women had equal status.[6] But, there seemed to have been categories of women of other nationalities who served as concubines and prostitutes to royal Egyptian men, while royal Egyptian women were banned from men of other nationalities.[7] All these contradictions existed long before the Persian invasion and conquest in 525 BC, and the final conquest, and destruction of African history and culture in Egypt by Roman conquest and colonial rule.

I seem to have castigated Egypt and not to have praised her. This is not to say that Africans should not acknowledge the positive achieve-ments of that flamboyant civilization which remains an integral part of our African past. Indeed, the West is unceasingly tapping from the cultures of ancients, especially Egypt. What I have tried to do, as an African woman who comes from a people with an ideal of modesty in material acquisition and a strong sense of social justice and democratic rights, is to introduce a critical approach to history; to establish that history is both a social and cultural construct. And as such, how events are recounted depends very much on both the gender and self-interest of the narrator.

This is why we see that even in this piecing together of the 'shattered diamond', in order to reconstruct Africa, men are constructing mascu-linist history contrary to social facts. This is the crux of the difference between my own and Cheikh Anta Diop's formulation of African matriarchy. Diop said that it was a 'harmonious dualism' between men and women (1989). I, on the contrary, argue that it embodied two oppositional or contesting systems, the balance tilting and changing all the time; that was the gender politics (Amadiume, 1987a). However, the peculiarity of the African gender language system was such that men and women could cross gender boundaries, and also share roles and status through genderless terms and pronouns. Gender was therefore a means of dividing, but also a means of integrating and co-opting (Amadiume, 1987b). This is not so in rigid European monologism and gender demarcation of men and women. We shall see that this has structural implications when we look at social structures and political systems in the following section.

Precolonial states in Africa: basis of power and transformation

I now shift the focus to hinterland Africa for an overview of precolonial states in Africa. How were they distributed geographically? What were the processes that led to their transformation? And how did women feature in them?

Even as Christopher Columbus, in the pay of the Spanish monarch, set out in 1492 to the Caribbean and the Americas, initiating a process that would result in a catastrophic devastation of native communities, Africa itself was undergoing fundamental economic, social, political and geographical changes as a result of inter-regional internal trade, wars, and the trans-Saharan commerce and slave trade with Berber nomads, Arabs, Asians and the Chinese. This led to unchecked material accumulation, and the disruption of the anti-centralist community-based traditional African social and political systems.

There were the ancient kingdoms with a history of huge cities, whose cultures stretched up far into North Africa. Europe, according to its historians, was still in the Dark Ages when Timbuktu and Gao were great centres of learning. Mali and Songhai are usually cited as great civilizations. However, its urbanized cities, as distinct from the rural areas where the grassroots population lived, were also centrepoints of accumulation, and occupational, economic and social inequalities. Although we can argue that they were no caste or class structures in the industrial capitalist sense, based on the feudalism and patriarchy of Islam, there was a differentiated educated elite: such as lawyers, jurists, priests and teachers.

There was so much wealth in these centres of accumulation in Africa during this period that when, in 1324, the famous King Mansa Musa of Mali stopped off in Egypt on a pilgrimage to Mecca, his expenditures and gifts were such that there was a surplus of gold. The consequence was a general price inflation in Egypt for a very long period.

After the breakup of the ancient kingdoms, with the new wealth, men acquired destructive military weapons and built new feudal states. In West Africa, these new states, based on wealth derived from taxes, trade and slaves, are usually referred to as the Savannah states. These were the Wolof, Mossi, Mende, Hausa and Fulani kingdoms. In East Africa, Ruanda was also an old Bantu kingdom. They became predatory feudal regimes plundering neighbouring communities, some of which disappeared completely while others were eaten up by these feudal states. Some became slave outposts or agricultural slave villages working for the enrichment of the kings and queens and other ruling elites. There were therefore dynamic social movements and social trans-formations going on all the time. Neither the societies nor the cultures were static, contrary to what European scholarship would have us believe.

Accumulation through appropriation of the fruit of other people's labour means that appropriators resort to more and more violence, since human beings – as history rightly shows – always rebel against oppression in one form or another. In Africa, irrespective of internal social contradictions and conflicts, the most effective and destructive instruments of oppression were imported from outside that continent:[8] horses and firearms, which were used to kill, capture and enslave. The ideology of violence was monolithic masculinist patriarchy, which, according to the great African scholar, Cheikh Anta Diop,[9] had roots in European social systems. It entered Africa gradually through Islam.

On this question of the source of patriarchy in Africa, I have some areas of difference with Diop, as I have expressed in my own work. However, it is generally agreed that it was Europeans who first domesti-cated the horse and used it as an instrument of war.[10] That is what they used to invade and conquer the Asians. This was also the case with gun powder, which the ancient Chinese and Egyptians in their concern with balance and harmony only used medicinally[11] and not for destruction and murder.

The important point is that with the introduction of firearms into Africa in the sixteenth century by European colonizers and slavers, by sea, the whole of the African continent became totally militarized. Human beings became commoditized as slaves and merchandise that could be captured, enslaved and sold, time and time again. The eco-nomies of all the later states from the sixteenth to the nineteenth century were mainly based on slaves.[12] They included the firearms forest states of Benin, Gonja, Dagomba, Nupe, Oyo, Ashanti and Dahomey in West Africa. Militarization in the southern African king-doms of the Sotho, the Nguni and the Zulu was more directly related to a balanced system of inter-group cattle raiding, as part of the mode of production.

For us Africans, the slave trade was our greatest tragedy, because it undermined the very powerful internal trade of real goods on which the continent could have taken off economically.[13] The internal trade was an autonomous economy based on agricultural and craft products, such as salt, grain, cloth, cotton thread, textiles, shea butter, dried fish, kola nuts, tobacco, iron and gold, spices, scents and perfumes, dyes, medicinal herbs, roots and fresh steriods from certain trees, medicinal and mystical knowledge, secrets, etc. Europeans had nothing to do with this extensive network of distribution and trade. Consequently, when historians refer to Europeans in Africa as traders, we wonder what they mean, since the evidence shows that what the Europeans exchanged for land and slaves were no more than gun powder, muskets, alcohol, and sometimes amber and coral beads.[14] These were goods directed at the local rulers. They were therefore exchanging nothing that was of benefit to African people; on the contrary, by the time the Europeans were through with their mission, they had appropriated the people's lands, flooded the place with European consumer goods, undermined the agricultual economy and colonized Africans.

In the ancient Southern African regions and its civilizations – including the great Zimbabwe kingdom, and stretching as far back as the first century – trade routes stretched from Madagascar right into the East African coast, to the Red Sea. They continued on to the Mediterranean, and along the Persian Gulf to India, South-east Asia and Indonesia. They therefore had a highly developed trade and monetary economy, which was linked to the economic system of the Old World. In this process of exchange, Arabs and Asians settled in Africa, sometimes as distinct populations. In some cases, they intermarried with the Africans that they met. There were also cases in which they wiped out African populations or pushed them further inland or kept them on the periphery of city states. These processes were more overt in Arab colonization and settlements in North Africa. This was also the case in European settlements in the Eastern and Southern African regions.

The Chinese were in the Southern African regions even before the Portuguese.[15] This history has meant that the African continent today comprises peoples of various cultures of the world who could now claim to be Africans, if they so wish. But, unfortunately, they do not see themselves as pan-Africanists, but as civilizers and colonizers of Africans – just as their forebears did. Many are still racist in their relations with Africans. In every single case, such settler communities identify culturally with their nation of origin, which enjoys superiority to Africa either through military might or finance capital.

However, with that ruthless militarization of the African continent, these coastal trading states were soon turned into slave states, and new highly centralized bureaucratic states became established, based on ivory trade and trade in slaves – examples are Buganda and Barotseland. Ruling class women played a totally different role in these highly bureaucratized political state systems[16] than the role they played in the traditional African non-state systems that I shall be referring to later on. In the slave state of Dahomey, women were active participants in the enslavement of people. Their ruling class women enjoyed the life style of leisurely palace culture.

Warfare had been made a business enterprise, which meant that there had to be a professional warrior class[17] and a merchant class. In 1850, the King of Dahomey's army consisted of around two thousand men and five thousand women. These were the famous Dahomean Amazons whom black women often recall today when enumerating women's achievements in African history. Yet they were professional soldiers who had nothing to do with motherhood and the rearing of children; and were effectively involved in the capture of slaves. Ruling class women, especially princesses and daughters of the royal families, lived a very privileged life, marrying within the family. The traditional African institution of woman-to-woman marriage had been corrupted into slave ownership. These royal women owned several girls whom they had the right to marry off to whichever man the ruling women chose.[18]

Buganda, another bureaucratized slave state had three kings – the king's mother, the queen sister, and the king himself. This was a common matriarchal tripartite system of power and kingdom sharing between a mother and her children in ancient African political systems which had grown into kingdoms, or more correctly queendoms,[19] since early Arab historians reported the rule of queens in most early African regions. In Buganda, each of these rulers had their own separate palace and estates. In both Buganda and Dahomey, these ruling women did not have their power base in the structures of formal women's organizations, which were a basic institution of traditional African social structures – as we shall see later – they were basically part of the male structure of power.

So far, we have viewed the political system from the top, showing the power base of a ruthless autocracy that was imposed on the African masses by external factors and also protected by the same external factors. However, it is important to stress that on the role of African rulers in the slave trade, some African scholars are in discord with

European scholars.[20] While some European scholars, out of guilt, avoid the issue of the role of Africans themselves in the slave trade, others stress the active role of Africans in enslaving and selling their fellow Africans.[21] Some of them, however, point out that Africans only enslaved their enemies.[22]

In addition to this, African scholars emphasize the detonating and corrupting effects of the social conditions created by the very presence of war and slave hungry Europeans on the continent: namely, their demand for slaves; their removal of those rulers who would not agree to trade with them or to their terms of trade; their installation of puppet dictators in their trading posts; and their effective use of Christianity and Western education to impose a self-hating, colonized mentality, leading to the erosion of a people's historical memory and a lack of sense of direction. Religion missionaries and colonizers were racists who saw themselves as civilizers and enlighteners of a 'dark and backward' continent. Thus, the colonialists set about reproducing their own cultures on the African continent. First, they had to produce a mimicking and colluding elite.

The fact still remains that for about five hundred years, Africa was continuously emptied of its people. She was the slave supplying continent to the North African Islamic countries, to Arabia and to India, to serve their ruling classes. European sources claim that almost twelve million (11.7 million) Africans were shipped to the Americas in a matter of only two hundred years (between 1600 and 1800) of the Atlantic slave trade.[23] But the National Coalition of Blacks for Reparation, supported by members of the Republic of New Africa Movement, put the figures at over a hundred million. Western capitalism was built on the sweat and blood of Africans.

By the nineteenth century, the African population had been dealt a great blow by the slave trade.[24] In some places, about thirty per cent of the population were slaves, while in others it was about sixty per cent. In the Islamized Sahel regions, slave populations could even reach over seventy-five per cent of the population, equalling that of ancient Roman patriarchal slavery. In mid-nineteenth-century Dahomey, ninety per cent of the population were slaves. The conditions of the majority of Africans in countries such as these were probably no different from those on the plantations in the Caribbean and America.

After the collapse of the external slave trade at the beginning of the nineteenth century, palm-oil had replaced slaves as an exchange commodity by the mid-nineteenth century. There were consequently palm-oil plantations worked by slaves in some of the slave states. As other cash crop plantations developed, some were also worked by slaves.

Africans were working for the same European companies both on the African continent as elsewhere. They too experienced the conditions of slavery.

Opposition to slavery

This history of slavery did not go unchecked in Africa. Villages rebelled against neighbouring feudal states by migrating. There are many fundamental differences between slavery in Africa and its operation in the European system. One of these was in the status and social mobility of slaves. In the European system, slaves were legally bound as property of their masters. There was no social mobility for the slave, any more than there was for the peasant class.[25] This was not the case in the African system in which a slave was more of a dependent. There was social mobility and slaves achieved impressive worldly success.[26]

In the feudal state systems, since slaves were not seen as an immediate threat, they tended to gain positions of trust or high office in the state hierarchy or the military. This meant that slaves sometimes headed the military, or in fact constituted the entire military force: the Egyptian Mamluks and the Wolof Tyeddo are good examples of this. They sometimes used the military to overthrow their oppressive rulers in a slave revolt. This process took place in Africa throughout the eighteenth century and intensified during the nineteenth century, leading up to the later Islamic jihadist movements, both in the Western Sudan and East Africa, and their wars of conquest.

As the Muslims were subduing Africans and expanding their Muslim states, the Europeans were also in hot pursuit in their own wars of territorial conquest. Finally, all the colonialists met in Berlin and in 1885 signed the Treaty of Berlin. By the terms of this treaty they divided up the land of the African continent – the shattered pieces of the diamond that was Africa – rather as pirates sharing the booty among themselves. From this resulted the imposition of nation states in Africa as we know them today.

Twentieth-century neo-colonial nation states in Africa

African history of the past five hundred years, if viewed solely from the top – that is, through the activities of kings, queens and state rulers – has only one simple structure to it: that of appropriation of labour and the violation of human rights. The very nation state systems that the colonialists instituted in the twentieth century, and through which they ruled Africans, also have the same basic structures. The African elites at so-called independence inherited the same structures of power, and have not yet dismantled the exploitative structures of the colonial state.

Gun salutes and flag flying were a symbolic act of performance, and part of the means by which the colonial powers demonstrated their power of weaponry. This was done in order to terrorize and instil fear, and therefore paralyse the African masses, stopping them from rioting and overthrowing dictators in our traditional fashion. With repetition, these acts of performance became a ritual. The African elite today use the same rituals to demonstrate their legitimacy. They are, when demystified, actually acts of violation of the rights of the masses. They are rituals of domination by violence. The fundamental structures of ruling class exploitation have not changed, despite the periodic changes of personnel.

In the next section, I move away from the tip of the pyramid to the base – that is, to the broad mass social structures of real African communities – in order to look at African political systems and the contribution of women in Africa over the past five hundred years.

Women and traditional African non-state political systems

There are two unique and specific contributions that African women have made to world history and civilization. The first is matriarchy as a fundamental social and ideological base on which African kinship and wider social and moral systems rest. The second is directly related to this matriarchal factor. This is the dual-sex character of African political systems, a characteristic uniquely African.

If self-rule, that is, sovereignty or autonomy, is the ultimate goal of social groups, African women achieved this autonomy through their social institutions of women's organizations and the Women's Councils. European women, it seems, never achieved this in their entire history, as their feminist scholars, who are now digging back into their social history, have discovered with bitterness and regret. They have consequently wondered why this 'apathy' and inability to have challenged patriarchy effectively, or at least kept it at bay, prevailed.[27] Patriarchy runs through the organizational principles of all European institutions.[28] Their history of women's struggle is no more than participation with men in working-class industrial strikes in the nineteenth century, and later, the suffragettes and the Women's Movement of the past thirty years.[29]

There is possibly an answer to this puzzle in the history of European women in Cheikh Anta Diop's theory of matriarchy, which is different from that of nineteenth-century European 'social Darwinists', such as Bachofen, Morgan and Engels. They had an evolutionist view of society and development. While Engels was probably not a racist, this cannot be said of Bachofen and Morgan whose theories of social development were definitely ethnocentric and racist. They put European civilization at the top of their graded ladder of superior and inferior, civilized and savage human beings. At the bottom of this ladder was savagery, primitive promiscuity and matriarchy; at the top was monogamous marriage, the nuclear family, and the patriarchy of Greece and Rome. Europeans, they theorized, had evolved beyond matriarchy a long time ago to the superior system of patriarchy. Africa, on the other hand, was still in savage chaos.

Diop (1989) reviewed the works of these men and showed the fallacy of their theories. He showed that the very material that Bachofen presented for Europe clearly revealed that the system was patriarchal right from its early history. Patriarchy did not stem from capitalism and its associated privatization of property and the family as Engels had argued (1891). For Diop, given the dialectical relationship between ecology and social systems, Africa and Europe generated different social conditions and associated social systems. The European system was characteristically patriarchal, while the African system was matriarchal.

Patriarchy and matriarchy are social and political ideologies which directly decide the role and status of women in society; how society is to be organized; and how social subjects are to relate to one another. They are also ideologies which decide the degree of violence and abuse of human rights that is permissible in society. Matriarchy, as was constructed by African women, had a very clear message about social and economic justice. It was couched in a very powerful goddess-based religion, a strong ideology of motherhood, and a general moral principle of love.

This is not the case with patriarchy, which seeks to control and rule women – indeed everyone. It always seeks to appropriate people's right to self-determination and to bring everyone under the rule of the male. It has a basic masculinist ideology which celebrates violence, valour, conquest and power in varying degrees. It is usually imperialistic. However, this patriarchal masculinist imperialism takes on different characteristics under different political economies, or under different social systems.

According to Cheikh Anta Diop (1989), the distinguishing feature of ancient and classical European civilization was the denial of basic rights to their women, who were subjugated under the private institution of the patriarchal, monogamous, nuclear family. Women were confined to the home, and did not have either a public role or much power, even during the period when the family was the unit of production. In this European patriarchal system, first a father, then a husband had the right of life and death over their women, whom they could chastise or sell at will. This is why European feminists say that marriage was the first form of slavery.

Africans, in contrast, were basically agriculturalists. Their basic matriarchal system meant that woman was the agriculturalist, while man was the hunter. For this reason, it was the woman who was the mistress of the house and keeper of the food. Husbands consequently used to go to wives at marriage, hence the bridewealth system and the strong mother-linked ties between brother and sister. This strong love among children of a mother was not undermined by an out-going marriage. In Africa, therefore, a woman's power was based on her very important and central economic role.

Strongly tied to this factor was the general belief in the sacredness of the mother and her unlimited authority, to the extent that this was given expression in the widespread goddess religion. In indigenous African religion, mystical powers and worldly prosperity are gifts inherited from our mothers. The moral ideals of this system encouraged the matriarchal family, peace and justice, goodness and optimism, and social collectivism; the shedding of human blood was abhorrent.

This was the background to women's economic and political prominence in African history. Their economic role was not confined to the household and wider kin-corporate units. They managed and controlled a very extensive market network where they were selling and buying. These marketplaces were also social places where outings were held after life-cycle ceremonies involving birth, marriage and death. Markets and marketing were not governed by pure profit values, but the basic need to exchange, redistribute and socialize. That is why traditional African systems were not capitalist economies. They have variously been described as subsistence, communal, and redistribution economies.

Even though women became wealthy through hard work and boosted their productive force in the household through such institutions as woman-to-woman marriage and through various social ceremonies, all this wealth was redistributed into society. The most women would gain from being wealthy was the right to belong to prestigious associations, such as titled societies, and leadership of the various women's organizations and the Women's Council.

These Women's Councils constituted the leadership of women's autonomous government to which all women of specific villages belonged. In most cases, these women leaders were crowned queens by women themselves. If they abused their power or authority, women themselves removed them. These queens reigned inside the marketplace, which they kept in order. In those anti-centralist or non-state societies which did not believe in having kings and queens, the leaders were simply titled men and women.

There were therefore two governments, that of men and that of women, which were supposed to respect each other's opinions. But, for general matters, everyone met at the village open assembly. Where there was a king, this assembly could be held at the king's court; similarly it was held at the queen's court if a queen ruled. The assembly could even be held inside the marketplace. However, most villages had a common open space where assemblies were held.

The democratic principles governing these assemblies meant that all social groups were present, including the youth, who were usually organized in age-grades or age-sets. Every human being had the right to voice an opinion. Those who showed a gift of oratory became very popular or spokespersons. The system was geared to work by consensus. If dictators emerged in the leadership, they could not monopolize both absolute power and absolute truth. There were devices of removing them through oracular decrees, prophetic movements, the Women's Council and women's movement, use of masquerades or popular mass action. These were social institutions which were embedded in the social structure. Of course dictators could equally hi-jack them for their own benefits, especially the oracles. But for dictators to succeed unchecked, the evidence shows that they had to have the support of outside forces. This means that political activity was intense; people were not necessarily living in bliss and innocence. The right to oppose dictatorship was, however, fundamental.

The majority of African societies were characterized by anti-centralist, non-state systems. They are not the state political systems that I descibed above, whose economic power base came to be solely dependent on slavery. In these anti-state systems, even when slavery became a strong feature of the overall African economy, it was still marginal in these societies as part of their kinship system of placement and replacement of people. This does not mean that this custom was not abused under the pressures of the slave trade. Indeed, these societies were themselves undergoing tremenduous changes as a result of pressures from slave mercenary armies and slave merchants. Protected by no militarily strong kings and armies, they suffered continuous raiding. The bulk of these African societies were constituted in areas from which slaves were captured.

The histories of women and queens who wielded power in these non-state systems is a legacy that African women should be proud of and refer to continuously as a model. Perhaps this is not the case with the women operating in masculine systems of oppression. African women, however, did not have this prominence handed to them on a platter of gold. They fought bravely to achieve it, and to maintain their power and self-esteem. They used every means and strategy available to them, from peaceful demonstrations to mass women's walkouts and exodus – even resorting to total war when all else failed. All these means were employed to oppose British colonial rule in Africa, the most famous of this opposition being the Igbo Women's War in 1929. Throughout our past history, because women rarely applied these extreme strategies of struggle, whenever they did, their demands were met. Women were regarded as the very embodiment of African society and custodians of African culture. They therefore commanded the highest respect. In the eyes of European colonialists, however, women were not sacred. They consequently shot and killed African women who protested against colonial rule.

This unique historical achievement of African women has been experiencing fundamental transformations, if not gradual erosion over the past five hundred years, beginning with the introduction of Islamic patriarchy into Africa by Arabs and Asians. This, as I have shown, was followed by European imperialism in Africa, and finally the present subjugation of African societies and people under European-imposed nation states. It has introduced a new gender politics, favouring men and undermining the traditional system of balance of power politics between African men and women. This European patriarchal system constructs power as solely male and subordinates the female to male rule.

The African elites are guarding these petty-nation states against disintegration at all cost. Their project is the same as that of the European colonizers: the 'civilizing' and 'enlightening' of the African masses! To assist them in this mission, there is the neo-colonial state and its masculine institutions, such as colonial legislation, land rights, naming after the father, monogamy, and other monolithic male institutions, especially the armed forces. They have all proved oppressive to African women. But most oppressive has been the narrowing, if not total closure, of avenues of opposition. As is generally known, African regimes, both military and civilian, monopolize absolute power and absolute truth. In this, they have the protection of the West. That has been their own achievement in the last five hundred years.

Notes

* Public lecture delivered at The College of Wooster, USA, 5 November 1990, sponsored by the Women's Studies Programme.

1. Van Sertima, at a conference which I attended in London, in June 1987.
2. Introduction to Van Sertima (ed.), 1984.
3. Well documented by Rashidi, 1984.
4. On the character of Ancient Egyptian colonialism, see Chapter 2 of this volume.
5. This is what I see in pictures of their wall paintings.
6. Lectures by Theophile Obenga on the theme Ancient Egypt and Black Africa, organized by Karnak House and the School of Oriental and African Studies, London, October 1990.
7. Claims made by Theophile Obenga at this same lecture.
8. See Jack Goody, 1971.
9. Cheikh Anta Diop, 1987; 1989.
10. See Jack Goody, 1971: 68.
11. See Van Sertima (ed.), 1983.
12. Robin Law, 1978.
13. See Claude Meillassoux, 1971.
14. Ibid.; and Robin Law, 1978.
15. See Jack Goody, 1971.
16. See Karen Sacks, 1979.
17. Claude Meillassoux, 1971.
18. Karen Sacks, 1979.
19. See D. Paulme (ed.), 1963.
20. See Walter Rodney, 1966; John Fage, 1969.
21. See Robin Law, 1978.
22. See S. Miers and I. Kopytoff (eds), 1977.
23. See Paul Lovejoy, 1983.
24. See Karen Sacks, 1979.
25. See Cheikh Anta Diop, 1987.
26. See S. Miers and I. Kopytoff (eds), 1977; C. Meillassoux, 1971; Cheikh Anta Diop, 1987.
27. Karen Sacks, 1979.
28. This is pursued further in the following chapters.
29. Lindsey German, 1989.

Bibliography

Ajayi, J.F.A. and Crowder, M. (eds), 1971, *History of West Africa*, 3 vols, Longman, London.
Akinjogbin, A.I., 1967, *Dahomey and its Neighbours, 1708–1818*, Cambridge University Press, Cambridge.

Amadiume, Ifi, 1987a, *Afrikan Matriarchal Foundations: The Igbo Case*, Karnak House, London.

— 1987b, *Male Daughters, Female Husbands: Gender and Sex in African Society*, Zed Books, London/New Jersey.

— 1989, 'Cheikh Anta Diop's theory of matriarchal values as the basis for African cultural unity', Introduction to Cheikh Anta Diop, 1989.

Asad, Telal (ed.), 1972, *Anthropology and the Colonial Encounter*, Cambridge University Press, Cambridge.

Bachofen, J.J., 1861, *Das Mutterrecht*, Benno Schwabe, Basel.

Batouta, Ibn, 1843, *Voyage au Soudan*, trans. Slane, Paris.

Beattie, John, 1959, 'Checks on the abuse of political power in some African states', *Sociologus*, 9: 92–115.

Ben-Jochannan, Yosef, Oduyoye, Modupe and Finch, Charles, 1988, *African Origins of the Major World Religions*, Karnak House, London.

Bernal, Martin, 1987, *Black Athena: the Afroasiatic Roots of Classical Civilisation. Vol. 1: The Fabrication of Ancient Greece 1785–1985*, Free Association Books, London.

Bloch, Marc, 1962, *Feudal Society*, Routledge and Kegan Paul, London.

Bohannan, P. and Dalton, G. (eds), 1962, *Markets in Africa*, Northwestern University Press, Evanston, Ill.

Brown, Judith K., 1970, 'Economic organisation and the position of women among the Iroquois', *Ethnohistory*, 7: 151–67.

Chinweizu, 1975, *The West and the Rest of us: White Predators, Black Slavers, and the African Elite*, Vintage Books, New York.

— 1987, *Decolonising the African Mind*, Pero Press, Lagos.

Cipolla, C.M., 1965, *Guns and Sails in the Early Phase of European Expansion, 1400–1700*, Collins, London.

Davidson, Basil, 1989, 'The ancient world and Africa: whose roots?', in Van Sertima (ed.), 1989.

Diop, Cheikh Anta, 1974, *The African Origin of Civilization: Myth or Reality*, Lawrence Hill and Co., Westport, USA.

— 1978, *Black Africa: The Economic and Cultural Basis for a Federated State*, Lawrence Hill & Co., Westport, USA.

— 1987, *Precolonial Black Africa: A Comparative Study of the Political and Social Systems of Europe and Black Africa, from Antiquity to the Formation of Modern States*, Lawrence Hill & Co., Westport, USA.

— 1989, *The Cultural Unity of Black Africa: the Domains of Matriarchy and of Patriarchy in Classical Antiquity*, Karnak House, London.

Engels, Frederick, 1891, *The Origin of the Family, Private Property and the State*, Foreign Languages Publishing House, Moscow.

Fallers, Lloyd A. (ed.), 1964, *The King's Men: Leadership and Status in Buganda on the Eve of Independence*, Oxford University Press, New York.

Fage, John D., 1969, 'Slavery and the slave-trade in the context of West African history', *Journal of African History*, 10(3): 393–404.

Forbes, F., 1851 (1966), *Dahomey and the Dahomans*, 2 vols, Frank Cass, London.

Forde, Daryll and Kaberry, P.M. (eds), 1967, *West African Kingdoms in the Nineteenth Century*, Oxford University Press, Oxford.

Fynn, J.K., 1971, *Asante and its Neighbours, 1700–1807*, Longman, London.

German, Lindsey, 1989, *Sex, Class and Socialism*, Bookmarks, London, Chicago and Melbourne.

Gluckman, M., 1960, 'The rise of a Zulu empire', *Scientific American*, 202: 157–68.

Goody, Jack, 1971, *Technology, Tradition, and the State in Africa*, Oxford University Press, Oxford.

Gray, R., and Gulliver, P., 1964, *The Family Estate in Africa*, Boston University Press, Boston.

Gugler, J. and Flanagan, W., 1978, *Urbanization and Social Change in West Africa*, Cambridge University Press, Cambridge.

Herskovits, Melville J., 1938, *Dahomey: an Ancient West African Kingdom*, 2 vols, Augustin, New York.

Hoffer, Carole, 1972, 'Mende and Sherbo women in high office', *Canadian Journal of African Studies*, 1: 151–64.

Ifeka-Moller, C., 1975, 'Female militancy and colonial revolt: the Women's War of 1929, Eastern Nigeria', in S. Ardener (ed.), 1975, *Perceiving Women*, Dent/Malaby, London; Halsted, New York.

James, G.G.M., 1954, *Stolen Legacy, the Greeks were not the Authors of Greek Philosophy, but the People of North Africa, Commonly Called the Ethiopians*, Philosophical Library, New York.

Jewsiewicki, Bogumil and Newbury, David (eds), 1986, *African Historiographies: What History for Which Africa?*, Vol. 12, Sage series on African modernization and development, Sage Publications, Beverly Hills.

Johnston, H.A.S., 1967, *The Fulani Empire of Sokoto*, Oxford University Press, London.

Khaldun, Ibn, 1854, *Histoire des Berbères et des dynasties musulmanes de l'Afrique septentrionale*, 4 vols, trans. Slane, Government Printshop, Algiers.

Last, Murray, 1967, *The Sokoto Caliphate*, Longman, London.

Law, Robin, 1978, 'Slaves, trade, and taxes: the material basis of political power in precolonial West Africa', *Research in Economic Anthropology*, 1: 37–52.

Lerner, G., 1986, *The Creation of Patriarchy*, Oxford University Press, Oxford.

Levtzion, Nehemia, 1973, *Ancient Ghana and Mali*, Methuen, London.

Lovejoy, Paul E., 1983, *Transformations in Slavery: a History of Slavery in Africa*, Cambridge University Press, Cambridge.

Meillassoux, Claude (ed.), 1971, *The Development of Indigenous Trade and Markets in West Africa*, Oxford University Press, Oxford.

Miers, Suzanne and Kopytoff, Igor (eds), 1977, *Slavery in Africa: Historical and Anthropological Perspectives*, University of Wisconsin Press, Madison, Wis.

Morgan, Lewis Henry, 1877 (reprint 1963), *Ancient Society*, ed. Eleanor Burke Leacock, World Publishing Company, New York.

— 1871, *Systems of Consanguinity and Affinity*, Smithsonian Institute, Vol. XVII.

Mudimbe, V.Y., 1988, *The Invention of Africa: Gnosis, Philosophy and Order of Knowledge*, Indiana University Press, Bloomington and Indianapolis.

Nadel, S.F., 1942, *A Black Byzantium: Kingdom of Nupe in Nigeria*, Oxford University Press, London and New York.

Okonjo, Kamene, 1976, 'The dual-sex political system in operation: Igbo women and community politics in midwestern Nigeria', N.J. Hafkin and E.G. Bay (eds), 1976, *Women in Africa: Studies in Social and Economic Change*, Stanford University Press, Stanford, Calif.

Omer-Cooper, J.D., 1969, *The Zulu Aftermath: a Nineteenth Century Revolution in Bantu Africa*, Northwestern University Press, Evanston, Ill.

Parpart, Jane L. and Staudt, A. Kathleen (eds), 1989, *Women and the State in Africa*, Lynne Rienner Publishers, Boulder, Colo and London.

Paulme, D. (ed.), 1963, *Women of Tropical Africa*, University of California Press, Berkeley, Calif.

Polanyi, Karl, 1966, *Dahomey and the Slave Trade*, University of Washington Press, Seattle.

Rashidi, Runoko, 1984, 'African Goddesses: Mothers of Civilisations', in Van Sertima, Ivan (ed.), (1984).

Rodney, Walter, 1966, 'Slavery and other forms of social oppression on the Upper Guinea Coast in the context of the Atlantic slave trade', *Journal of African History*, 7(4): 431–43.

Roscoe, John, 1966, *The Baganda*, Barnes and Noble, New York.

Sacks, Karen, 1979, *Sisters and Wives: the Past and Future of Sexual Equality*, Greenwood Press, Westport, Conn.

Sweetman, David, 1984, *Women Leaders in African History*, Heinemann Educational, London.

UNESCO, 1985, *General History of Africa*, 8 vols, UNESCO, Paris.

Van Sertima, Ivan, (ed.), 1983, *Blacks in Science: Ancient and Modern*, The Journal of African Civilisations, New Brunswick and London

— (ed.), 1984, *Black Women in Antiquity*, Journal of African Civilisations/Transaction Books, New Jersey.

— (ed.), 1989, *Egypt Revisited*, Transaction Publishers, New Brunswick and London.

Vasina, Jan, 1962, 'A comparison of African kingdoms', *Africa*, 32: 324–35.

Wilks, Ivor, 1975, *Asante in the Nineteenth Century: the Structure and Evolution of a Political Order*, Cambridge University Press, London and New York.

5 Gender and social movements in Africa: a West African experience*

In this chapter, I examine a different concept of social movements which distinguishes between two concepts of power. The dominant approach has been to see power in terms of individuals, interest groups or social groups seeking to control the state or seeking effective citizenship in a state system, even if the objective of the movement is also ideological, that is, to change the ideology of the state. Most social movements in contemporary African societies have been seen in this light, whether bourgeois, youth/students, labour or women's movements.

In these movements, whichever faction or group succeeds in seizing power forms a government in order to rule others. Generally these movements have not succeeded in establishing the concept of self-government by the masses or peasantry. They have always thrown up an elite class or so-called vanguard party, thus constructing a new imperialism over and above socially viable groups or communities which do not necessarily want to be part of a state system.

In relationship to massive African communities who never wanted to be part of a state system, there is another movement – the one least written about. It involves another concept of power – the anti-power movements which simply seek to defend and maintain their autonomy. This seems to me to have been the central characteristic of indigenous women's movements in Africa. This implies that traditionally, African women had autonomous organizations, structures or systems of self-rule that they needed to defend. Their histories are consequently full of experiences of struggle against processes leading to a gradual loss of this tradition. Here, I look at a specific Nigerian experience. But first, is it possible to formulate a specific African model of gender and social conflict?

Gender and African political systems: a theoretical debate

In trying to distinguish traditional African political systems from Western systems, Kamene Okonjo (1976) had used the concept of a 'dual-sex' system to characterize the African system, using the Igbo example. She described the European system as 'single-sex'. According to Okonjo, in the 'dual-sex' systems, 'each sex manages its own affairs, and women's interests are represented at all levels'. In contrast, in the European 'single-sex' system, 'political status-bearing roles are predominantly the preserve of men ... women can achieve distinction and recognition only by taking on the roles of men in public life and performing them well' (ibid.: 45).

This historical political importance and autonomy of African women's organizations was also confirmed by Annie Lebeuf's (1963) general survey of the role of women in the political organization of African societies, particularly their practical participation in public affairs. Like Okonjo, Lebeuf saw public participation of women as the distinguishing factor between African political systems and European state systems. Her historical survey covered the rule of queens and queen mothers among the Lovedu, the Swazi and the Lunda in the southern African region.

In West Africa, similar systems of female rule and power sharing with men are recorded from the Bamileke of Cameroon, the Chamba of Benue in Northern Nigeria, and the Ashanti of Ghana. In Muslim Nigeria and Chad the same practice obtained among the Nupe, the Bolewa (a Kanuri people), the Kotoko of the Chari delta and the Bagrimi. It was the same among East African societies such as the Bemba of north-eastern Zimbabwe, the Bushongo of the Kasai and the Loango, the Kitara, Ankole and the Bateke. Further more, David Sweetman's (1984) and Ivan Van Sertima's (1984) accounts of very prominent and powerful women leaders, queens and empresses in African history go back into antiquity, covering the ancient empires including Nubia, Ethiopia and Egypt. These were ruling women in the centralized political systems which were in complex economic and social relations with other decentralized African political systems at the community level or within the same regions. These relationships would involve some contradictions and, therefore, conflict due to the historical economic dependence of centralized systems on the communities – the people.

However, female leadership was not confined to the centralized systems – but extended to the community level, resulting in varying

levels of formal and informal women's organizations. Most African
societies therefore had women's organizations which controlled or
organized agricultural work, trade, the markets, and women's culture
and its relevant ideology. Some of the African societies famous for
their women's organizations include the Igbo, the Kikuyu, the Lunda
group, the Ekoi of Southern Nigeria, the Bini, the Ube, Gere, Wobe
of the Ivory Coast, the Mende, the Yoruba, and so on. Her knowledge
of the public importance of African women led Lebeuf to pronounce
this indictment of her own society and its anti-female history and
values:

> By a habit of thought deeply rooted in the Western mind, women are
> relegated to the sphere of domestic tasks and private life, and men alone are
> considered equal to the task of shouldering the burden of public affairs.
> This anti-feminist attitude, which has prevented political equality between
> the sexes from being established in our country until quite recently ... should
> not allow us to prejudge the manner in which activities are shared between
> men and women in other cultures, more particularly, so far as we are con-
> cerned, in those of Africa (1963: 93).

Here then are two contrasting historical experiences which influenced
the character of women's movements in different political systems.
While European women have struggled to gain power in their formal
political structures, colonial imposition of European systems in Africa
has undermined the traditional empowering structures of African
women's socio-cultural systems. African women have been losing the
power of autonomy as European women have been gaining power in
the hegemonic European system.

Cheikh Anta Diop (1989) has tried to explain these historical differences in the structural positions of women through his theory of
African matriarchy. He has argued that, historically, European societies
have been patriarchal (totalitarian male rule and oppression of women)
and, in contrast, Africa is the cradle of matriarchy (a pro-female
mother-focused society). Comparing the economic, social and political
practices in both systems, he showed the degree of power which African
women have had since the time of antiquity.

The main forces of change in this archaic matriarchal system,
according to Diop, came first from Islam which introduced patriarchy
into Black Africa in the tenth century. However, he maintained that
Islam did not lead to a total erosion of indigenous African cultures. In
many cases, Islam existed side by side with African customs for over a
thousand years. It was Christianity, Western education, and the secular
European state system in Africa which, in less than a hundred years,

forced wide-ranging radical changes through the colonial imposition of a male-biased ruling system. Male bias was reflected in legislation, land rights, naming after the father, monogamous marriage and the moral values of a ruling European-produced elite class. It was therefore the introduction of a Western system which led to the erosion of centuries of political gains which African women had achieved.

Diop's theory of matriarchy is largely based on rules of succession and inheritance through the female line, and the reigns of queens in African kingdoms. I, on the contrary, have preferred to define matriarchy in terms of deeper ideological structures which have wider socio-political expressions in a well recognized viable women's system.[1] However, I have no quarrel with Diop on the central importance of the concept of motherhood.

The traditional power of African women had an economic and ideological basis, which derived from the importance accorded motherhood. I have argued that this issue of the structural status of motherhood is the main difference between the historical experiences of African women and those of European women.[2] This is directly linked to the histories of the family in these different systems. Frederick Engels (1972) argued that the European patriarchal family has been both the root and seat of women's oppression. I believe that it also explains why European women never achieved women's organizations and self government as African women did.

The ideology of gender

So far, in this chapter, women have been presented simply as constituting only a single analytical category on the basis of biological sex gender. I have shown this to be a weakness in Okonjo's 'dual-sex' and 'single-sex' formulations and in earlier theories on women and power, since in terms of social classification biological sex does not necessarily correspond to ideological gender.[3] Depending on gender systems, men can be reclassified as females and vice versa.

Due to linguistic and historical differences between the European and African systems, gender appears to be manipulated differently in these systems. We find in African gender systems a flexibility which allows a neuter construct for men and women to share roles and status. The rigidity of the European gender system allows for only male or female. Its historically male-gendered power structure has consequently kept females out of power. Power in this system has been monolithically masculine gendered and valued. This has consequently raised the question of the gender values of women who successfully wield power in this type of system. The masculinism of this system – its male charactered spaces, clubs and public houses – seems to force an outward appearance of maleness on these women, such as deepened voices and tailored suits. What is the gender classification of, say, the British ex-Prime Minister, Margaret Thatcher? Whose interest did she serve?

These questions have become fundamental issues in the stock-taking exercises on the losses and gains of the Western women's movement in the past few years. There has resurfaced a debate on the class and gender question, with veteran Marxists and socialist feminists reclaiming the analytical primacy of gender and patriarchy in the sense of cultural and political values. These feminists have admitted that class alliance alone did not safeguard their personal interests as women, with many of their male class allies remaining oppressive to women.[4] These same accusations have been made by African women against their male comrades in the various liberation struggles (Jaywardena, 1986; Rama-zanoglu, 1989).

The class/gender debate

If gender is a fundamental principle of social organization, it is a fundamental contradiction which predates class and is carried over into class formations. But Marxist and socialist feminists thought differently, seeing gender domination only as one aspect of class dominance. Consequently, when the socialist feminists and Marxists threw out the concept of patriarchy (Barrett, 1980), they underplayed the very principle or logic behind male privilege, the oppression of women, class, capitalism and violent and oppressive masculinism.

Perhaps because European women never had a history of matriarchy, it was impossible for them to see oppositional systems to patriarchy, hence their focus on class – that is, workers as the opposers of the bourgeoisie. But, they have again come full-circle to the gendered class, which again tends to lean on gender as a biological distinction and not gender as an ideological system that could be manipulated by men or women.

In the West, where gender distinction is rigid and dichotomized, there are two genders: he or she. In Africa, which has a history of matriarchy, there are three systems: male, female, and a non-gendered collective pronoun in place of the discriminatory gender pronouns – he/she/his/hers/him/her. With this possibility of a non-gendered status and role, a woman need not be masculinized in order to wield power.

With the Oedipal logic and paradigm (destined male rule: the father rules the mother, and the son is destined to kill the father, then marry and rule his mother) behind European culture, patriarchy has been constructed as the superior and supreme system. When women push into power in this system, they therefore operate a system which is oppressive to other women. Class is not just a neutral or cultureless or valueless collection of people violating another group of people; there is a logic, reasoning or structure behind violence. This is why we talk of symbolisms of power, or jural reasoning governing modes of production.

Matriarchy, essentialism and motherhood

Can it therefore be that I am looking at matriarchy as an ideal system without its own contradictions? Yes I am. But, instead of contradiction in this system, I acknowledge conflict, since the logic of patriarchy is to steal 'the wild fruit of women' (Meillassoux, 1981: 44). According to the domestic mode of production theorists, women are the producers of the producers and patriarchy appropriates from them. Meillassoux may have been right about the exploitation of the domestic mode of production by the centre, but he was blind to gender as an ideology. This is a major flaw in the Marxist mode of production theoretical formulations (Rubin, 1975; Leacock, 1981).

There is no doubt the works of Marx and Engels represented the perspective of the industrial proletariat, as did those of their later disciples in the French school of Marxist anthroplogy such as Meillassoux and others. But they all lacked a gender perspective since their pivotal axis was the male. Woman was seen as the filiated or commoditized exchangeable female. Thus they failed to look at the evidence of women as heads of corporate production units, using the ideology of motherhood in relations of production, and widening their social base on the same logic.

The very thought of women's power being based on the logic of motherhood has proved offensive to many Western feminists. It is easy to see why this is so since in the European system, wifehood and motherhood was a means of enslavement of women. In the African system of matriarchy, it was women's means of empowerment. Rejecting the concept of innatism, Karen Sacks wrote: 'it is an unfortunate position for feminists to take because it is virtually impossible to make a logical case for equal rights from innatist premises' (1979: 25). Sacks herself shows how meaning was manipulated over time in European philosophical thought – for specific economic and political reasons – continuously to redefine the qualities and capabilities of woman, from innate inferiority to the place of motherhood and the domestic sphere as separate from the public, that is, production relations.

In the European innatist construct, a fabrication was constructed to justify male rule. The fabrication is a false one and imposes gender rigidity. The African situation was different. Yet Western women used their ethnocentric understanding and experiences to interpret the experiences of African women. What African women constructed in matriarchy was not innatist but essentialist, a logic based on concrete facts generated by the production and reproduction roles of the core production unit in the kinship system – the matricentric unit. It is this concrete fact that is at issue. Patriarchal claims and matriarchal claims, which of these proximate the material reality most?

African women had no problem with difference, since they could contribute to the social construction of difference. They had a collective neuter gender that could mediate this difference for role and status fulfilment in the course of social relations, with the result that their social system was not based only on an indefinite separation of the sexes. The problem for European women is that they did not construct the difference; it has been imposed on them because, according to Cheikh Anta Diop, patriarchy was the rule since their earliest history.

Socialist feminists, like Linsey German (1989), have argued that Marx's usage of patriarchy related to the rule of the father in the Western domestic household system of production in a specific historical context in the European family system. Their point is that Marx did not use it as a general phrase meaning women's oppression as feminist theorists are doing and thereby reaching the conclusion that it continues or would continue to exist even after a socialist revolution. According to Marx and Engels in *The German Ideology* (1964) and *The Communist Manifesto* (1967), women's oppression arose alongside the division of society into classes and the development of private property. To Engels, this resulted in the world-historic defeat of the female sex – the defeat of mother-right and the establishment of the family.

How do I relate this to the African context? This European unilinear evolutionist view of history does not fit the African experience, where there was no outright defeat of matriarchy in spite of distinct class inequalities in the centralized political systems and the ancient empires. Matriarchy and patriarchy were juxtaposed in a system based on contending gender ideologies. In this context, patriarchy is associated with the construct of family as opposed to the matricentric kinship unit – that is, the female-headed household in the African context. With family, there is filiation and appropriation and therefore privatization or ownership in relation to the autonomy of the household matri-centric unit. Thus this potential for gender antagonism was in the kinship structure long before class formations.

Contending ideologies and systems in contest

In the African context, following Marxist materialism, there are two production units within the family. Tension arises as a result of the relations of production involving these two spheres. According to functionalists, this tension is articulated in jural as opposed to moral rules. For the structuralists, the tension is also symbolically demonstrated in ritual and religious practices. My approach has been to demonstrate the dialectical relationship or dynamics involving all these interactions.

This in essence is the politics between gendered groups, interest groups, or classes. These terms shift situationally. The issue is therefore to determine when and how change or transformation results because of tensions from within a polity or from external factors introduced into a polity, and the character of such change. What are the differences between social change, social transformation and radical change? Social movements do not necessarily lead to any of these changes, but they can, and this is what interests conflict, dissent and liberation theorists, who place emphasis on contradiction, cleavage and the possibility of change and transformation.

I now return to the issue of the under-analysed female-headed household and its implications for the history of marriage in Africa. In the European concept, there is an assumption that marriage is transacted by men, and that women are the passive objects in that trans-action. Yet the widespread social practice of woman-to-woman marriage in Africa and female-headed households means that we can retheorize woman marriage in the context of historical materialism. Woman-centred, mother-focused or matricentric socio-economic formations suggest that woman marriage could have been the first marriage pattern. The early practice of suitors coming to work for mothers in return for sexual access to daughters would support this theory.

Now, if we reconsider the general accounts of mass women walk-outs or cases of exodus in which women left the villages en masse taking only suckling babies during periods of extreme social conflict in Africa, we can ask more relevant questions. Were these conflicts always resolved? Did the women always return? Could they not have formed new settlements? Did they in fact form new matriarchal settlements? Why are African riveraine settlements usually matrilineal (so-called) or goddess worshipping? Lack of a gender perspective has meant that these very important issues have not been taken into consideration in the formulation of frontier theories, theories of socioeconomic formations or of social transformations.

We know that African communities formed and disintegrated in constant social movements. The moral values of matriarchy seem to have generated anti-state and anti-centralist tendencies, while patriarchy is about control, rule, and subordination, hence we talk of male bias and male dominance. There is a major social contradiction based on the pull or tension between these tendencies as a result of their juxtaposition in the social structures of African societies. In short, what was the gender politics and how can we look at change historically without falling into the danger of the racism and imperialism embodied in the concept of unilinear evolutionism.

This imperialism constructs a hegemonic unipolar centre to which every head must bow, and into which every system must transform. This has been the imperative of the racist European model (Bernal, 1987; Mudimbe, 1988). In a recent reassessment of African political systems,[5] I used the term anti-state decentralized political systems to characterize traditional African polities that have in the past been classified as non-state, stateless, or acephalous societies – terms which imply that these societies lack something, that is, a state. The politics of the past hundred years has been the imperialism of the subjugation of these societies under a European state system.

To define these societies as anti-state poses a challenge to the racist and imperialist European concepts of unilinear developmental evolutionism, because we would be able to recognize the fact that not all societies and cultures want to develop states. We would also recognize the struggles that communities have made to challenge centralism, state intervention and state dominance. We would, therefore, be compelled to bring into focus moral philosophies and political consciousnesses which are anti-dominance, anti-power and anti-state. It will enable us to shift from the state–civil society paradigm in European political philosophy to other possibilities of socio-political organization. It allows us the freedom to recognize difference, and to examine and analyse systems in contest. How then can we historically contextualize social movements in Africa?

Contextualizing social movements in Africa: the processes of militarization and masculinization

It goes without saying that the late Cheikh Anta Diop remains the foremost African scholar in the project of comprehensive reconstruction of what he called an 'African history of sociology'. His work has covered the social organizations of ancient Pharaonic Egyptian civilization, the African empires of the Old World such as Ghana, Mali and Songhai of the Middle Ages. For Diop, the Moroccan War of 1593 and the destruction and occupation of Timbuktu, which led to the decline of Songhai, marked the beginning of the modern period in Africa. The modern period, therefore, came about as a result of Africa's encounter with the Arabs and the consequent Islamic experience. The modern African period did not result from the experience of European colonialism and the establishment of European state systems in the twentieth century, as is generally claimed by Eurocentric African scholarship.

What interests me here is not so much the chronology of events – important as they are in establishing certain facts about what took place, where and when – but the ideas behind events and the structures of economic, social and political relations between African states and subject and non-subject communities in specific regions.

Historically, there appears to have been a common feature to centralized political systems in Africa: the fact that they have been centrepoints of accumulation of wealth. There is, however, disagreement as to whether this wealth at the centre always derived from exploitation of subjects. Diop has been most vociferous in claiming that the authentic, that is pre-colonized African empires did not exploit their subjects. Even though subjects paid specified taxes, these empires were not feudal systems based on land ownership by the feudal lord – unlike the European system where both land and a subject peasantry belonged to the feudal lord (Diop, 1987: 103).

The religious character of indigenous African kingship itself ensured relative stability. It was under the secular kings of Songhai, as a result of the last phase of Islamization, that radical change took place in Africa. Africa was then thrown into violent upheaval due to endless intrigues for succession (ibid.: 50). Diop therefore saw state violence in Africa as resulting from external influence, not being caused by internal contradictions in the state system.

Although Diop acknowledged the wide practice of slavery even in the eleventh-century empire of Ghana, he did not analyse patterns of relations between the state systems and the communities. He saw both systems as dichotomized, and the centralized system as the superior system. Social transformation was consequently seen as a question of 'detribalization'. Here, I would like to quote Diop extensively. Citing Robert Vigondy's 1795 map of Africa, Diop wrote:

In the precolonial period the entire continent was indeed covered by monarchies and empires. No spot where man lived, even in the virgin forest,
escaped monarchic authority. But we must recognize that not all peoples
living under the same political regime had the same cultural level. Some
outlaying populations still lived in a scarcely shaken or liberalized clanic
organization, where the large numbers in the cities were detribalized. A
striking example of this is the empires of Ghana, Mali, and Songhai. One
can indeed contrast, on the basis of the remaining documents (Al Bakri or
Khaldun), the teeming city life of Timbuktu, Gao, Ghana, Djenne, or Mali,
which contained only isolated individuals, with the collective life that still
held sway in the outlaying clans of the goldbearing regions to the southwest,
located on the Upper Senegal, and even farther south, where detribalization
was scarcely even beginning. (1987: 73)

First, we learn that it is the region of these clan-based communities
which contained the gold that was the principal medium of exchange
in both the Ancient World and Old World. Then Diop goes on to
point out that it is also in this region that empire city dwellers went
slave hunting. Again, slavery was the main method of acquiring labour
both in the Ancient and Old Worlds.

Diop did not go into the issue of violence in these structures of
relations in the acquisition of slaves and labour to work the mines for
the rulers. He did not, therefore, focus on the contradictions and
possible areas of antagonism between these systems. He argued instead
that the abundance of wealth in Africa during these ancient times,
confirmed by Arab sources, meant that there was no need for monopoly
and exploitation. He consequently stressed consensus and stability. His
approach was therefore formalist. Other scholars more concerned with
the relations of production have, however, pointed to the social, economic and occupational inequalities between the ancient cities and
their rural villages (Law, 1978; Hart, 1982).

Historically, Africa was the source of most of the gold for the
Mediterranean world before the Americas came into the picture in the
fifteenth century. It was also a major source of tropical products, such
as ivory, gum and slaves, throughout history. Africa has, therefore, had
centuries of a dynamic history of international commerce. The ruling
classes needed external trade to acquire prestige and luxury goods for
its differentiated life style. Slaves, trade and taxes were therefore an
important material basis of their power in precolonial Africa. Direct
taxation by all these states is well documented, even in ancient Ghana
where mining was taxed; all gold nuggets found went to the king. In
certain cases, the king took all gold nuggets plus a large share of gold
dust (Law, 1978).

Keith Hart's (1982) references also confirm the great wealth of the ancient Savannah empires. From Arab sources (Levtzion, 1976), it is recounted how Ibn Hawqal, in 951, saw a bill of credit made out to a trader from Awdaghust in Ghana, the sum of which (42,000 diners) was unheard of in the Muslim world at that time. But at the same time, great contrasts were exhibited between these urban cities and the surrounding villages. There was clear indication of an Islamized urban elite, including merchants and mercenary armies, and a ruling class which was busy with taxes and slavery. In the occupational differentiation, slaves were food producers, administrators and soldiers. Even though Arabs – living in their Arab quarters – were subjects of Black African kings, Islam itself produced a literate elite class of lawyers, priests and teachers.

The history of Africa before the Europeans was not that of a gradient centralization, or a transformation from small-scale polities to large-scale centralized states. Empires seem to have come and gone; for example, some nations that we know today, such as the Mande, the Wolof, the Hausa, the Mossi and the Fulani, derive their history from the ancient Savannah empires. Bands of nomadic Tuareg warriors also occupied the southern fringe of the Sahara in a predatory existence with the savannah sedentary agriculturalists whom they raided for food and slaves. These large pockets of uncentralized peoples (Horton, 1971) who resisted centralism lived between the forest and the savannah.

These were areas of dynamic social movements in communities and societies which were plundered for slaves. They were anti-state people who refused to have kings as a result of what has been described as their 'egalitarian' worldview. The Dogon of Mali, who told French anthropologists (Griaule, 1948; Graule and Dieterlen, 1965) that they know the meaning and purpose of life, moved up to the hills to resist Islamic colonialism and dominance. The Tiv of Nigeria also put up the same struggle for many years. Thus we find among these peoples authentic African communities whose only experience of direct colonization has been under the European state system for less than a hundred years.

Gender, political systems and violence

I want to pick up again Diop's thesis that the Arabs introduced state violence, patriarchy and radical change into African political systems, referring particularly to the Moroccan War of 1593. Other scholars (Goody, 1971; Law, 1976) who have tried to trace the relationship between military technology and different patterns of political organizations in precolonial Africa would appear to support Diop's thesis to some extent. There is, however, a basic difference between the European scholars and Diop. Diop's position is that states in Africa preceded ownership of means of war and destruction; that the pre-colonial African states had enjoyed relative stability for centuries.

For the Europeans, it was the introduction into Africa of the more advanced weapons of war, such as horses and firearms, which led to centralization and feudalism in African political systems. Goody argued that it was the ownership of these 'higher technology' weapons of violence which supported state power in Africa, since centralization was impossible with the democratic weapon of bow and arrow of the so-called acephalous African peoples. He thus seems to be supporting the idea that instruments of destruction and subordination came from outside the continent. While in the savannah states horses became the basis of military organization, the forest kingdoms depended on the power of gun fire.

Diop had traced the origin of patriarchy to the ancient and classical European systems of Greece and Rome, stressing their relatively violent, exploitative and oppressive character in relation to women, slaves and the peasantry. He saw patriarchy as being in contrast to the more compassionate and egalitarian system of African matriarchy.

Historically, it appears as if both the ideology of state violence and the instruments of state violence have their origins in the European systems. It was the Indo-Europeans, the Hittites, who first domesticated the horse and used it to extend their domination into the Near East. The Egyptians in turn got the chariot from the Hyksos who invaded Egypt in 1500 BC. From Egypt, horse-drawn vehicles spread into the Eastern Sudan in the first millennium BC, then to Western Sahara (Goody, 1971: 68). Robin Law's (1976) references also confirm the use of archery in West Africa in the first century AD, and the introduction of horses into the Nile Valley in about 1675 BC in Nubia, and from there to North Africa. There was a change from the use of chariotry to cavalry in the Maghrib, that is, North-West Africa in about 300 BC.

Law, however, maintained that chariots never spread into West Africa. On the date of the appearance of the horse in Africa Law differed from Goody, claiming that horses preceded the Islamic era in West Africa, since Arabs refer to the presence of horses in the Kanem area and in ancient Ghana. These were, however, small horses, and horses were of limited military value. Since there were no saddles, cavalry fighting was limited. It was in about the fourteenth century that a revolution occurred in West African warfare with the introduction of larger breeds of horses and the introduction of the saddle and bit.

In 1324, the famous emperor of Mali, Mansa Musa, is reported to have been given horses equipped with saddles and bridles by the Sultan of Egypt on his stopover in Egypt during a pilgrimage to Mecca.

Thus began a history of militarism in Africa, and the gradual militarization of the continent. The period of the fourteenth to the nineteenth centuries was one of heavy cavalry in Africa. Also in the sixteenth century, firearms were introduced into Africa by sea by European traders, and from across the Sahara. The importation of both horses and firearms were financed by the export of slaves. Many cavalry states and slave states emerged during this period – the Southern West African cavalry states which depended on imported horses included Gonja, Dagomba, Nupe, Oyo. The military power of Dahomey and Asante in the eighteenth century was based on firearms. This was the period that enthroned violence and monolithic masculinism. Anti-state communities and African matriarchal systems came under attack from the new patriarchal systems.

Gendered values The difference between Cheikh Anta Diop and the Europeans on the question of the character of state power in precolonial Africa has something to do with gendered moral values. Goody had argued that Africans never seemed to have learnt to make firearms as good as those of the Europeans because Africans 'did not possess the requisite level of craft skill in iron-working' (1971: 28). Here Goody's unilinear Eurocentric evolutionism results in the assumption that all moral systems favour the acquisition and use of destructive weapons for the same military ambitions. Diop argued that a different moral system meant that indigenous African rulers did not need to rely on violence. In which case, they did not need to develop weapons of mass destruction; they did not have an imperialist colonial history.

I am arguing that traditional African matriarchy, an oppositional system of checks and balances, had something to do with why Africans did not value advanced military weapons and did not domesticate wild animals (as Goody affirms). The matriarchal values and moral system which generated the concepts of love, harmony, peace and cooperation, and forbade human bloodshed, imposed a check on excessive and destructive masculinism. As a result of their concentration on the top strata of centralized masculinist states, Europeans tend to see the control of force in equally masculinist items such as guns and horses. They tend not to consider that certain social organizations and moral systems might determine whether or not guns and horses should be acquired in the first place, or whether guns and horses should be seen as objects of violence.

Consequences of violence What were the consequences of this massive violence and appropriation on social transformations in Africa? Various scholars have proposed theories for the so-called underdevelopment of the African continent, seeing it as a direct result of European imperialism in Africa, especially the social, economic and political consequences of the history of slavery (Rodney, 1966; Fage, 1969; Inikori, (ed.), 1982). They have argued that there is a relationship between economic backwardness and the slave trade; that, for example, while fifteenth-century observers are said to have noticed no discernible differences among the Africans that they visited, nineteenth-century observers noted obvious differences in comparison to earlier accounts. Unlike earlier accounts of teeming markets, trade and commerce, in the nineteenth century there appeared to have been a low level of market development in sub-Saharan Africa and a predominance of subsistence production. The Europeans did not develop commodity trade in Africa, but only traded slaves and weapons of violence.

With the rise of slave kingdoms and empires between the fifteenth and mid-nineteenth centuries there was increased social conflict, warfare and violence. The numerous consequences for the African economy included: the withdrawal of labour and skills to military production, which resulted in lowered efficiency of production; loss of labour through the slave trade and death as a result of war, raids, famine, epidemics and starvation; a general anti-economic development atmosphere; widespread insecurity which raised transport cost; communities moved to inaccessible areas; transport was not developed and the community walked.

With the militarization of the African continent, Goody (1971) has given some insights into some of the devastating effects of slave raiding and general violence on so-called acephalous peoples by state systems. Instead of choosing to be subordinated to state systems, acephalous people resisted centralism by moving. They are therefore mostly found deep inside the forest, in hill areas or straggled across a major river (Horton, 1971). They have remained Earth people, custodians of the Earth religion; the Earth is usually a goddess in African religion. Instead of desiring the horse, there is a widepread taboo against the horse among autochthonous African people.

It seems that in the kingdoms of the Western Sudan, there was a traditional practice of the ruling estate recognizing the superior wisdom of the autochthones concerning anything about the Earth, while the conquering Muslims held a superior position on things about God – that is, the secular polity. Therefore a dual moral system obtained which allowed the autochthones to cling to their own religion. Such examples can be cited among the Gonja, the Mossi, the Tallensi, etc. However, other evidence suggests an intolerant Islamic imperialism resulting in unceasing attacks, eschatological and military, on African religion and indigenous social institutions (Hiskett, 1973; 1984). Women's resistance to Islamic patriarchal oppression appears to have taken the form of spirit possession, during which the possessed women adopted male garments and acted as men (Boddy, 1989; Lewis, 1971; Strobel, 1976; Onwuejeogwu, 1969; Berger, 1975).

Gender and transformations under the European state system: a Nigerian experience

The pre-1500s had witnessed a relatively stable period in African history when the labour of grassroots Africans and African gold built and sustained the pomp and glitter of empires, courts, palaces and gigantic sculptures at home, in the Mediterranean region, and in the Orient as far as China and India. The exploitation of African resources intensified with unbelievable violence between 1500 and 1830, the period of European mercantilism and the Atlantic slave trade, when Africans were commoditized and became merchandise to be captured and sold again and again as slaves (Lovejoy, 1983; Meillassoux, 1971; Inikori (ed.), 1982; Miers and Kopytoff (eds), 1977).

The nineteenth century saw the dismantling of the Atlantic slave trade since it was no longer economical to Europeans due to the Industrial Revolution and the economic devastation caused by African resistance and rebellions. What was needed by Europe was vegetable oil; consequently in the 1830s there began the production of vegetable oil for export. European economic interest led to a need for direct control and management, and therefore European imperialism in Africa intensified with military violence. There were massive anti-European riots and wars, especially in 1917, the year of revolts in Africa, and a violent and ruthless suppression and subordination of rebellious Africans from the late nineteenth to the early twentieth century.

With the carving out of rigid frontier states, all types of African societies were forcibly brought under direct European colonial rule between 1900 and 1960, even though the Europeans like to refer to their rule as indirect rule through African rulers. After 1960, a European reproduced African elite took over where the colonialists left off. The project of the African elite has not been the transformation but the management of the successor states in the context of a world political economy. They have therefore occupied the same racist and imperialist position *vis-à-vis* the autonomy and self-expression of grassroots communites, constructing a relevance as civilizers and modernizers of village Africans, as did the European, using the same basis of colonial state power-violence (Fanon, 1967).

In the following case study, I look at the transformations in gender relations in a specific rural community in the context of the contemporary Nigerian psuedo-state system.

Local administration in Nigeria The disastrous consequences of Lugard's universal system of local administration in the form of indirect rule in Nigeria has been well documented and analysed (Afigbo, 1972). This indirect rule was in the form of a warrant chief system from 1891 to 1929. Fundamental to imperialism is the insistence on control and 'order'. For this reason, the mentality of developmental evolutionism ruled British policy in Africa. Anti-state decentralized African communities had to be brought under state control, and kings and chiefs had to be imposed on them. Where there were none, the British picked their allies and gave them certificates of recognition and authority called warrants. Men who hitherto were 'nobodies' in their communities were made chiefs, and they acquired both executive and judicial powers previously unknown in their communities. This policy proved disastrous practically everywhere in Africa, and African women in particular, whose traditional power bases were the first institutions to come under attack, revolted against this new system of male dominance and oppression. All accounts of the women's revolts show consistent attacks on the colonialists and the collusion or cowardice of local African men.[6]

In what was then Southeastern Nigeria, there were several demonstrations by women against British imperialism. There was the Dancing Women's Movement in 1925 and the Spirit Movement in 1927, which were all about genuine rejection of colonial rule and Western culture. Following a series of localized protests, rebellions and demonstrations throughout the region against the imposition of a poll tax, the women rioted en masse in 1929 and told the colonialists to leave. This became known as the Women's War.[7]

The causes of the war included the economic disadvantages that women felt under the new system, the marginalization of their social organizations, the banning of their religion, and the new economic and political advantages that their men were gaining under the new system. The traditional balance of power had been disrupted and tilted to favour men.

What is of interest here, however, is the organization and strategy of the Women's War. How was it that illiterate grassroots women could mobilize and organize crowds ranging from hundreds to over ten thousand women across an area of six thousand square miles, involving several villages and towns, and involving non-Igbo women such as Ibibio and Calabar women? This is something that the urban-based contemporary national women's organizations seem unable to achieve. A second point of interest is the fact that colonial soldiers opened fire on unarmed near naked women and shot many of them dead, thus introducing an unheard of practice in Igboland – the shooting of women – a practice that contemporary European-produced elites in Africa inherited from the colonial masters.

As a direct result of the Women's War, there followed a series of unpopular ordinances aimed at native court reforms, before the idea of democratic government in Africa was finally accepted by the colonial legislators. In 1946, a section of the educated elite had mounted a powerful criticism of the whole structure of native administration. By this time, the nationalist movement for so-called independence had also begun.

It was against this background that, in 1947, directives for a grassroots democracy were given to the African colonialists by the then Secretary of State for the Colonies, Arthur Creech-Jones, as a prerequisite for African independence (Kirk-Greene (ed), 1965: 245). The directive was for a democratic system of local government in which participation would be through elected councils, as in Britain. What was therefore adopted was the English local government model. Since it was pro-educated elites, the emergent county councils and district councils became incompetent bureaucratic administrative institutions, which were far removed from the illiterate grassroots. As pointed out by Bello-Imam (1983), local government did not become the primary base where potential politicians were trained for national leadership. It did not have resources to attract educated people, who went to the urban centres, where the resources and power were concentrated. As local governments covered very wide areas and lacked funds, development efforts were consequently left to initiatives within specific communities.

Participatory local government remained an illusion in the rural communities since, for the majority of rural people, their administrative local government headquarters were far beyond their reach in distant towns. The rural communities had, therefore, been subordinated to a psuedo-state which in reality was a burden upon them – extracting taxes and levies but providing nothing in return.

This brief background explains the emergence and importance of Improvement and Town Unions in rural Igbo communities, which were formed to fill the huge vacuum in the provision of services by the local government. Focusing on a specific rural Igbo community, Nnobi, I

examine the processes of change and transformation in the gradual
erosion of the traditional power base of women in this community. I
look at the character of a new gender politics and social conflict around
two issues: the structure and autonomy of the traditional women's
organizations, and women's traditional control of the marketplace, both
of which were indigenous power bases of matriarchy.

Nnobi case study[8] Unpublished researches by the government
appointed Directorate of Mass Mobilization and Social Economic
Recovery (MAMSER), has established that Nigeria has 99,400 rural
communities. Nigeria is supposed to be the most highly populated
African country, yet in the ancient empire of Ghana, population density
was such that the region of Djenne alone had 7,077 villages in close
proximity to one another (Diop, 1987: 141). Today, Nigeria cannot claim
to have recorded the social history of even one-tenth of its component
communities. How real is the state to these communities? What services
does the state provide to these communities from which it extracts so
much in taxes and levies? How do the communities see themselves in
relationship to the state? Are there anti-state tendencies in these communities? To what extent are the powers of factions in the communities
dependent on external factors beyond the communities?

These and several other issues make it imperative that we decentre
our minds from statism and focus on the people, the very basis of the
state. It does not therefore matter which of the component communities
we choose to study, since everyone of them has a structural significance
in indicating how the British-fabricated Nigerian state works or does
not work for a particular community, several communities or all the
communities. It is imperative that we look at the structures of these
communities.

The traditional social structure of Nnobi   Nnobi is one of the
many rural Igbo villages in the Idemili Local Government Area of
Anambra State. With a population of well over twenty thousand in
1982 in an area of about nineteen square kilometres, it is in the most
densely populated and least fertile areas of Igboland. Traditionally, the
people have been farmers and traders. Their deteriorating ecology has
meant that outward-migration, trade and commerce have a strong
influence on their political economy.

Igbo people in general claim an autochthonous origin, but most
communities have a history of migration. Significantly, all the communities along the Idemili River worshipped the river Goddess, Idemili,
in a religion dominated by women. Several interrelated factors here

need to be researched and analysed further in order to take into consideration the full importance of gender factors in the processes of socioeconomic formations and social transformation. We need to understand the settlement histories of these communities; were they first settled by rebellious women in exodus, following their traditional strategies of mass walkout from their villages when serious conflicts were not resolved? Did the settlements have something to do with the general atmosphere of insecurity during the period of slavery?

In any case, we know that these were among the anti-state decentralized African communities which were raided for slaves by neighbouring slave states. They were in fact derided by slave state Igbos as people without kings. We also know that this is an area where petty states came and went, as communities centralized and fell apart again, following changes in the economy and patterns of accumulation and redistribution of wealth. The Igbo themselves, as a nation of about fourteen million people, also became one of the first African people to rebel against the neo-colonial state of Nigeria, thus fighting a bitter war of secession – the Biafran war – which lasted from 1967–70.

As far as it was possible for me to reconstruct the indigenous social structure of pre-colonial Nnobi society, that is the structures before British colonial rule, the economic patterns showed that the traditional division of labour was gender based. It was a society structured on descent and kinship, like all African communities; even in the centralized states, the communities or villages always had a kinship structure.

Nnobi productive units were based on two ideologies which were paradigmatically in structural opposition, and thus generated dual moral and social systems. The minutest productive unit was the matricentric unit – the *mkpuke* structure, a distinct mother-focused social category which occupied a distinct space in the form of a self-contained compound of mother and children. It had an economic base, since it produced for itself; it was a production and consumption unit of those who ate from one pot or one plate. This unit also had an ideological base as it was bound in the spirit of common motherhood, in the ideology of *umunne*, with its strong moral and spiritual force binding members in love, care, compasion, peace and respect, and forbidding incest and bloodshed.

A step removed from the matricentric productive unit, was the *obi*, involving the social (but not necessarily biological) construct of fatherhood and family head, a status role which can be played by women through the practice of woman-to-woman marriage. The Igbo term for husband, *di*, is not gendered; both a man or woman can be husband. Historically, we do not know when the status of husband assumed a male gender in the history of marriage in Africa. Male gendering of husband is definitely the case in Islam and Christianity, and in European culture in general. Since these were the key positions for the command of labour and economic management, whether a woman could be husband or not had structural implications for women's access to power.

In the indigenous social structure of Nnobi, we thus see a parallel or dual-system of social organizations based on what seems on the surface a sexual division of labour, but is in practice a flexible gender system, and a third non-gendered classificatory system mediates the apparent dualism. An indefinite gender contrast and conflict is thus minimized by the third non-gendered system, a system which allowed men and women to share the same status and play the same roles without social stigma. Thus the monolithic masculinization of power was eliminated.

Thus in practice in the traditional social structure of Nnobi, the female matricentric unit, the *mkpuke*, and what became a male family headed compound, the *obi*, would appear to be in dual opposition. This opposition is mediated by the fact that females can head an *obi*. A daughter can also go through a ceremony whereby she becomes a male and a son and may then replace her father in the *obi*; she thus becomes a male-daughter.

Step by step, at every level in the wider descent group organizations, again we have these parallel dual-sex social organizations, all with specific social and formal political roles. This is why these systems have been described as decentralized political systems, for there is a diffusion of authority and power. Power is not concentrated at the top as in centralized political systems. Patrilineage men, *umunna*, constituted a formal organization with specific duties and powers. Patrilineage daughters, *umuokpu*, on their part constituted their own formal organization with specific duties and powers. Patrilineage wives, *Inyomdi*, again constituted a formal organization with specific duties and powers. Since in the gender classification daughters were classified as males in relation to wives and had authority just like their brothers over wives, their formal political organization also had its own areas of superior authority over the organization of wives. But there is a major difference between the organizing of men and women. Whereas all the women of Nnobi collectively constituted a formal organization – *Inyom Nnobi*, Nnobi Women's Council – the men did not come under an equivalent overall organization.

With this structure of organization combined with economic power and a mother-focused ideology, and a goddess-worshipping religion which forbade bloodshed and prescribed fighting only with clubs and stones, we begin to see that there was a matriarchal construct – not in the sense of queen rule, but in the sense of a viable female-controlled autonomous system. The women had a socioeconomic base from which they could accumulate, and prestigious titles were open to them. For example, economically successful women could be possessed by the goddess Idemili to take her title of *ekwe*. This gave them leadership in their various organizations. It was their all-embracing goddess Idemili who reigned above all the other deities and the ancestors; she provided an overall administrative system, embracing the organization of the periodic markets, the days of the week and the seasonal festivals.

All these activites linked up Nnobi with surrounding communities, forming a regional system. Through the rotating periodic markets, shared ceremonies, marriage, organizations, trade and other cultural activities,[9] women enjoyed a very extensive communication network which men did not. They were more mobile than men, and enjoyed multiple identities in different communities as daughters, wives and mothers. They were therefore very well placed to mobilize women across several communities over a short space of time. This is why thousands of women could be mobilized during the Women's War, Women's Movement and Mobilization Under Colonialism.

One of the African institutions which suffered the greatest onslaught from both Islam and Christianity was indigenous African religion. It was the first thing that the British banned in the areas that they invaded. In Nnobi, the worship of Idemili was banned, and the new converts to Christianity exercised their new found power in attacks on ancient religious symbols. It is significant that, generally, it was elderly women who defended these symbols and refused to be converted to Christianity.

In the 1940s, there took place a huge mobilization and march by Nnobi women which women today often recall with pride as perhaps the last show of strength by the matriarchs. A Christian fanatic called Nathaniel, Natty for short, had deliberately killed the holy symbol of the Goddess Idemili, a python, a sacrilegious act in the native moral philosophy. Knowing the protection and power that the new elite enjoyed from the colonial administrators, the elderly matrons and titled women mobilized the whole of Nnobi women and marched en masse to the provincial headquarters at Onitsha, which was dozens of miles away. They demanded that the man be arrested and executed. As the District Officer failed to act, the women returned to the village and erased the man's house. They put a curse on him and the following morning, he was dead.

The significance of this incident is that, in spite of the new divides of class and religion, the leadership of the Women's Council was still controlled by the old leadership which continued to exercise authority over all the women of Nnobi. They also controlled the strategy of spontaneous direct action and the autonomy of their organization was maintained. They therefore still directed their organization themselves. During this period, in spite of colonial violence on traditional cultures, a European-reproduced African elite was emerging, but had not yet inherited the colonial state and its machinery of violence with which it would eventually divorce itself from the traditional systems of accountability.

Transformation of the Women's Council The nature of traditional popular struggles changed as soon as the new African elites got control over the military forces, especially the police and the army, which were introduced by the colonial imperialists. When the popular forces were being mobilized to fight the colonial imperialists, little did they realize that they were fighting to enthrone a ruthlessly violent elite capable of violating women and abusing the democratic rights of the rural grassroots more thoroughly than the colonialists.

Christianity and change in the Women's Council In the contemporary women's organizations in Nnobi, the greatest contradiction is between values and aspirations derived from Christian ideologies of womanhood, wifehood and motherhood, and those derived from traditional Nnobi values and norms associated with the African ideology of matriarchy.

The values guiding the church-based associations, such as the Catholic Christian Mothers and the Anglican Mothers' Union, have preached the suppression of self, self-sacrifice, and concern with order and peace. This kind of concern was only one aspect of the complex moral system associated with the ideology of motherhood in the indigenous matriarchal culture in which motherhood had its social rewards in a whole moral system generated by women. Pro-female values were encouraged through songs, folktale and myth to motivate, on the one hand, the tender values of love and compassion, and, on the other, competitiveness in economic pursuit – for it was women who fed their children. These mores also promoted positive aggression and militancy without bloodshed in the defence of self, women's rights, children's rights, the pursuit of public peace, and the defence of the traditional matriarchal religion itself.

In the church-based and church-controlled modern women's organizations, it is the suppressive and inhibitive aspects of Christian ideologies of motherhood which are most prominent. The male-biased patriarchal family laws of the Old Testament, with their strong anti-female notions of pollution, have been most effective in eroding the historical memory of these African women. The ideal Jewish and Victorian models of womanhood teach the acceptance of a place directly under the authority and rule of husbands, with obedience and servitude. Consequently, one finds that the attitude of the new usurpers of the leadership of the Women's Councils is characterized by ambivalence and contradictions.

As I showed earlier, in the traditional political system the indigenous women's organizations were political and recognized at every level of the political structure. The new church-based women's organizations claim to be non-political. Their membership is not even open to all women, but only to the women who have been married in church, and 'screened' for their good Christian character. This is unlike the traditional system in which every female belongs to a women's organization as part of the social structure.

These church unions have select committees where a few particular women make decisions for the rest of the members. The leadership of the church organizations is selected on the same principles as that of the Women's Council, which consists of representatives from all the village wards in Nnobi. However, while the indigenous organizations are descent- and town-based, the church unions are simply branches of wider national and international bodies, with headquarters in London, Rome and the USA. Thus, Western imperialism no longer needs to assume a colonial presence, having debased Other (African culture) and reproduced Sameness (European culture) in an elite class (Mudimbe, 1988).

Leadership in indigenous organizations was based on titles and seniority. In the church organizations, wives of the petty bourgeoisie, the clergy, lay readers, wealthy traders or prominent men in Nnobi tend to assume leadership positions. Some of the conflicts with the new leadership of the Women's Council were highlighted during the incident of the women's arrest of 1977 (see p. 135–6). This arrest is a landmark in the political history of Nnobi as it dealt a great blow to the confidence of the women, exposed the weakness of the new leadership of the Women's Council, and led to its loss of autonomy.

Colonialism and the construction of a new monolithic masculinization of power in Nnobi politics In order to have representation in the House of Chiefs, which the Eastern Region had established in 1951, there followed a general revival of kingship and chieftaincy titles. Business tycoons quickly claimed chiefly titles. In

Nnobi, the *Igwe*, the installed colonial local ruler later removed by the
Nnobi people, was reinstated. This title was not indigenous to Nnobi,
as Nnobi did not have an overall male chief. There were *Ozo* or *Eze*
titled men who were associated with specific lineages or villages. Oc-
casionally, however, there emerged 'big men' who, for a short period of
time, could attract overall recognition through influence, might and
wealth. As a result of the goddess religion and the Women's Council, it
was the most senior *Ekwe* titled woman, the *Agba Ekwe*, who had overall
political power, in the sense of veto rights in public assemblies of all
Nnobi. With the clamping down on traditional religious practices by
the colonial administration and the church, the *Ekwe* title was banned.
Colonial rule, on the other hand, instituted a ruling male chieftaincy,
the *Igwe*, as a result of the warrant chief system. The *Igwe* council is
made up of the *Igwe* and other titled men appointed by the *Igwe*. Their
sitting is referred to as *Igwe*-in-council. They are supposed to deal
mainly with traditional matters, and native law and custom.

The policy of the colonial administration which encouraged self-
help based on ethnic associations, resulted in the formation of Patriotic
and Town Unions in Igbo towns and villages in the 1940s. This trend
was started in Nnobi in 1942 by urban traders and merchants. In 1951,
the Nnobi Improvement Union had become known as the Nnobi
Welfare Organization (NWO). It has an all-male central executive,
elected at the general meetings of all Nnobi people, resident at home
and outside. Like all other ethnic associations, NWO has branches in
all the towns in Nigeria where Nnobi people reside. However, the
central focus is the home town, where annual general meetings are
held. For these annual general meetings, each branch is expected to
send two representatives. Each village in Nnobi is also expected to be
represented (Nnobi consists of three villages). NWO therefore appears
democratic in its composition. But an examination of methods of
selection of representatives, the social status of representatives and the
decision-making processes of NWO show both gender and class contradictions within NWO, and a lack of grassroots democracy.

The NWO was by far the most powerful of all the governing bodies
in Nnobi, since it was self-financing and also appeared widely representative. Most community self-help and development projects were
initiated and supervised by the NWO. Levies for these projects were
also imposed and collected by NWO. However, for major projects and
levies, NWO liaised with *Igwe*-in-council and sought its sanction. Final
decisions regarding specific projects were, therefore, taken at the joint
meeting of NWO and *Igwe*-in-council, where committees for specific
projects were set up. Such consultations were also supposed to take

place between ward councillors and *Igwe*-in-council for the discussion and execution of local government projects.

In this new political structure, therefore, we see that at all levels of local administration and government, suggestions and decisions were made by an all-male caucus, without mass consultation and participation. It is thus not surprising that the history of town unions is riddled with alleged cases of mismanagement, incompetence and embezzlement of funds.[10] Government policy of self-help and the system of matching grants meant that there was no uniform or consistent pattern of giving grants to the local communities. This obviously left room for partisan politics and patron–client relationships between voters and politicians. Communities received government help and finance according to the party they voted for, or if one of their sons happened to be in government.

The incompetence of the Nigerian state system resulted in the growth of the power of the urban elites *vis-à-vis* the rural communities, as the urban elites financed development projects. Through such contributions, the urban elites sought reward, fame and power in electoral politics from 1960. Thus developed a political culture of wealth, conspicuous display of affluence and political power. The resultant class and gender conflict has been most strongly felt in the rural communities, where the ruling elites have exercised their new powers with unbelievable violence and contempt for accountability.

Loss of autonomy of the Women's Council By 1977, class and gender conflict had reached crisis point in Nnobi when the urban-based leadership of NWO was challenged. The NWO's response, instead of tackling its own internal problems, was to attempt to curb the political autonomy and powers of the Women's Council by arresting its leaders (see Amadiume, 1987b: 147–61).

As the indigenous social organizations were embedded in the descent and kinship systems of Igbo societies, colonial rule and political administration were unable to wipe out the traditional kinship- and descent-based organizations. Even though some of the legislative and judicial powers and roles of these native organizations were appropriated by government and church institutions, the organizations remained in control of the routine management of life-cycle ceremonies concerning birth, marrriage, death and the distribution of property and wealth; indeed, things to do with the very *raison d'être* of a community or society *vis-à-vis* its members. This suggests that these communities are still viable without government presence, and in fact Igbo communities identify themselves as 'autonomous communities'.

The Women's Council in Nnobi was indeed still in control of the daily affairs of the local women, and they sometimes extended this control to men. With the increased control of formal politics by men, and the concentration of legislative, executive and judicial powers in the hands of modern male-controlled organizations like the NWO, the Local Council, and *Igwe*-in-council, a clash with the Women's Council over the exercise of rights and duties was bound to take place.

In 1977, the leaders of the Women's Council were arrested and taken into detention in Onitsha, a town a few dozen miles away. The Onitsha police had acted on the strength of an anonymous letter which they had received. It claimed that the women's government was up-setting Nnobi; that leaders of the Women's Council no longer took heed of anyone, including the traditional ruler; that the women's institution was too powerful and was like a state within a state, and therefore, their wings had to be clipped. The actual problem was, in fact, that the Women's Council had judged and fined two women who had fought at a public water pump. Some men in Nnobi, who had already intervened to settle the quarrel, felt that the Women's Council had no right stepping into the case. The men consequently resorted to anonymity in organizing the arrest of the leadership of the Women's Council.

For the first time in their memorable history, Nnobi women thus assaulted found themselves denied their spontaneous militant strategy. Instead of demonstrating solidarity in resistance to bullying and in-timidation by men, selected women were being mobilized and organized by men to travel to Onitsha to protest. But at the same time, their leaders were collaborating with other men by settling the dispute without having consulted with the rest of the women.

In the precolonial social values, the arrest and detention of elderly women, especially leaders of the Women's Council – who would have been *Ekwe* titled women, the earthly representatives of the Goddess Idemili, the ultimate matriarchs – would have been sacrilege. But values were changing as some people felt that the new women leaders were corrupt and used their powers dishonestly, conspiring in secret and fining people unjustly in order to enrich themselves. To them the arrest was a sanction against excessive use of power. While some looked to the Bible and Hebrew culture, others distorted facts about traditional culture in their definition of the proper status of women *vis-à-vis* men. The Christian and Western influenced elites condemned the women's 'headstrongness' as unfeminine, as all women ought to bow their heads to their husbands; women should be seen as helpmates and sub-ordinates.

The 1977 arrest ushered in a new era of politics in which representatives of organizations could be mobilized by others – men or women – to demonstrate. Protests and demonstrations became manageable events, like ceremonies that can be planned, rehearsed and acted out or performed. A new era had emerged in which hitherto autonomous women's organizations began to act on directives from elsewhere or from 'above', and no longer in the context of the women's system.

After this arrest, meetings and activities of the Women's Council were banned. It was not until a year later, through pressure from individuals in Nnobi who had been embarrassed by the incident, that the NWO reorganized the Women's Council. Their method of representation was altered. They were given a constitution. The NWO cut down the offences which the women could fine. In effect, the NWO put the Women's Council under its supervision and guidance.

In the same year, men were having their own problems in the NWO as a result of a general demand that its accounts be rendered to the public. The youth attacked the dominance of the elders, calling for the setting up of a committee to draw up a constitution for the town and for a general election. They demanded a new NWO in which women, the youth and social organizations would be given seats on the executive committee. When this general election was finally held at the end of 1977, these demands for wider representation had not been heeded. When a constitution was finally written and published, the Women's Council had no representation on the central executive. Thus, in terms of its organizational autonomy and political relevance, the traditional powers of the Women's Council and therefore Nnobi women had been altered. The same processes took place in their historically economic power base, the marketplace.

Striking at the heart of matriarchy: loss of control of the marketplace In Nnobi, the major commercial centre, the central marketplace called Afor Nnobi, has traditionally been under women's control. Women still occupy the centre or heart of the market, while both men and women trade on the peripheral areas. As a result of colonialism and the introduction of a market economy, economic transformation has resulted in significant changes in the balance of economic power. Whereas most Nnobi women's economic and commercial activities end up at this marketplace, the majority of Nnobi men have greater economic choices in a wider network involving other urban centres in Nigeria, through paid employment, trade and commerce, industry, agriculture, consultancy, etc. This has had a direct effect on social transformations and patterns of social relations in contemporary

Nnobi society. These wider networks have given men a lot of advantages over most women in Nnobi, who remain confined to the marketplace economy. Yet, this marketplace, the traditional power base of Nnobi women, has come increasingly under male control.

Among its other problems of loss of autonomy, in 1982 the Women's Council found itself fighting to maintain control of the marketplace. The *Igwe*'s council had appointed a special market committee to take over the policing of the marketplace without the consent of the Women's Council. The Women's Council had to confront these men who were sent to reorganise and police the central market. Following agitations by the women, a compromise solution was reached whereby the market masters would be jointly appointed by the NWO and the Women's Council. Duties were then shared out between the Women's Council and the market masters. The women were to clean the markets, while the market masters would allocate stalls and police the market.

Within the confines of the marketplace, it seems that the women remained very strong and powerful. Even in the 1977 arrest, during which Nnobi women failed to act collectively, in the marketplace they had booed and insulted those whom they knew to have been responsible for their arrest. However, instead of the traditional Nnobi women's strategy of strike action and mass walk out, *isi nta*,[11] they used the strategy of satire and innuendo. It was in the marketplace that they felt strong enough to do so.

In 1987, the politics around Nnobi central market came into the open again as a result of a new government rural development policy. With the biting effect of the International Monetary Fund (IMF) prescribed Structural Adjustment Programme (SAP), the local and state governments have found it necessary to generate revenue. Yet they find it difficult to contribute money towards rural projects. There is, therefore, a situation in which government wants villages to build markets and hand them over to government. This was the case with the planned Afor Market Project, whereby the NWO decided to construct a modern market at the present central market. To this effect, a committee of experts was set up consisting of a designer, surveyor, and architects and chaired by an engineer.

Everyone in Nnobi acknowledged the fact that the markets have been the responsibility of the Women's Council ever since Nnobi was born, and agreed this to be the most important function of the Women's Council. The president of the NWO claimed that the Women's Council recommends any further development in the market to the Town Union and that the Town Union works in close cooperation with the women. But my investigations with members of the Women's Council did not corroborate this claim, especially in the plans to modernize the central market. The institution of a market master was, in fact, an attempt to reduce the power of the Women's Council in the controlling of the marketplace. Again Nnobi women were not consulted over the decision to institute toll collection at the central market in 1983. Both Nnobi women and other people from neighbouring towns who used the marketplace raised objections to the toll.

Since certain elements in one of the neighbouring towns tried to cash in on the discontent around the toll levy, the NWO quickly appealed to the leaders of the Women's Council for support – which they got and thus averted upheaval in Nnobi. In the toll conflict, the NWO saw the role of the Women's Council as that of convincing Nnobi women that the money collected from the market toll would go into the central purse of Nnobi. They reasoned that since women make up about ninety per cent of the market population, winning them over meant an end to the conflict. With this new strategy, when the NWO set up the Market Improvement Committee, six representatives of the Women's Council were nominated onto the committee – but they were not invited to the meetings. The male experts from the urban elites who made up the committee felt that they had nothing to say to illiterate village women.

In an interview in 1987 the president of the NWO, who was very aware of the powers of the Women's Council, admitted to me, and in the presence of the leader of the Women's Council, that women have always controlled the marketplace. He stated that it was only recently that men have come into the market, the reason being that development requires a lot of money. Other than this, everything – even the construction of the market stalls, including those in the periphery occupied by men – was done by women. The structures are constructed by women in groups. Each group usually collects money and constructs one line of market stalls.

We thus find that the cost of modernization has made it necessary, as a result of an ineffective government and lack of clear policies to safeguard women's traditional rights, for men to come into the marketplace. The new market has to be designed and planned, larger buildings have to be constructed – all requiring an expertise lacking in village women. Yet there is a tragic irony in the fact that these women will contribute money towards this modernization which will result in the erosion of their traditional power base, the economic heart of African matriarchy.

In this contemporary history and its structures, the forces against women's traditional rights seem to be coming from all directions, including government policies. Such policies which have, for example, made local organizations the primary vehicle for rural development at the grassroots have only strengthened the powers of Town Unions, social clubs and the private sector.

There is a problem in the fact that the body through which the stated main priorities of the government – that is, rural development – are to be achieved, is instituted as a separate Community Development Committee (CDC), and not as an integral part of the structure of local government councils. Yet the CDC is expected to comprise representatives of all local organizations in each community in Anambra State: for example, Town Unions, clubs and associations, age-grades, women and youth organizations, religious organizations, elders and traditional rulers. Indeed, it is vaunted as a popular front, based on assumptions of a common interest. Yet we know that this is not the case from the detailed analysis of the conflicting interests which I have presented in this case study of the rural community of Nnobi.

Conclusion

This chapter has attempted to shift the focus from the usual state–civil society paradigm to the concept of anti-power, anti-state movements. By this, I mean political struggles which are not out to wrest power from anyone, but simply wish to defend and maintain their autonomy – that is, their right to stand against domination and violation. I have argued that apart from decentralized African societies which have historically resisted incorporation into state systems, and fought and rebelled against state domination, indigenous women's movements in Africa have also been anti-power. They have struggled to defend their autonomous organizations, their structures or systems of self-rule.

I have argued that states are not self-sufficient entities in themselves, but are economically dependent on component or other communities. The contradiction is the fact that in many cases, particularly the historically decentralized societies, the communities themselves are organizationally and economically viable without state presence. From their point of view, the state is in fact a burden to them. It is not a question of integration since these communities do not want to be part of a state system; they do not need to be part of a state. State power thus seems to be based on appropriation, domination and violence.

On the history of this state violence in Africa, I highlighted the differences between the work of Cheikh Anta Diop and those of European scholars. Diop maintained that precolonial states in Africa did not need to use violence, since their matriarchal moral philosophy did not necessitate it. In any case, resources were abundant. This position was reached as a result of Diop's dichotomization of the states and community systems, thereby failing to analyse the structures of relations between these systems. The evidence, however, shows that the material wealth of the states was dependent on exploitation of wealth from the surrounding communities in the region and beyond. The practice of slavery is, of course, based on violence; and all the states practised slavery.

I showed that although some European scholars argued that the evolution of states in Africa was dependent on the acquisition and control of weapons of war and violence, their own evidence showed that these instruments of violence – horses and gunfire power – were imported into Africa during specific historical periods. The kind of masculinist patriarchal ideologies which validated violence also came into Africa as a result of violent invasions. From the time of these invasions to the present day, state power in Africa has been based on violence, domination and exploitation of the communities.

Having formulated a specific African model of gender and social conflict, which establishes the analytical concept of gender, I traced the processes of the subordination of women in a specific Igbo community, Nnobi, which itself became subordinated under a European state system. I contrasted the character of women's organizational autonomy under the indigenous matriarchal system with their gradual fragmentation and loss of autonomy and solidarity under the leadership of a European-reproduced elite. With a new male-biased political system, under such a masculinized power structure, women in power could no longer be said to be serving women's interests.

In looking at conflicts and social movements, one is therefore faced with level upon level of contradictions, or changing situations of contradictions, between the state and the community, and within the community itself. This study has concentrated on the most fundamental and perennial contradiction of gender.

Notes

* This chapter was first written as a paper for the CODESRIA project on Social Movements, Social Transformation and the struggle for Democracy in Africa. It was published in Mahmood Mamdani and E. Wamba-dia-Wamba (eds), 1995, *African Studies in Social Movements and Democracy*, CODESRIA Publications.

  1. See Amadiume, 1987a; 1989; and the introductory chapter of this volume.
  2. See Chapter 8, this volume.
  3. See Amadiume, 1987b.
  4. See *Feminist Review*: Socialist-Feminism, Out of the Blue. Special Issue, No.

23, Summer 1986; *Feminist Review*: The Past Before Us, Twenty Years of Feminism. Special Issue, No. 31, Spring 1989; Judith Evans, Jill Hills, Karen Hunt, Elizabeth Meehan, Tessa ten Tusscher, Ursula Vogel, Georgina Waylen, 1986, *Feminism and Political Theory*, Sage, London.

5. See Chapter 4 in this book.

6. See, for example, R.E. Ritzenthaler, 1960, 'A Woman's uprising in the British Cameroons', *African Studies*, 19 (3); S. Ardener, 1975, 'Sexual insult and female militancy', in Shirley Ardener (ed.), *Perceiving Women*, Dent, London; Audrey Wipper, 1982, 'Riot and rebellion among African women: three examples of women's political clout', in F. Jean O'Barr (ed.), *Perspectives on Power*, Duke University Press, Durham, NC; Cora Ann Presley, 1986, 'Labour unrest among Kikuyu women in colonial Kenya', in Claire Robertson and Iris Berger (eds), *Women and Class in Africa*, Africana Publishing Company, New York.

7. See H. Gailey, 1971, *The Road to Aba*, University of London Press, London; S. Leith-Ross, 1965, *African Women*, Routledge and Kegan Paul, London; M. Perham, 1937, *Native Administration in Nigeria*, Oxford University Press, London; Nina E. Mba, 1982, *Nigerian Women Mobilized: Women's Political Activities in Southern Nigeria, 1900–1965*, University of California, Berkeley, Calif.; C. Ifeka-Moller, 1975, 'Female militancy and colonial revolt: the Women's War of 1929, Eastern Nigeria', in Shirley Ardener (ed.), *Perceiving Women* (see note 6 above); and S.N. Nwabara, 1977, *Iboland: a Century of Contact with Britain 1860–1960*, Hodder & Stoughton, London.

8. Information in this section is based on my fieldwork in Nnobi during the following periods: 1980, 1981–82, and 1985–87. Some of these data are published in detail in Amadiume, 1987b.

9. On periodic markets, market networks and the social functions of the marketplace, see Hodder and Ukwu, 1969.

10. This was also the conclusion reached by H.N. Nwosu and G.O. Nwankwo in their case study of local governments in Anambra State. Their research covered ten Local Government Areas and ten communities for the period 1980–83. Their report is contained in a paper entitled, 'The effectiveness of local governments in social and economic development of the rural areas: a case study of local governments in Anambra State', final report on I.D.S. Research Project No. 9 on Self-Reliance and Development in Nigeria, Institute of Development Studies, University of Nigeria.

11. See Ifi Amadiume, 1987b for a description of this traditional method of picketing; see also J. Van Allen, 1972, 'Sitting on a man: colonialism and the lost political institution of Igbo women', *Canadian Journal of African Studies*, 6 (2).

Bibliography

Afigbo, A.E., 1972, *The Warrant Chiefs: Indirect Rule in South-Eastern Nigeria, 1891–1929*, Longman, London.

Amadiume, Ifi, 1987a, *Afrikan Matriarchal Foundations: The Igbo Case*, Karnak House, London.

— 1987b, *Male Daughters, Female Husbands: Gender and Sex in an African Society*, Zed Books, London.

— 1989, 'Cheikh Anta Diop's theory of matriarchal values as the basis for African cultural unity', Introduction to Cheikh Anta Diop's *The Cultural Unity of Black Africa* (1989).

Barrett, Michele, 1980, *Women's Oppression Today: Problems in Marxist Feminist Analysis*, Verso, London.

Bello-Imam, I.B., 1983, *Local Government Structure in Britain and Nigeria – a Study of Structural Evolution*, Nigerian Institute of Social and Economic Research (NISER), Lagos.

Berger, Iris, 1975, 'Rebels or status-seekers? Women as spirit mediums in East Africa', in Shirley Ardener (ed.), *Perceiving Women*, J.M. Dent, London.

Bernal, Martin, 1987, *Black Athena: The Afroasiatic Roots of Classical Civilisation, Vol. 1: The Fabrication of Ancient Greece 1785–1985*, Free Association Books, London.

Boddy, Janice, 1989, *Wombs and Alien Spirits*, University of Wisconsin Press, Madison, Wis.

Diop, Cheikh Anta, 1987, *Precolonial Black Africa: a Comparative Study of the Political and Social Systems of Europe and Black Africa from Antiquity to the Formation of Modern States*, Lawrence Hill & Co., Westport, USA.

— 1989, *The Cultural Unity of Black Africa: the Domains of Matriarchy and of Patriarchy in Classical Antiquity*, Karnak House, London.

Engels, Frederick, 1972, *The Origin of the Family, Private Property and the State*, Lawrence & Wishart, London.

Fage, J.D., 1969, 'Slavery and the slave-trade in the context of West African history', *Journal of African History*, 10(3): 393–404

Fanon, Frantz, 1967, *The Wretched of the Earth*, Penguin Books, Harmondsworth.

German, Linsey, 1989, *Sex, Class and Socialism*, Bookmarks, London.

Goody, Jack, 1971, *Technology, Tradition, and the State in Africa*, Oxford University Press, London.

Griaule, M., 1965, *Conversations with Ogotemmeli*, Oxford University Press, London.

Griaule, M. and Dieterlen, G., 1965, *Le Renard pale* (The Pale Fox), Tome 1, Inst. Ethnol., Paris.

Hart, Keith, 1982, *The Political Economy of West African Agriculture*, Cambridge University Press, Cambridge and New York.

Hiskett, Mervyn, 1973, *The Sword of Truth: The Life and Times of the Shehu Usman Dan Fodio*, Oxford University Press, London and New York.

— 1984, *The Development of Islam in West Africa*, Longman, London and New York.

Hodder, B.W. and Ukwu, U.I., 1969, *Markets in West Africa*, Ibadan University Press, Ibadan.

Horton, Robin, 1971, 'Stateless societies in the history of West Africa', in J.F.A. Ajayi and M. Crowder (eds), *History of West Africa*, Vol. 1 (2nd edn), Longman, London.

Inikori, J.F. (ed.), 1982, *Forced Migration: The Impact of the Export Slave Trade in African Societies*, Hutchinson, London.

Jaywardena, K., 1986, *Feminism and Nationalism in the Third World*, Zed Books, London.

Kirk-Greene, A.H.M. (ed.), 1965, *The Principle of Native Administration in Nigeria: Selected Documents, 1900–47*, Oxford University Press, London.

Law, Robin, 1976, 'Horses, firearms, and political power in pre-Colonial West Africa', *Past and Present*, 72: 112–32.

— 1978, 'Slaves, trade, and taxes: the material basis of political power in precolonial West Africa', *Research in Economic Anthropology*, 1: 37–52.

Leacock, Eleanor, 1981, *Myths of Male Dominance*, Monthly Review Press, New York.

Lebeuf, Annie, 1963, 'The role of women in the political organization of African societies', in Denise Paulme (ed.), *Women of Tropical Africa*, University of California Press, Berkeley.

Levtzion, N., 1976, 'The early states of the Western Sudan to 1500', in A. Ajayi and M. Crowder (eds), *History of West Africa*, Vol. 1, Longman, London.

Lewis, I.M., 1971, *Ecstatic Religion*, Penguin, Harmondsworth.

Lovejoy, Paul E., 1983, *Transformations in Slavery: a History of Slavery in Africa*, Cambridge University Press, Cambridge.

Marx, Karl and Engels, Fredrich, 1964, *The German Ideology*, Lawrence and Wishart, London.

— 1967, *The Communist Manifesto*, Penguin, Harmondsworth.

Meillassoux, C., 1981, *Maidens, Meal and Money: Capitalism and the Domestic Community*, Cambridge University Press, London.

Miers, Suzanne and Kopytoff, Igor (eds), 1977, *Slavery in Africa: Historical and Anthropological Perspectives*, University of Wisconsin Press, Madison, Wis.

Mudimbe, V.Y., 1988, *The Invention of Africa: Gnosis, Philosophy, and the Order of Knowledge*, Indiana University Press and James Currey, Bloomington and Indianapolis.

Okonjo, K., 1976, 'The dual-sex political system in operation: Igbo women and community politics in Midwestern Nigeria', in N.J. Hafkin and E.G. Bay (eds), *Women in Africa: Studies in Social and Economic Change*, Stanford University Press, Stanford, Calif.

Onwuejeogwu, M., 1969, 'The cult of the Bori Spirits among the Hausa', in M. Douglas and P. Kaberry (eds), *Man in Africa*, Tavistock Publications, London.

Ramazangolu, C., 1989, *Feminism and the Contradictions of Oppression*, Routledge, London.

Rodney, Walter, 1966, 'Slavery and other forms of social oppression on the Upper Guinea Coast in the context of the Atlantic slave trade', *Journal of African History*, 7(4): 431–43

Rubin, Gayle, 1975, 'The Traffic in Women', in R. Reiter (ed.), *Towards an Anthropology of Women*, Monthly Review Press, New York.

Sacks, Karen, 1979, *Sisters and Wives: the Past and Future of Sexual Equality*, Greenwood Press, Westport, Conn.

Stroebel, M., 1976, 'From Lelemama to lobbying: women's associations in Mombasa, Kenya', in N.J. Hafkin and Edna Bay (eds), *Women in Africa*, Stanford University Press, Stanford, Calif.

Sweetman, David, 1984, *Women Leaders in African History*, Heinemann Educational, London.

Van Sertima, Ivan (ed.), 1984, *Black Women in Antiquity*, Transaction Books, New Brunswick, NJ.

6 Gender and the contestation of religion: a historical perspective on African societies*

I hope by the wording of the title of this chapter to demonstrate a departure from the traditional male-focused approach to the study of religion. In the classical patriarchal approach, females are usually seen as good or mad and bad, either as controlled women saints and mystics or uncontrolled witches and prostitutes. In short, females are seen as polluting objects to be controlled by taboos and negative representation, giving rise to the term misogyny in feminist theology and feminist philosophy of religion. Religion in this Judeo-Christian approach is seen as an abstract, unquestionable body of beliefs and practices relating to the worship of one supreme universal God. This has, of course, given rise to a huge debate on the place of monotheism in traditional African religions, which I am not going to concern myself with here.

For the sake of brevity, I am also not going to go into various critiques of the anthropological evolutionist approach to what has variously been called tribal, autochthonous, indigenous, traditional African religions, which assume a progressive development from inferior primitive magic and superstition to superior civilized religion proper in the worship of one universal God.

I prefer here to present a specific self-named African religion in its social and historical context, showing the primacy of gender in both the construction and contestation of religious claims. I also hope to show that social subjects in their specific interest groups play an active role in the reproduction and use of ritual, the symbolic and communicative expression of religion. Also, I aim to highlight specific historical experiences which have led to the redefinition of ethics and the consequences of these on gender relations, identity, status and African women's traditional power systems. By so doing, I would be adding my contribution to a recent widened scope focusing on women's religious involvement and experiences.

In his important text book, *African Religions*, Benjamin Ray (1976) claims to have reviewed various perspectives and controversies in the study of African religions. Yet he neither mentioned nor considered the relevance of gender. He, however, acknowledged the continuing centrality of the question of perspective in the study of African religions. Moving beyond theological concerns with phenomenology, Ray suggests a polymethodic and multidimensional approach, due to the very nature of African religions. He, like many other scholars, reaffirmed African religion as 'part and parcel of the whole fabric of African cultural life. Religious phenomena are thus closely interwoven with social, psychological, and moral dimensions' (1976: 16). Ray was therefore proposing a multi-disciplinary approach.

Not far removed from Ray's position, Evans Zuesse in his book *Ritual Cosmos* (1979) calls African religion the religion of structure as opposed to Christianity which he calls the religion of salvation. Since religions of structure are concerned with 'the norms and eternal relationships which structure all process and change in this world' (1979: 7), Zuesse points out the importance of the rich data and insights of ethnography, particularly the use of structural anthropology for the study of African religions. I have consequently found it more useful to focus on specific societies for context.

The specific society that I am going to look at is a Nigerian Igbo village, Nnobi, where I have carried out fieldwork periodically for over ten years. It is also my father's hometown. Most of these data have been published in my book, *Male Daughters, Female Husbands* (Amadiume, 1987).

I set out to do fieldwork knowing religion only as either god-centred or God-centred. I had no previous knowledge of religion as possibly being goddess- and female-centred. Also, my area of fieldwork had been classified as patrilineal by the few social anthropologists who had some knowledge of the place. Most of my subsequent findings, which went contrary to received knowledge, were completely new to me. I was not born and brought up in Igboland, but in Muslim Hausaland. However, I spoke Igbo well and had some knowledge of Igbo culture through family and relatives. From this short personal background, I turn to some background on African political systems, to facilitate a better understanding of the dynamics of gender in Nnobi society.

Gender and African political systems

It was Kamene Okonjo (1976) who first used the concept of a 'dual-sex' system to characterize traditional African political systems, citing the Igbo as an example. In contrast, she described the European system as 'single-sex'. According to Okonjo, in the 'dual-sex' systems, 'each sex manages its own affairs', while in the European 'single-sex' system, 'political status-bearing roles are predominantly the preserve of men … women can achieve distinction and recognition only by taking on the roles of men in public life and performing them well' (ibid.: 45).

This historical political autonomy of African women's organizations was also confirmed by Annie Lebeuf's (1963) general survey of the role of women in the political organization of African societies, particularly their practical participation in public affairs. Like Okonjo, Lebeuf saw public participation of women as the distinguishing factor between African political systems and European state systems. Her historical survey covered the rule of queens and queen mothers in the Southern African region, and similar systems of female rule and power sharing with men in West Africa. This was also the case among East African societies. Furthermore, David Sweetman's (1984) and Ivan Van Sertima's (1984) accounts of prominent and powerful women leaders, queens and empresses in African history go back into antiquity, covering ancient empires including Nubia, Ethiopia and Egypt.

In Chapter 5, I pointed out the privileged position of these ruling women in the centralized political system, and the fact that female leadership was also present at the community level in both the centralized and non-centralized political systems. African women were therefore involved at various levels of formal and informal organizing of economic, social, cultural and political activities. As Annie Lebeuf eloquently stated, the West should not use its anti-feminist attitude and misogyny to judge gender relations in other cultures, particularly in Africa (1963: 93).

While Lebeuf showed the prominence of African women in social and political activities, debunking the supposition in Western feminist theory that all women were enslaved in domesticity, Cheikh Anta Diop (1989) persevered to demonstrate a historical explanation for these differences in women's experiences of power. Diop's theory derives from his notion of African matriarchy, which, as I pointed out in the previous chapter, is based on rules of inheritance and succession, and thus gives great prominence to the rule of queens in centralized political systems. In my own work, I have been more interested in the economic and ideological evidence of matriarchy in the social structure; indeed as a distinct social system.

In my research I have found that the traditional power of African women had an economic and ideological basis, and derived from the sacred and almost divine importance accorded to motherhood. This has led me to argue that the issue of the structural status of motherhood is

the main difference between the historical experiences of African
women and those of European women. It explains the differences in the
histories of the family in the different systems. Frederick Engels (1891)
argued that the European patriarchal family is both the root and the
seat of women's oppression. This has led me to suggest that the atom-
ization of women in this privatized family probably explains why
European women did not achieve structural women's organizations as
African women did.

We do need to develop a more comprehensive theory about African
women's social organizations and their cultural models. A lot more
work is needed on the history of marriage, the widespread social
practice of woman-to-woman marriage, female-headed households, and
matricentric socio-economic formations in Africa. What were the first
marriage patterns? What new kinship and social arrangements were
formed at the end of the women's sex-strike and mass women walk-
outs described in the previous chapter? We have yet to explain the
predominance of matriarchy symbolism in myths and goddess-worship
in the study of religions in Africa, and the juxtaposition of patriarchal
and matriarchal tendencies in the social structures of African societies.

From a recognition of plural-gendered systems, I am able to retheorize the moral philosophies and political consciousness which are
anti-dominance, anti-power and anti-state. This enables me to shift
from the state–civil society paradigm in European political philosophy
to other possibilities of socio-political organization – for example, the
case study of Nnobi presented in Chapter 5, which showed Igbo
women's indigenous socio-cultural models and the power they had,
and how they lost that power under a new European-imposed model. I
described a society structured on descent, but based on a gender
division of labour, whereby men and women pursued different types of
economic activities. However, with wealth accumulation and certain
liberal social institutions, ideological gender reclassified biological
gender. In kinship and descent groups, we find ideological gender
crossing biological gender divisions in the definition of social roles and
statuses and the rights and power that went with these. The system was
not monolithic and rigid, since gender-bending and gender-crossing
were practised.

In the smallest reducible units of kinship, we find that Nnobi productive units were based on two ideologies which were paradigmatically
in structural opposition, and thus generated dual social systems and
morals. As I showed, the minutest productive unit was the matricentric
unit, the *mkpuke* structure, a distinct mother-focused social category
which occupied a distinct space in the form of a self-contained com-

pound of mother and children. It had an economic base, since it produced for itself. It was a production and consumption unit of those who ate from one pot or one plate. This unit also had an ideological base as it was bound in the spirit of common motherhood in the ideology and ritual of *umunne* – children of one mother – with its strong moral and spiritual force, binding members in love, care, compassion, peace and respect, forbidding incest and bloodshed within the group. In the *umunne* ritual, the focus of worship and spirituality was a successive line of mothers to whom an *okwu*, an altar or shrine, was built inside a woman's kitchen or bedroom.

Above the matricentric productive unit was the *obi*, the ideologically male-focused ancestral house, involving the social (not necessarily biological) construct of fatherhood and family head, a status which can be occupied by women through the practice of woman-to-woman marriage. Just as the *mkpuke* was the ideological seat for motherhood-generated religion, so was the *obi* the ideological seat for the male-generated ancestor religion, which was controlled by men. However, whereas male ancestors were not represented in the temples to the mothers, the symbolic objects of the mother-religion were also represented in the male ancestor temples or shrines.

In practice, in the traditional social structure of Nnobi, the mother–sibling unit – that is, the matricentric unit, the *mkpuke* – and what became a male-headed compound, the ancestral house, the *obi*, would appear to be in dual opposition. This opposition is mediated by the fact that women can head an *obi*. A daughter can also go through a ritual whereby she becomes a male and a son and thus replace her father in the *obi*. She thus became a male-daughter.

At the wider organizational level, patrilineage men, *umunna*, constituted a formal organization with specific duties and powers which were symbolized in specific ritual practices. Patrilineage daughters – *umuokpu* – for their part constituted their own formal organization with specific duties and powers. Because they are the same blood as patrilineage men, they too had specific duties in lineage rituals. Patrilineage wives, *inyom-di*, again constituted a formal organization with specific duties and powers. In their status as daughters and mothers, they conducted specific rituals and religious worship, which was quite distinct from the religious practices of patrilineage males, both in symbolism and in objects or subjects of worship, in a successive line of mothers and the Goddess Idemili.

Since in socio-cultural gender construction daughters were classified as males in relation to wives and had authority just like their brothers over wives, their formal political organization also had its own areas of superior authority over the organization of wives. But there is a major difference between the organizing of men and women. Whereas all the women of Nnobi collectively constituted a formal organization in *inyom Nnobi*, the Nnobi Women's Council, the men did not come under an equivalent overall organization. There were of course exclusive male interest groups, such as titled associations like the *ozo*. But wealthy women could buy themselves into these associations.

With this structure of organization combined with economic power and a mother-focused ideology manifested in a goddess-worshipping religion which forbade human bloodshed, and prescribed fighting only with clubs and stones, we begin to see that there was a matriarchal construct. This is not in the sense of queen rule (although the matriarchs sat like 'queens' in the marketplaces, monopolizing such space as women only and excluding anything male in some cases), but in the sense of a viable female-controlled autonomous system, both complementary and juxtaposed to the male or patriarchal system.

The women had a socio-economic base from which they could accumulate wealth. They could also transform material wealth into prestigious titles and political power. For example, economically successful women could be possessed by the Goddess Idemili to take her title of *Ekwe*. In this system, spirit possession is not an articulation of subordination and powerlessness resulting from invasion by alien spirits, but a direct call to leadership and power. Titled *Ekwe* women became the matriarchs proper, with the most senior *Ekwe*-titled woman, *Agba Ekwe*, having the right of veto in village assemblies. This gave them leadership in their various organizations. They were also next in rank to the Goddess Idemili. It was the Goddess Idemili who reigned above all the other deities and the ancestors. She provided an overall administrative system, embracing the organization of the periodic markets, the days of the week, and the seasonal festivals.

However, this obvious supremacy of the goddess was not left uncontested. I am not going to go into the complex genealogy of Nnobi, naming all the villages and lineage groups. Briefly, these lineages operate on the principles of primordialism (origin) and seniority. However, as several ethnographies have shown, dominant immigrant or conquering lineages usually hijacked the senior political or secular headship, leaving autochthones custodians of the widespread goddess religion, in her manifestation as either earth goddess or river goddess. In Nnobi, for example, we find that while the whole of Nnobi worshipped the Goddess Idemili, only Umuona, the most senior patrilineage, worshipped the male deity Aho, who is represented as the husband of Idemili. Thus the structural contradiction in kinship categories between the *mkpuke* (matriarchal structure) and the *obi* (patriarchal structure) was reproduced in a religious superstructure, as complex and comprehensive as the society itself. Neither society nor religion was monolithically male in the articulation of power, nor monologically reductionist in the proposition of truth.

In order not to present Nnobi as an isolated primitive 'tribe', as would the more negative classical anthropological traditions, I would like to emphasize the fact that all social and cultural activities linked Nnobi with surrounding communities, forming a regional system. Through the rotating periodic markets, shared ceremonies, marriages, organizations, trade and other cultural activities, women enjoyed a very extensive communication network which men did not. They were more mobile than men, and enjoyed multiple identities in different communities as daughters, wives and mothers. This is also true of most Igbo societies, and was the main reason why they were well placed to mobilize women across several communities over a short space of time. This explains how thousands of women could be mobilized over hundreds of kilometres during the Women's War against British colonialists in 1929.

Igbo women opposed colonialism with their lives because it meant a great loss of power for them. The titled women rejected the new White man's religions and his schools, which were against the society and culture of the African Goddesses.

Gender, African religions and social change

Among the African institutions which suffered the greatest onslaught from both Islam and Christianity were indigenous African religions. They were the first thing that the British banned in the areas that they invaded. In Nnobi, the worship of Idemili was banned, and the new converts to Christianity exercised their new-found power in attacks on ancient religious symbols. It is significant that, generally, it was elderly women who defended these symbols, and refused to be converted to Christianity.

In the indigenous system, pro-female values were encouraged through songs, folktales and myths to motivate, on the one hand, the tender values of love and compassion, and, on the other, competitiveness in economic pursuit, for women fed their children. They also promoted positive aggression and militancy without bloodshed in the defence of self, women's rights, children's rights, the pursuit of public peace, and the defence of the traditional matriarchal religion itself.

With structural changes introduced by Christianity, there were changes in the systems of women's leadership. Leadership in indigenous organizations was based on titles and seniority. In the church organizations, wives of the petty-bourgeoisie, the clergy, lay-readers, wealthy traders or prominent men in Nnobi tend to assume leadership positions. This all means a new system in which women in positions of leadership and power can be manipulated by men to whom they owe their access to power. The result is the gradual loss of organizational autonomy and women's indigenous power systems.

On the ethics of gender and power

I have shown how in Nnobi social structure there was a flexibility which allowed a neuter construct enabling men and women to share roles and status. The rigidity of the European gender system allows for only male or female. Its historically male-gendered power structure has consequently kept females out of power. Power in this system has been masculine-gendered and valued. This has consequently raised the question of the gender values of women who successfully wield power in this type of system; that is, the question of gender ethics of power.

These questions have become fundamental issues in the stock-taking exercises on the losses and gains of the Western Women's Movement in the past few years. A debate has resurfaced on the class and gender question, with veteran Marxists and socialist feminists reclaiming the analytical primacy of gender and patriarchy in the sense of cultural and political values in feminist revisionings, feminist ethics and feminist retrievals in the search for knowledge, truth and identity, with women seeking alternative role constructs, and exploring their spiritual and inner nature. Feminists have admitted that class alliance alone did not safeguard their personal interests as women. Many of their male class allies remained oppressive to women. These same accusations have been made by African women against their male comrades in the various liberation struggles in Africa.

My thesis has been very much based on a redefinition of matriarchy and an associated female-generated moral and political philosophy. This gender perspective involves a refocusing on the one constant factor in kinship, the mother. Whether a woman is called daughter or sister, it seems to me, would depend on the gender focus. If mother is the focus, she is daughter. If son is the focus, the same mother's daughter becomes sister, thus giving rise to the term matrilineality, which incorrectly shifts focus from mother to her son. Thus in matrilineality there is already a power shift from matriarchy.

In matriarchy, the matriarchal structure of kinship, manifested in the matriarchal triangle of power, was reproduced in African queen-doms as the tripartite power-sharing system. The names of the queens were uttered jointly with those of the kings on the throne to be occupied. Cheikh Anta Diop refers to Ibn Battuta's testimony on the fourteenth-century West African empire, Mali, that men were not named after their fathers; that genealogy was traced through the maternal uncle; that sons of the sister inherited to the exclusion of his own children (1991: 107).

Other anthrolopologists, such as Wendy James (1978), have pointed out the continuing relevance of matriliny as a metaphor (biological connection between generations), and matriliny as a moral system. However, it is on the structural analysis of the metaphorical symbolism of matriliny (biological connection between generations or motherhood) and the matriarchal ideological construct generated from this symbolism that Eurocentric scholarship has failed to enrich African Studies and studies of religions in general.

The importance of Diop's comparative historical perspective is in his understanding of matriarchy/matriliny as a shift of focus from man at the centre and in control, to the primacy of the role of the mother/sister in the economic, social, political and religious institutions (Diop, 1989). In the anthropological framework, these are the in-stitutions which make up a society, or a social system. The European writers were affected by their patriarchal bias in their understanding and interpretation of African data; James called it the 'patrifocal syndrome'.

Famous anthropologists such as Claude Lévi-Strauss (1969), E.E. Evans-Pritchard (1965), and I.M. Lewis (1976) were perplexed by the imagined 'conflict between male domination and citizenship traced through women', as Lewis put it. Since they assumed male dominance, citizenship traced through women was a strange phenomenon. The general position was that the seizure of political control by women would transform matriliny to matriarchy, and artificial insemination would make things very different.

Unlike the Europeans, Diop as an African had no difficulty in talking about a 'matriarchal regime'. James in contrast rejected the application of matriarchy, suggesting an alternative view of matriliny which focuses on ideas of citizenship and identity, authority, status and ties of loyalty, instead of focusing on structures of power, and therefore contradictions and conflicts. She goes on to provide examples of the centrally creative role of women in production and reproduction in African societies, namely, founding a family, building a household, and the respected and honoured role of motherhood.

Despite acknowledging that this motherhood is 'represented as a central social category, from which other relationships take their bearing – particularly connections with the next generation', James does not describe the organizational unit for the sociocultural construction of these roles, because she is avoiding an analysis of power and conflict – she is avoiding analysing the politics. The result is an inhibited analysis of matriarchy. This is evident in the interpretation which she gives to specific case studies. On Rattray's 1920s Ashanti data, James points out the prevalence of matriliny, the primacy of the mother as a central fact on which Ashanti ideas focus, and the physiology of reproduction as the metaphorical symbol. Consequently, James settled for the term 'matrifocality' as 'an indigenous view of the moral primacy of biological motherhood in the definition of social relations' (1978: 150). In Ashanti society, matrifocality was expressed in socioeconomic terms and a jural framework of matrilineal descent groups.

This so-called matriliny is therefore both concrete and ideological. It is through their mothers and not through their mothers' brothers that men trace status, rank and rights. The matrilineal group holds and transmits property. Had James included a study of the political organization, she would have seen the reproduction of the matricentric unit, the tripartite matriarchal triangle at the superstructural level in the centralized political systems, as pointed out by Annie Lebeuf (1963). This would again bring back the much-dreaded term: matriarchy.

In her second case study, the Uduk of the Sudan-Ethiopian border, James again points out the relevance of matrifocality in the reckoning of status and the social structure, 'in personal and moral terms the mother is the key figure in the kinship world of the Uduk' (1978: 153). Behind the seemingly patrilineal organization there is a matrifocal logic. Having listed several so-called patrilineal societies in Africa in which it is possible to perceive underlying matrifocal ideas, James concludes: 'patrilineages are artificial constructs built up from the fragments of many natural matriline' (ibid.: 156).

This was an important statement which needed to be developed for an analysis of the socioeconomic basis of the ideological construct of matrifocality. Matrifocality is a cultural construct even if the metaphor used derives from the female reproductive role. It throws into question the derogatory dismissal of these ideas by European feminists as essentialist and limiting to women's choices. It seems to me that the important thing here is the ideological message generating the notions of a collectivism of love, nurturance and protection derived from womb symbolism. As James says of most African societies, whether patrilineal or matrilineal: 'there is a deeper and historically more enduring level at which the nature and capacity of women are given primacy in the definition of the human condition itself' (ibid.: 160).

James acknowledged that the European experience and fundamental theory of the family is patrifocal. This has led to biased comparisons and caused difficulties in the present analysis of matriliny, just as it affected the nineteenth-century debate on matriarchy. Significantly, James saw bridewealth and the exchange of woman as the key factor responsible for patriarchal formation. If there is no bridewealth, the system shifts back to matriliny.

Contrary to James, I am arguing that with matriliny, there is already a shift of focus or power in the matriarchal triangle from mother to son, who in matriliny is seen as the all-important uncle. Yet he is a son, a brother, a husband, an absentee/invisible father, as well as an uncle.

I have argued that the recognition of the motherhood paradigm prevents the error of taking patriarchy as given, or as a paradigm. Both matriarchy and patriarchy are cultural constructs, but patriarchy is one step above the motherhood paradigm. This is the basis of my distinction of household as the matricentric unit and family as a wider construct involving the head of one or more household matricentric units. As I have already argued, the matricentric unit does not need to be dismantled for the purpose of reproduction. Also, with the practice of woman-to-woman marriage, the family need not be male headed.

In order further to press my point about the structural presence of a basic matriarchal system in the social structures of traditional African societies, I re-examined three ethnographic texts on contrasting African societies, showing through local terms gender structures of kinship and associated ideological oppositions which are expressed and acted out in ritual (see Chapter 1). I present a summary of this comparison here.

The non-discriminatory matriarchal collectivism acts as a unifying moral code and culture, generating affective relationships, as opposed to the political culture of patriarchy and its strong potential for violence.

In Meyer Fortes's data on the agricultural Tallensi of Northern Ghana (1959; 1987), the contradictions in the kinship system can be glimpsed, in spite of the suppressed and fragmented nature of the information suggesting that there is a missing system in dialogue with the male-centred patriarchal system. But as a result of the ethnocentric bias of the European ethnographer, the partial and monologic experience of the son became a model for the whole society. Yet a dual-gendered system was in operation. Thus, we see a masculinization of data.

The structural significance of female ancestresses and spirits were not analysed from the *soog* kin ideological system, which appears to provide an alternative matriarchal kinship-based moral ideological system. The *soog* kin concept, we are told, extended beyond the framework of the lineage and clan; it was in complementary opposition to clan relations and was based on trust and amity. There was, therefore, another ideological system in opposition to patriarchy, but its socio-economic base and the processes of its reproduction were not described.

Similarly Paul Riesman's (1977) data on the Jelgobe, a pastural Fulani people living between Mali and Upper Volta, who practice a mixed economy of cattle-rearing and agriculture, provide a whole set of gendered symbolism in binary opposition in *wuro* (house) equals female equals woman, and *ladde* (bush) equals male equals man. *Wuro* and *ladde* appear to constitute the basic paradigmatical structures of matriarchy and patriarchy. Structurally, the father remains as an outsider to the *wuro* structure. The woman builds and owns the hut, and as such was addressed as head of the house, *Jan suudu*. From this structural unit is derived a whole set of matriarchal meaning and ethics symbolized in the concept of *suudu* – a place of shelter, hut for people, nest for birds and bees, envelope for a letter, a box or case, where anything rests or sleeps. Customs, rules, morality binding wider patrilineage of *Suudu baaba*, father's house, were derived from this womb symbolism.

In Maurice Bloch's (1986) data on the agricultural Merina of Madagascar, we again see two gendered systems of kinship. The matricentric kinship was considered the biological kinship linking children to their mothers and their siblings. At birth, therefore, humans were only matrilineally related. There was a close bond between the children of two sisters. The other kinship system is that of descent, which was determined by elders. In accordance with these two distinct systems, two systems of belief were reproduced or elaborated in ritual, forming a symbolically gender-valued opposition. Under female, we have woman, the house, household, dispersal, south, division, kinship and heat; under male, we have man, the tomb, the clan, unity, north-east, sanctity and order.

A third category was the Vazimba autochthonous category – considered to be the original owners of the land and natural fertility. Vazimba cults were usually dominated by women. There were therefore three ideological systems: the matricentric system dominated by a motherhood ideology; the descent system dominated by elders and a patriarchal ideology; and an invisible/inverted/externalized matriarchy in the Vazimba category. In these four ethnographic texts there is a juxtaposition of systems. The matricentric structures generated alternative moral systems available to social subjects, male or female, in the course of social relations, producing several local oral texts and a local epistemology. The presence of these fundamental matriarchal systems generating love and compassion also means that we cannot take the classical Greek Oedipal principle of violence as a basic paradigm or given in the African context, as Meyer Fortes unfortunately introduced it into African Studies. The ameliorating matriarchal system acted as a constraint on the patriarchal structure, checking the development of the totalitarian patriarchy and monolithism which seem typical of the Indo-European legacy. Out of the European legacy emerged the concept of cultural or moral society as a solid monolith glued together by ritual. That ritual meant patriarchal ideology which was equated with society, power and the state. From a gender perspective, I have attempted to show a different construct and a different experience of religion in African societies. This raises a number of questions.

Issues raised by the matriarchal structure for African Studies

1. What is matriarchy in the African context?
   a) Is matriarchy to be defined as rules of succession and inheritance and the reign of queens?
   b) Or is it to be defined as the deeper structure of the matricentric unit and its ideological and cultural reproduction in the social structure?
2. What is the history of marriage in Africa, given the fact that men have not always controlled the movement of woman?
3. How relevant is the Eurocentric paradigmatical theory of patriarchy for the study of the social structures of African societies?
4. How can we reformulate gender models and socioeconomic formations in the light of the centrality of the basic matriarchal triangle in the social structure of African societies?
5. Given the frequently cited histories of women's mass walk-outs in African villages, what are the implications of matriarchy for frontier theories?
6. If my theory is right that the matricentric structure is present in some form in our varied African societies, what are the implications of the absence of this system in African studies?
7. What are the implications of the matricentric system as a female generated paradigmatical cultural construct for the man is culture and woman is nature theory in anthropology and social studies? This theory sees woman as the voiceless/muted/chaotic/unordered object to be classified or ordered, in the same way that it is assumed that science controls and orders nature.

8. What are the implications of a matriarchal moral philosophy for a comparative historical perspective on state ideologies?

9. What important role does a matriarchal moral philosophy play in the construction of an African identity in contemporary politics and society?

10. How do we restructure the study of indigenous African religions to reflect the relevance of matriarchal moral philosophy and gender in social structure, social processes, in the context of change, and in resistance and social movements in general?

Bibliography

* Open lecture at the Department of Religion, Dartmouth College, USA, February 1993.

Amadiume, Ifi, 1987, *Male Daughters, Female Husbands: Gender and Sex in an African Society*, Zed Books, London/New Jersey.

Bachofen, J., 1861, *Das Mutterrecht*, Benno Schwabe Co. Verlag, Basel.

Bloch, Maurice, 1986, *From Blessing to Violence: History and Ideology in the Circumcision Ritual of the Merina of Madagascar*, Cambridge University Press, Cambridge and New York.

Diop, Cheikh Anta, 1987, *Precolonial Black Africa: A Comparative Study of the Political and Social Systems of Europe and Black Africa from Antiquity to the Formation of Modern States*, Lawrence Hill, Westport, USA.

— 1989, *The Cultural Unity of Black Africa: the Domains of Matriarchy and of Patriarchy in Classical Antiquity*, Karnak House, London.

— 1991, *Civilization or Barbarism: an Authentic Anthropology*, Lawrence Hill Books, Brooklyn, New York.

Engels, Frederick, 1891, *Origin of the Family, Private Property and the State* (4th edn), Lawrence and Wishart, London.

Evans-Pritchard, E.E., 1965, *The Position of Women in Primitive Society and Other Essays in Social Anthropology*, Faber, London.

Fortes, Meyer, 1959, *Oedipus and Job in West African Religion*, Cambridge University Press, Cambridge.

— 1987, *Religion, Morality and the Person*, Cambridge University Press, Cambridge.

James, Wendy, 1978, 'Matrifocus on African women', in Shirley Ardener (ed.), *Defining Females: the Nature of Women in Society*, Croom Helm, London.

Law, Robin, 1976, 'Horses, firearms, and political power in pre-colonial West Africa', *Past and Present*, 72: 112–32.

— 1978, 'Slaves, trade, and taxes: the material basis of political power in precolonial West Africa', *Research in Economic Anthropology*, 1: 37–52.

Lebeuf, Annie, 1963, 'The role of women in the political organization of African Societies', in Denise Paulme (ed.), *Women of Tropical Africa*, University of California Press, Berkeley.

Lewis, I.M., 1976, *Social Anthropology in Perspective*, Penguin, London.

Lévi-Strauss, C., 1969, *The Elementary Structures of Kinship*, Eyre and Spottiswoode, London.

Maine, Henry, 1861, *Ancient Law*, John Murray, London.

— 1871, *Village Communities in the East and West*, John Murray, London.

McLennan, J.M., 1865, *Primitive Marriage*, Black, Edinburgh.

— 1876, *Studies in Ancient History*, Quaritch, London.

Morgan, L.H., 1871, *Systems of Consanguinity and Affinity of the Human Family*, Smithsonian Institute, Washington.

— 1877, *Ancient Society*, Macmillan, London.

Okonjo, K., 1976, 'The dual-sex political system in operation: Igbo women and community politics in Midwestern Nigeria', in N.J. Hafkin and E.G. Bay (eds), *Women in Africa: Studies in Social and Economic Change*, Stanford University Press, Stanford, Calif.

Ray, Benjamin, C., 1976, *African Religions: Symbol, Ritual, and Community*, Prentice Hall, Eaglewood Cliffs, NJ.

Riesman, Paul, 1977, *Freedom in Fulani Social Life*, The University of Chicago Press, Chicago.

Schneider, D., and Gough, K., 1961, *Matrilineal Kinship*, University of California Press, Berkeley.

Schlegel, Alice, 1972, *Male Dominance and Female Autonomy: Domestic Authority in Matrilineal Societies*, HRAF Press, New Haven.

Sweetman, David, 1984, *Women Leaders in African History*, Heinemann Educational, London.

Van Sertima, Ivan (ed.), 1984, *Black Women in Antiquity*, Transaction Books, New Brunswick, NJ.

Zuesse, Evans M., 1979, *Ritual Cosmos: the Sanctification of Life in African Religions*, Ohio University Press, Athens, Ohio.

PART TWO
Decolonizing History

7 African women and politics: a history of transformation*

This chapter looks at contemporary women's organizations in Africa and the transformations which have taken place since the colonial period, especially with regard to women's representation and participation in politics. The chapter begins with a general overview of indigenous women's movements and then shifts to a a specific Nigerian case study. My overview draws on the work of Cheikh Anta Diop and his theory of African matriarchy as a way of reopening the matriarchy debate in women's studies

In his book, *The Cultural Unity of Black Africa* (1989), Diop theorized that precolonial Africa had an 'organic cultural unity' based on matriarchy. He showed that matriarchal institutions united Africans and were more important than superficial differences, which were imposed as a result of Arab and European colonialism. Indeed, he went as far as to argue that Africa is the cradle of matriarchy, typical of the southern system, while patriarchy is essentially Indo-European in origin and typical of the northern system. He went on to point out some general distinguishing characteristics of each system, which he suggested were the result of ecological influences.

In African marriage custom, Diop argued, husbands came to wives. Wives were mistresses of the house and keepers of the food. Women were the agriculturalists, and men were hunters. African women derived their power from this central agricultural role. What made this system unique was the sanctity of the mother and her ultimate authority. Oaths invoked the power of the mother in the ritualization of the matricentric unit, mother and child, and the spirit of common motherhood, which is generally symbolized in African religions. From this derives belief in magical gifts and powers, including worldly prosperity.

My own studies have corroborated Diop's ideas (Amadiume, 1987a; 1987b) and it appears to me that all unadulterated African myths, stories, and legends provide additional confirmation. Diop maintains that the ideas

> go back to the very earliest days of African mentality. They are thus archaic and constitute, at the present time, a sort of fossilization in the field of current ideas. They form a whole which cannot be considered as the logical continuation of a previous and more primitive state, where a matrilineal heritage would have ruled exclusively. (1989: 41)

Diop dismissed the evolutionist matriarchal theory of Bachofen (1861) and Morgan's (1871) equally racist theory of marriage and the family, which saw the patriarchy and monogamy of Greece and Rome as the ultimate civilization. Diop's book is in fact a devastating critique of the work of these two men. He argued that the (northern) Indo-European patriarchy, which was nomadic, denied women rights and subjugated them under the private institution of the patriarchal family. The system was characterized by dowry, fire worship and cremation. The ethnocentricism, racism and imperialism of Indo-Europeans resulted in their judgement of other civilizations by their own standards, which resulted of course in a false and racist classification and ranking of social systems and values. This racist notion of 'high' and 'low' civilizations equated feudal, pyramidal, bureaucratic and imperialistic political systems with high culture, while democratic, decentralized political systems, where power was diffused, were regarded as low and primitive.

As Diop pointed out, the northern patriarchal civilization, as exemplified by Greece and Rome, was characterized by the city state. Its literary ideals were tragedy, war, violence, crime and conquest. Guilt, original sin and pessimism pervaded its moral ethics, which were individualistic. Africa, on the other hand, was characterized by the territorial state. It valued the matriarchal family, peace and justice, goodness and optimism, and social collectiveness.

Diop argues that the introduction of patriarchy to Africa occurred as a result of external change: principally the coming of Islam in the tenth century, Christianity, and the secular presence of Europe in Africa, as characterized by colonial legislation, land rights, patronymics, monogamy, a class of Western-educated elites, and moral contact with the West.

The point I argued in *African Matriarchal Foundations* (1987a), where I tried to substantiate some of Diop's theories, is that one need not go back to ancient history to discover African matriarchal ideology and its socio-political institutions. In the Igbo case – Igbo being a society which received Western anthropological theory has classified as strictly patriarchal – I showed clearly that, despite its colonial heritage and subsequent distortion of its history, African matriarchal heritage is still present in the deeper structures of the kinship systems: in women's rituals, women's institutions and indigenous women's organizations.

Diop's view of society appears to be formalist, and I have quarrelled with his position, which leaves little room for dissent and conflict (Amadiume, 1989). A view of society as dynamic in itself and therefore capable of internal change, given its inherent contradictions, prompted me to disagree with Diop's thesis of a 'harmonious dualism' between men and women. I argue that patriarchy and matriarchy have always been contesting systems which have been articulated and manipulated in the power struggle between interest groups in indigenous African societies. Economic, social, and political groupings have continually manipulated the ideologies of sex and gender.

As a result of this struggle, many indigenous African societies developed a system of checks and balances. If African women were the economic backbone of the continent (and still are today in the subsistence economy and informal sector), they must have been well organized in very effective women's organizations, institutions, rituals and religions. If women were used to defending their economic position and fighting the ever-present, controlling and oppressive forces of patriarchy, they must have developed a very strong sense of female solidarity.

In my reconstruction of traditional African women's organizations in Igbo society, I showed how language and the manipulation of gender resulted in a system which made it possible for men and women to share roles and status in the power hierarchy, through certain titles and institutions such as 'male daughters', woman-to-woman marriages, or 'female husbands'. Gender crossing was flexible enough to mediate what would have been a rigid system separating men and women and a perpetual situation of sexual conflict, with the main contradiction being the simple sexual division of labour.

What did operate in this 'democratic', decentralized political system was the diffusion of power among various interest groups and their formal organizations. In these decentralized political systems, women in their various organizations – which were based on status, economic achievement, or secret or mystical knowledge – retained a great deal of autonomy. This is, of course, the essence of decentralization. Power is not concentrated at the centre, as is characteristic of the Western state systems which have bred horrible dictatorships in Africa.

In a subsistence redistributive economy based on agriculture and trade – the case with most traditional African economies – the degree to which women controlled the proceeds from their labour seems to have depended on the status and the strength of their organizations. The important point is that Women's Councils were controlled by women. Whether as lineage daughters, as daughters of a specific village or town, or as wives, the women achieved the right of formal recognition as a political group with recognized and guaranteed economic, social, political powers and ritual force. Members knew the rules of the game and broke them with full knowledge of the consequences. With economic achievement or ritual approval, it was also possible to belong to various title societies – some open, some restricted.

Thus African women's organizations traditionally enjoyed the privilege of ritual autonomy, a factor which was important for any exclusive political organization to function autonomously and effectively. Women made their own rules, sanctioned their own members, and devized their own strategies of action. I would argue that these institutions mirrored ancient African matriarchy, from which we have inherited goddess religions and mother-focused myths, legends and folktales. We have also inherited an ideology of motherhood and its social rewards, and, more importantly, the structure of our primary kinship system and its matricentric units as well as our kinship morality of the all-binding 'spirit of common motherhood' – the closest bond of love and trust in our descent or clan systems.

I believe that the reverence of motherhood that this system has generated in African culture is also related to the fear of women's anger in indigenous African societies. The material reality of African women – that is, the economic and social role that women played – meant that the leaders of women, who were the workers and feeders of society, held the right of veto in traditional community assemblies – what Chinua Achebe called 'the court of last resort' in *Anthills of the Savannah* (1988). Collectively the women also held the power of opposition through strikes, non-cooperation, or mass exodus. We have not yet completely worked out what these possibilities mean or their implication for social formation and transformation. We have a great deal of data on African women challenging formal patriarchal authority. However, most of the studies have been about African women applying traditional strategies of rebellion to protest against patriarchal systems imposed by either Islam or Christianity.[1]

In opposing colonialism all over Africa, women acted in the traditional manner to defend the society of which they were the embodiment, irrespective of their struggles against patriarchal control, abuse and oppression. Over the ages, they had perfected a strategy of self-defence that did not rely on destructive weapons. In situations of extreme oppression, danger and anger, women fought with their bodies by exposing that which is held sacred and throwing excrement on themselves.

The greatest insult to an African is to curse his or her mother or to refer to his or her mother's vagina (which explains the angry reactions of many Africans to the insults heaped on Africans by bourgeois women on the issue of women's circumcision). I believe this is true for Arabs and Asians as well. Is this attitude to be attributed to zones of matriarchy or goddess-worshipping cultures? It is through this heritage that we should analyse and explain the general strategy of the 'sexual insult' used by African women during protest and war.[2] The strategy was most effective during the precolonial and colonial periods, when traditional African women's organizations were still autonomous and the traditional systems of checks and balances obtained.

Audrey Wipper (1982) examined three cases where this strategy was applied – namely, Kom women of Cameroun, Gikuyu women of Kenya, and Igbo women of Nigeria. In all three societies women were organized into something like a dual political system. The women's organizations generated their own methods of protest and sanction, which their menfolk had learnt to fear and respect. There was unity of purpose. The women had economic, ritual and political power. Where they did not own land outright, they worked that land and controlled the markets and the subsistence economy. Grassroots women were quick to recognize the new colonial class formations, and the economic and political loss inherent in the changes taking place. They directed their attacks towards the appropriate symbols of imperialism, whether buildings or people.

The sell-out by African men is the reason why, in all three cases, the women cursed the men. Kom women spat in the face of the elite man who came forcibly to teach them about hygiene and agriculture, and they told him that he was 'shit'. Gikuyu women called their men cowards and demanded a change of gender symbols – trousers for skirts – when the men failed to stand up to the White men for imprisoning and banishing their anti-colonial campaigner, Harry Thuku. Igbo women took their grievances against British colonial practices and local collaborators to warrant chief Okugo, who slighted them. They retorted that had he not been protected by the White man, they would have chewed him up like peanuts (Nwabara, 1977: 188).

All three societies had traditionally had a decentralized democratic political system with a grassroots-based leadership, and women had their own self-government. Women also had economic power, strong organizations, and a deep sense of female solidarity. They were involved in the ideology-making processes and could generate positive images, models, symbols and signs, which they could manipulate in the course of social relations. The fact that there was a popular women's movement meant that women knew when and how to demonstrate, protest, abuse or insult. These were 'uneducated' women who, at that time, were reported to have been 'untamed' by Islam, conquest or Christianity. Missionary imperialism had not eroded their historical memory, as Diop would put it. This of course brings up the question of whether this process is reversible.

What is interesting is the fact that it was under colonial, patriarchal systems that traditional African women's organizations began to undergo change and transformation, based on the reproduction of men's organizations and the use of male symbols of power, in aspiring to masculine roles and status. *Omu* women, 'queens' in Onitsha society, for example, began to wear men's colonial helmets and to tie up their breasts (Amadiume, 1987b). This aping of men is more evident in societies colonized by the Arabs and Islam – as, for example, the symbolic articulations in the Bori cult of the Hausa (Onwuejeogwu, 1969), Iris Berger's (1975) analysis of women as spirit mediums in East Africa, and Strobel's (1976) account of the transformation of the Lelemama in Mombasa, Kenya.

Contemporary women's organizations: a Nigerian case study

Contextual political economy The structures, aims and objectives of the national women's organizations are best analysed in the context of the continuing presence of Western imperialism, whose interests the organizations articulate – wittingly or unwittingly. In the national women's organizations we see the processes I described (Amadiume, 1987b) in the formation and structure of modern church-controlled women's organizations in Nnobi – namely, the role of women of the petty bourgeois classes, the guiding principle of Christian morality, and the cooperation or collaboration with the state or the establishment. To understand fully the current situation among women's organizations, however, it is necessary to look briefly at the political history of Nigeria to see the political context in which the organizations are functioning and out of which they grew.

The British amalgamation of northern and southern Nigeria in 1914 meant the imposition of what I have described as a pseudo-state in a forthcoming book entitled *Daughters of the Goddess and Daughters of Imperialism: African Women Struggle for Power and Democracy*. The British sought to unify their colonial administration, not the Nigerian people, since different policies were applied in the north and south. This was especially true of education and religion, which became the two great divides to be manipulated by the colonialists, the new elites and politicians. After amalgamation, the economic and political activities of all sections of the new elites centred on control of the state apparatus and the resources of the country. British imperialist interests sabotaged the first nationalist and pan-African movements with the 1946 Richards Constitution, which arrested efforts toward true unification by encouraging differentiation based on regionalism, ethnicity and sectionalism.

The issue of class was downplayed and manipulated in inter-party clashes. Politicians thus did not concentrate on rejecting the whole capitalist socioeconomic and political systems that were being handed over by the colonialists. Politics became a scrambling for the national cake, not an equitable system of participation, representation and redistribution. The new elites found 'relevance' as representatives of the rural masses and ethnic groups and not as representatives of a new emerging class, with its own class consciousness and class interests, which in fact would prove to cut across religious and ethnic lines. The new elites continued to act as representatives of ethnic groups and communities, which had lost control as a result of colonial disruption and erosion of the traditional systems of checks and balances. These new elites also used inherited colonial state agencies to oppress, terrorize and exploit the masses that they purported to represent. In this way, minorities' fears and state creation became part of the Nigerian political language and culture.

Post-independence political instability cannot be divorced from the centralization of resources, leadership, and development planning. The scramble to get to the national capital and take control – that is, to control the centre – generated the corruption that Nigerians have found too ingrained to eradicate. Ethnicity became the ideology which determined national policy, and this of course obscured the presence of class formation and its inherent cleavages. With the transition from a redistributive to a capitalist economy, the sectors of agricultural production, food production and the subsistence economy, which had been traditionally dominated by women and small farmers, became less important than cash crops for export and foreign exchange. Intensification of a capitalist development strategy led to a mono-economy based on oil exports. Through the same processes, there evolved a political economy based on a capitalist appropriation of land and labour, and profit by a small minority with links to international capital.

There now emerged a new and well-consolidated class of elites which took control of the means of production and the right to determine the movement of capital, either directly or through those in power. Men in government, whether civilian or military, became the wealthiest Nigerians. They also controlled the national women's organizations through their wives, who dominated and directed those organizations.

National women's organizations: co-option

The National Council of Women's Societies As men's political parties emerged, based on ethnic or national affiliations, so too did women's organizations. Beginning in the 1950s, southern women, as a result of their socialization in Western religion and education, began to form organizations and linkages based on group and class interests. The role of Creole women and Creole culture was very important in the development of contemporary women's organizations in southern Nigeria. Their Western ideas spread through individual women who had been trained in the Christian church and through various associations linked to Christian ideology, especially the Young Women's Christian Association (YWCA). It was out of this background that the Women Cultural and Philanthropic Organization was born in Enugu in eastern Nigeria in 1958, for example, as an 'umbrella embracing all women's organizations'. According to a first-hand account by a founder member, with the sponsorship of the British Council in Enugu, she attended a YWCA social welfare course in London on how to organize women. On her return, she suggested the idea of an umbrella organization for women.[3]

Prior to this, the General Strike of 1945 had led to the formation of the Enugu Women's Association (EWA) in an effort to assist the men who were jobless because of the strike. The 1949 massacre of trade unionists at Enugu, on the other hand, saw the presence of female activists in the regional capital. In the western region, it was the abolition of women's flat rate tax in Abeokuta that led to the mass meeting of the Abeokuta Women's Union (AWU), where Mrs Fumilayo Ransome-Kuti proposed the formation of Nigerian Women's Union (NWU) to bring together all Nigerian women to fight for their rights. Mrs Ransome-Kuti suggested that it affiliate with the International Federation of Women.

All the women's organizations of this period were actively and militantly committed to the anti-colonial movement, and Mrs Ransome-Kuti was in fact a socialist, with a socialist agenda. However, as a result of state harassment, she lost the leadership of the emerging women's movement to women of the petty bourgeoisie. Her campaigns had been for women's autonomy and economic power, as embodied in the resolutions of the Federation of Nigerian Women's Societies (FNWS), which were identical with those of NWU.

In 1959, Mrs Adekogbe wrote to the Women's Improvement Society, which had been founded in Ibadan in 1948 as a social welfare scheme. It worked with the YWCA and the women's section of the Ibadan Progressive Union. Leaders of both these societies were teachers, as was Mrs Adekogbe. They inaugurated the National Council of Women's Societies (NCWS) in Ibadan in 1959, with the wife of the Chief Justice of Western Nigeria, Lady Ademola, as president. Mrs Ogunsheye, a lecturer at the University of Ibadan, was secretary, and the treasurer was Mrs Akran, wife of the western region's Minister of Social Welfare.

The NCWS claimed to be the only true national women's organization. From the outset it also claimed to be non-political, concerned solely with welfare and educational matters. This new women's organization received an annual government subvention and became the organization representing Nigerian women. It had branches in the capital towns of the (then) three regions, including Lagos, which was the capital then. Membership was on an individual basis or as members of organizations. Lady Oyinkan Abayomi was head of the Lagos branch, which was composed of elite women, market women, and activist members of the two southern political parties. Other branches were made up primarily of elite, educated, and wealthy women, many of whom had been co-opted by the new political parties. The organizations thus came under party – and men's – control.

During its first national conference, held in Ibadan in 1961, the NCWS called on the government to get women on to boards and into corporations, and to set up employment bureaus for women. They demanded a place in the establishment. From the background of these women and the organizations from which they emerged into the NCWS, we can see the influence of the Ladies Progressive Club and its concern with welfare, charity and philanthropy, on the one hand, and, on the other, the political activism of the militant market women and those from the Women's Party.

Some of the founding members, such as Janet Mokelu, believed that the fusion in the NCWS marked the beginning of group articulation of women's interests and a recognition by the government of women's groups as part of the political process. This claim, in my opinion, is questionable if one considers the issues of class, representation and participation, and, consequently, the effect that this trend has had on traditional women's organizations and women's participation in politics.

What we find is that the new organization provided elite women with an extensive network through which they could participate as individuals in politics, the economy, and the new elite culture. They could also pursue careers, albeit in the name of the female masses. This is not to suggest that individual women did not sometimes participate in women's protests and demonstrations. What we find, however, is that instead of the spontaneous mass actions which had previously led to political gains for the female masses, the leadership role of individual elite women became publicized. The establishment had found a way to 'shut up' the female masses through the co-option of these self-appointed leaders (in reality, they were usually establishment-appointed leaders). The establishment was now able to speak to the female masses through these 'leaders'. With both economic and political interests in the establishment, the 'leaders' saw themselves as accountable to the establishment and not to the women in the rural villages, from whom they are now cut off or shielded by state agencies. It marked the beginning of the present era, with its female tokenism in an establishment which is basically male.

Rather than insisting on collective participation by women in large numbers, these daughters of the establishment began to enjoy their solo performance. They learnt to end their speeches with 'thanks to our men, who stood behind us'. In much the same way, Margaret Thatcher of Britain never thanked the Women's Movement or the feminists on whose gains she rode, but she always thanked her Methodist socialization and the Conservative Party. With the formation of the NCWS, women's protest strategies changed dramatically. Petty bourgeois women wrote letters of appeal or summoned representatives of women's organizations to the town halls and appealed for a 'return to peace'.

Nina Mba concedes that the NCWS lacked the communal, broad-based support that Abeokuta and Ibadan gave the NWU, the FNWS, and the Women's Movement. Those organizations did not survive, but the NCWS, in spite of its ineffective leadership and lack of broad-based support, continues to enjoy the support of each regime and to work for every government that Nigeria has had. As Mba says, 'They bought recognition from government of their claim that they represented the women of Nigeria and that therefore they should be consulted by government on all decision-making which concerned women' (1982: 192). Every government in power has used the NCWS as its outreach to women, since its maternal self-image and philanthropic concerns are not threatening to the establishment.

Critics have relentlessly pointed out, however, that the organization is non-representative and elitist. Some have felt that it has little relevance outside the urban centres, since rural women are still exploited sexually and economically. As examples, they cite the tax laws, *purdah* (Islamic seclusion of women) and neglect. The urban leaders of the NCWS have been accused of ignorance about the plight of rural women. Other critics see the problems of Nigerian women as rooted in religion, customs, and male chauvinism. Nonetheless, the NCWS concerns itself with the interests of a few professional women.

The Council's tactic of 'waiting for government to act' has also come under fire. Some feel that on issues such as child marriage, the NCWS should press for eradication through massive campaigns. Others point out that the NCWS has not made any impact on societal discipline. An older generation of women have been criticized for monopolizing the Council even when they have achieved nothing, and have refused to make way for younger women who hold a different view of wifehood and motherhood. The Council, perceived as not acting but talking, has been told not to lecture rural women from Lagos. Critics have also pointed out the need for the NCWS to become more oriented towards community service, designing programmes for the organization and for the enlightenment of women.

The Council, according to its leaders, is a forum for women of diverse interests and professional background. Instead of empowering women in general, however, we find that elite women do very well financially. They act as missionaries *vis-à-vis* rural women under their so-called rural enlightenment campaign.

Despite the criticisms of the NCWS, officials of the organization are reluctant to give up their posts. The collaboration of the NCWS and the state has been ensured through the practice of having the wives of heads of government assume patronage of the Council. The NCWS continues to be a stepping stone to government appointments for women. Most of the state and federal presidents of the Council have at one time or another served as ministers of state or state commissioners.

In the struggle for control of the NCWS, elite women have often adopted some of the political strategies of male party politics – thuggery, for example. Instead of women's solidarity, there is a vicious rivalry for control, power and supremacy within the context of a political economy based on capitalism and state patriarchy. In order for women to succeed in this system, they must be tokens and act as ladies of the establishment, imitating men or servicing them. There is no true partnership of men and women in such a system. This imitation of those in a dominant position or imitation of the dominant culture can be stretched to include the role of Nigerian elites under the colonial government and that of civilian elites under the military governments. Western imperialism in Africa nurtured an imitative culture in the African elite in the pseudo-state that was imposed.

The NCWS monopoly extended to its relationship with other women's organizations, especially those with a potential for broad-based mobilization or those with the potential for emerging as a true national women's vanguard, in the sense of a pressure group, or those that might officially enjoy government recognition and financial support. For example, it felt threatened by the government-appointed National Committee on Women and Development, which was formed in 1984. Even though the Committee was not set up as a voluntary organization and was mandated to deal with the development needs of rural women, the NCWS saw itself in competition with the Committee and found it necessary to reiterate its status as an umbrella for all women to speak with one voice. The NCWS stressed unity and condemned women who portrayed Nigerian women as 'disunited'. While the NCWS was canvassing for money and power, however, the Committee was consulting with rural women and highlighting their problems.

The Federation of Muslim Women's Associations of Nigeria (FOMWAN) In 1985, as a result of Muslim women's reaction to the non-representative nature of the NCWS, its Christian concerns and orientation, the Federation of Muslim Women's Association of Nigeria (FOMWAN) was formed. Muslim women's organizations in Nigeria have usually been seen as a female wing of Islamic fundamentalism, since they seem to promote *sharia* laws (total obedience of women to Islamic concepts of propriety). In this sense, FOMWAN can be said to be the northern or Islamic equivalent to the NCWS. With FOMWAN, however, we find the same trend as in the other women's organizations in that members who speak on behalf of the organizations or officials of the organization make statements according to their level of political awareness. Hence, while certain members of FOMWAN are reactionary, others are radical or progressive in their pronouncements.

Women in Nigeria (WIN) WIN grew from university campus politics into an indepenent national organization. Its *Document* states that the organization originated in the interest and enthusiasm sparked

by the First Annual WIN Conference at Ahmadu Bello University
(ABU) in Zaria in 1982.[4] Men and women who attended the conference
had, by 1983, established an organization committed to working for
improvement in the condition of Nigerian Women. It is clear that
WIN is different from other contemporary women's organizations in
Nigeria in the sense that it is officially committed to change and is
ideologically oriented, even though the Marxist-Leninist or socialist
leanings of some individual members are not explicitly stated. Some
members claim that this is for strategic reasons. This loophole, I shall
argue, has posed a problem for WIN, as it means that the organization
is really not self-defined.

WIN is urban based in its organizational structure. Even though it
is elitist in its membership, it is essentially anti-establishment. In addition to sponsoring conferences, research work and publishing, WIN is a
campaign group which fights the cases of individual women – for
example, rape cases and women's rights and benefits. In 1985, WIN
began discussions on shifting its focus from academic and urban
concerns to project work at the grassroots level. It decided to undertake
development work with rural women, such as adult education, setting
up income-generating projects, housing and shelter groups. Women's
awareness and mobilization therefore formed its theme for the 1986
annual conference.

There are many problems faced by WIN, according to one of its
representatives, including the fact that its members work full-time and
thus have only a part-time commitment to the work of the organization. The organization also has problems with financing since, unlike
the NCWS, it is not state funded, but dependent on membership dues.
Its radicalism has caused registration problems at the national level
and in some states, where it has encountered threats and opposition.
There is also an issue regarding male membership, which is opposed
by some female members (although the initial high male membership
is said to have declined). Another serious issue dividing the organization
is the question of affiliation to the NCWS. However, a much more
problematic issue is the non-involvement of working-class, peasant,
and grassroots women. The reason is, of course, the origin of WIN
among the university elite and its initial concern with research and
conferences.

In the face of all these problems, including the general accusation
of elitism, WIN has found itself in a dilemma in defining the scope of
its ambitions – that is, should WIN act as a voice for women, or should
it enable women to organize and speak for themselves? I would argue
that the dilemma stems from the fact that WIN's membership is un-

defined. Side-stepping an explicit, self-defining ideology has resulted in irreconcilable differences in views, orientations, and ambitions of some WIN members. Many members seem to be better candidates for the NCWS, and some of WIN's more radical aims and objectives are constantly called into question by less radical members. These young ambitious women are more likely to find a congenial position in the WIN hierarchy or gain higher public recognition through WIN than the NCWS, which is dominated by older women. Thus WIN's lack of ideological self-definition has left room for elite opportunism.

Regarding the difference between WIN and the NCWS, indications are that there are generational, educational, and ideological differences among members in both organizations. This came sharply into focus in Nairobi in 1985 at the conference to mark the end of the UN Decade for Women. The NCWS, which sees itself as an umbrella organization for all Nigerian women, went to Nairobi as a governmental body. It was led by the Minister of Information, who was a senior Air Force officer. (This contradiction prompted Nigerian cartoonists to add a headtie to his uniform.) NCWS delegates objected to the presence of WIN members at the Nairobi conference, even though WIN is not affiliated with the NCWS. The confrontation exposed WIN members to harassment by Nigerian security agents and caused them a great deal of hardship (which again illustrates my contention that the NCWS tries to maintain its monopoly at any cost).

Unlike NCWS, which went to Nairobi to represent the Nigerian government, WIN went to Nairobi to report the Nigerian government's anti-female policies to the UN and the world. To do this effectively, it carried out research into various aspects of the conditions of women in Nigeria. The findings were compiled into a 195-page document which included policy recommendations to the year 2000. WIN believes that these policy recommendations, if implemented, would better the conditions of Nigerian women. The recommendations included: acknowledging and remunerating the value of women's work; the abolition of all flat-rate taxes; the removal of obstacles to women's access to land use and ownership; the improvement of healthcare, agricultural and technical training for peasant and other rural women; ensuring that women have access to and qualification for credit; that women in all sectors should organize and fight for their rights; that directives from women should be considered in formulating policies relating to women; that women should be involved and employed in all aspects of national development plans and programmes; compulsory and free education of women; that rigid gender divisions of roles and jobs should be discontinued for a more positive and egalitarian society; the restructuring of curricula and reorientation of teachers toward the elimination of gender bias; a mass adult education programme for rural women to acquire skills which will lead to the ability to earn higher incomes; minimum age for marriage; abolition of brideprice/dowry; and so on.

Since the Constitution overrides all other laws in Nigeria, WIN went on to quote the sections which guarantee sexual equality. According to Section 39 (11) of the 1979 Constitution, there should be no discrimination or favour on the basis of ethnic origin, sex, political or religious opinion. The WIN *Document* also cited some discriminatory laws. The law against loitering, for example, is used against women and not against male clients and pimps, who perpetuate female prostitution. It is noteworthy that the twenty-six recommendations made by women workers during the 1986 political debate on a new political system for Nigeria are very similar to the WIN recommendations.[5]

Nigeria Labour Congress/Working Women's Wing (NLC/WWW) Women workers in Nigeria had demanded an NLC women's wing because of discrimation against women. In spite of these demands, however, the initiative for setting up the women's wing did not arise out of local processes but as a result of a directive from the Third Ordinary Congress of the Organisation of African Trade Union Unity (OATUU) in Somalia in 1980. Thus it was that the NLC in 1983 decided to permit the formation of women's wings. Even then, permission was slow in coming and limited to a few states, due to the different levels of political awareness and trade union consciousness. The role of the NLC has been in providing women with venues and inviting them to participate in seminars. The NLC Women's Wing remains handicapped by financial and organizational problems, as well as NLC chauvinism: the NLC insists on controlling, supervising, and directing its activities and relations with other women's organizations. Its activities and programmes are subject to ratification by NLC national headquarters (and it is of note that there is not a single woman in the hierarchy of the NLC). The Women's Wing is not even co-opted into the central working committee of the Congress. The general problems of the state branches range from lack of financing to low involvement of women, since various individual unions do not permit their members to participate in the Women's Wing. This is also the case with employers.

The NLC Women's Wing is similar to WIN in its stated objectives. However, while the NLC Women's Wing stresses that it is mobilizing and fighting for women workers in particular, WIN is fighting on behalf of all women in general. Unfortunately, even in this concern with women workers there are problems of elitism and tokenism, as grass-roots women remain uninvolved. The orientations of officials of the NLC Women's Wing range from a focus on female respectability in modern trade unionism to those drawing inspiration from the traditional unionism of Nigerian women, referring to the 1929 Women's War and the Abeokuta Resistance of 1948. Both struggles involved economic and political rights for women, and focused on the tax on women and the excesses of local rulers.

But even with the NLC Women's Wing, we see that the 'performance syndrome', a disease of the colonized elite, also holds sway; one again witnesses the contradiction of male chauvinism, the opportunism of elite women, and their lack of ideological clarity and consistency, even on trade union platforms. As with all general public occasions in Nigeria, wives and daughters of the establishment occupy the high chairs of trade union platforms, and the press focuses on them, as these copy-cat dramas are acted out. More contradictory, however, is the presence of senior men of the NLC at the high chairs during these women's events – and more bewildering yet are the sexist statements made by these male trade unionists.

Conclusion

Given the effects of colonialism and neo-colonialism on African societies, the most urgent project in African scholarship – as many African scholars have argued – is deconstructing and decolonizing received colonial 'African history'. In its place must be constructed a more relevant African history and scholarship. I have found the work of Cheikh Anta Diop and his theory of African matriarchy extremely useful, in contrast to the patriarchal fabrications that characterize a lot of the so-called traditional claims and reconstructions by elite African men. Cheikh Anta Diop comes out in defence of women and their true heritage, deconstructing what he terms 'masculine imperialism' and patriarchy. He takes on the fundamental issue of matriarchy from an Afrocentric perspective, as opposed to a compromised struggle for women's rights in patriarchal systems. Unfortunately, African men who claim to be followers of Diop simply quote those aspects of his work which suit their purpose. The main thrust of his thesis, which rests on African matriarchy, is the least cited or applied.

From the Diopian perspective applied in this study, we have been able to gain a general understanding of African social, cultural and political systems and the place of women in these systems, including other dimensions of traditional gender relations. The most important facts that emerge from the analysis of older systems, which explain African women's traditional power base, centre around three factors: control of the subsistence economy and the marketplace, self-government, and control of their own religion or culture. These were the three most important resources that African women were organized to control and maintain. The contradictions inherent in this mode of production generated a sexual politics which resulted in well-developed women's organizations and a women's movement in Africa, as women had to be well organized to maintain control over these resources. The old systems of checks and balances began to disintegrate as a result of our colonial experiences. Thus Diop's theory, which attributes radical change in Africa to external factors, appears to stand.

It was not the colonialists who dealt the final blow to the traditional autonomy and power of African women, however, but the elites who inherited the colonial machinery of oppression and exploitation, which they have turned against their own people. The nature of traditional popular struggles changed as soon as the new African elites gained control of the military forces introduced by the colonial imperialists, especially the police and the army.

A new system now encroached as the society controlled by the elites began to 'call the tune' with impunity. Illiterate women found themselves bound under a system which needed a kind of expertise that poor villagers lacked. This marked the end of traditional, spontaneous, and popular women's movements in Africa, for this new struggle – with baton-, teargas- and gun-wielding police of the pseudo-states managed by the new African elites – is the current experience of peasant and grassroots women everywhere in Africa.

In Nnobi, for example, grassroots women have been struggling on two fronts – namely, to maintain or retain the autonomy of their organizations and their traditional control of the marketplace. The greatest force against them has been the Town Union – the Nnobi Welfare Organization – a conglomerate of the core male elites from the urban towns and from Nnobi itself. The new system of 'representation' has functioned as a means of co-option and not participation. Representatives of the Women's Council can be summoned, bribed, or told what to do. The absence of a financially viable and participatory local government, with open and local assemblies, has given unbridled powers to male-controlled NGOs and Community Development Committees (CDCs). The same contradictions are reproduced with women's organizations *vis-à-vis* state machineries or male-controlled state agencies at every other level of government, from the state to the federal capital.

In this contemporary system, representation has become synonymous with democracy. Hence the assumption that women can be represented through such fabrications as umbrella organizations. The idea of an umbrella organization representing the interests of all women is ridiculous. Women have been part of the elite and class structures of contemporary African societies and have manifested the fundamental contradictions in these socio-political formations. Their orientations are varied; their interests have been conflicting.

As we have seen from the Nigerian case study, none of the national organizations is representative of grassroots women – least of all the NCWS, which has acted as a buffer between the popular front of grassroots women and their exploiters and abusers. Not even the radical organizations, including WIN and the NLC Women's Wing, are representative of grassroots women. Given its background and its composition, the limitations of WIN, which was the most radical of the national organizations, were self-defined. It could have acted as a protest group, a campaign group, a vigilante group, an awareness group, but not a national vanguard, since events everywhere have shown that such a vanguard – if it is not to result in a revolution which enthrones the elites – must evolve from the grassroots, who must also decide policy after the revolution.

The NLC Women's Wing, on the other hand, is still firmly under the thumb of the Labour Congress, which is government appointed and government regulated, and ridden with sexism and a struggle for position in the hierarchy. It cannot mobilize working women, let alone grassroots women. It is possible that the creation of a government-regulated National Labour Congress marked the end of popular mass movements in Nigeria. Had the NLC made all the traditional women's organizations unconditional members, one wonders what the story of mass movements would have been in Nigeria today.

What then is the answer? How can we achieve a participatory democracy for grassroots women? Is it to be representative or partici-patory? If it is to be participatory, then all indications are that the post-colonial pseudo-state in Africa has crumbled. What we should be considering is what to construct in its place. That, really, is the current political thinking in Africa and in African studies, as opposed to Western constructs of African studies. Diop in fact proposed a bi-cameral system of two assemblies, allowing an independent consultative assembly for women (Diop, 1978). How can we effect this? And how can African feminist scholars theorize this? This could be considered within the framework of a plural system in which there will be community self-government which would again regenerate its own system of checks and balances.

Happily, this trend of stock-taking is worldwide and not confined to Africa. Many of these issues are included in the study of social movements, social transformation, and democracy in Africa being co-ordinated by the Council for the Development of Economic and Social Research in Africa (CODESRIA) based in Dakar, Senegal. Similarly, Western feminists have been involved in a stock-taking exercise on the achievement of set objectives over the years.[6] The arguments have revolved around the issues of race, class and sexuality – that is, differences and internal contradictions. There are, for example, such questions as: To what extent has socialist feminism lost its initial commitment to class struggle? To what extent have feminist academics 'sold out' on the Women's Movement as a whole and become part of the privileged class of the male establishment? To what extent has academic feminism been diverted from serious study to the general women's struggle and movement? Are the traditional tools of political analysis, as embodied in the subject of political science, able to contribute to a feminist political theory?

In this debate, middle-class White feminists have dismissed essentialist feminist theory or essentialism as limiting and stereotyping. Unfortunately, their arguments do not fit well with the African reality. For example, the traditional African women's movement thrived on essentialism, using women's bodies and social roles as ideological and political symbols. That collective and solidarity-based construction of essentialism worked for women at that time, given their political economy and socio-political systems. In contrast, one sees that it is not working for women today because they are deeply divided by class and sexuality under a capitalist system. African women used an essentialist matriarchal ideology to forge a culture for a women's world that was controlled by women. Some of this reality is still true for women in African villages. However, the manipulation of that essentialism has been taken over by elites and used against women. This, of course, prompts the question whether, if motherhood was socially rewarded in an African past, is it still rewarded today?

With elite women in the cities and other world centres, women's demands have become diverse and contradictory. Yet elite women, more than ever before, exploit the concept of networking and umbrella organizations to make inroads into male systems. Working-class and grassroots women are concerned with basic needs and remain on the periphery; bourgeois women are concerned with issues of privilege – for example, higher places in the civil service, education and government. Networking and umbrella organizations have served their ambitions and empowered them, not those of poor women. American White women have now, in 1997, got their political reward in having Madeleine Albright as the first woman secretary of state in the history of the United States. British White women had their own reward in Mrs Margaret Thatcher as the first woman prime minister in the history of Britain. But all these women function in a male environment. Often too, they have taken a male route to power, cutting their political teeth like middle-class boys.

Anna Coote and Polly Pattullo (1990) sought to answer the following questions. Why do so few women exercise real power in mainstream British politics? Why are so many powerless, and what is holding women back? They contrasted the lives of two British women from similar poor working-class backgrounds. The two women were Margaret Thatcher and Jan Burrows. Margaret Thatcher had no brothers. Alfred, her father, was the dominant character in her family and she was close to him. She thus had a male model. She succeeded as a result of a remarkable mix of single-minded ambition, discipline, the social mobility of her family and the family's capacity to educate daughters as though they were sons. Margaret Roberts married a tycoon and, although a mother of twins, had a first-class nanny-housekeeper. She took an individual route to power, her support base being family and class.

In the case of Jan Burrows her family was a hindrance to power as they remained in a working-class industrial setting, where the doors never opened to them. Jan worked in dead-end office jobs. Then she set up a nursery school, informal self-help groups, before setting up a community centre. She was, therefore, a local political activist and organizer. By manipulating and beating the system to gain access to facilities and social benefits, Jan improved her social status, but saw herself as something of a 'class traitor', since the doors remained closed to many in her community. Her movement towards power was due to her working-class access to a job, the influence of a trade union and the political education of the Labour movement. Jan therefore had a collective route to political power. Jan Burrows's approach to politics was female, that is, woman-centred, and she remained community based. Margaret Thatcher, on the other hand, used her mighty power as prime minister against the trade unions and welfare rights, and imposed burdens on the community that hurt mostly the poor.

The factors of race, gender and class differences must be taken into account in the formulation of new theories and alternatives, and in rethinking socialism and alliances with popular fronts and movements. Is not the ultimate goal that of correcting social inequalities so that we can respect and celebrate difference and variety? In the current rethinking of socialism, which tends to lean on populism these days, are we not taking popular movements out of their historical context and interpreting them to mean progressive? We may be fighting for autonomy – that is, to create and control our communities – but, within the context of struggle at the community level, the contradictions of patriarchy and other social inequalities, including gender, race and class, also exist.

Struggle is continuous. The project of deconstruction, demystification, and decolonization must continue.

Notes

* Public lecture for Women's Studies, University of Toronto, Canada, 22 January 1990 and for the Centre for Women's Studies and Feminist Research, The University of Western Ontario, London, Canada, 26 January 1990.

1. Such studies include: I.M. Lewis, 1971; M. Strobel, 1976; M. Onwuejeogwu, 1969; R.E. Ritzenthaler, 1960; S. Ardener (ed.), 1975. For references on Igbo women, see C. Ifeka-Moller, 1975; Ifi Amadiume, 1987b.
2. See Shirley Ardener (ed.), 1975.
3. Janet Mokelu, 'Women's political mobilization', *Daily Star*, 11 June 1986.
4. Women in Nigeria, 1985, *WIN Document: Conditions of Women in Nigeria and Policy Recommendations to AD 2000*, Ahmadu Bello University, Zaria.
5. See *The Guardian* (Lagos), 30 July 1986.
6. *Socialist-Feminism. Out of the Blue,* Special Issue of *Feminist Review*, No. 23, Summer 1986; *The Past Before Us. Twenty Years of Feminism*, Special Issue of *Feminist Review*, No. 31, Spring 1989; Jill Evans et al., 1986.

Bibliography

Achebe, Chinua, 1988, *Anthills of the Savannah*, Heinemann African Writers Series, London.
Amadiume, Ifi, 1987a, *Afrikan Matriarchal Foundations: The Igbo Case*, Karnak House, London.
— 1987b, *Male Daughters, Female Husbands: Gender and Sex in an African Society*, Zed Books, London.
— 1989, 'Cheikh Anta Diop's theory of matriarchal values as the basis for African unity', Introduction to Cheikh Anta Diop, *The Cultural Unity of Black Africa: The Domains of Patriarchy and of Matriarchy in Classical Antiquity*, Karnak House, London.
Ardener, Shirley (ed.), 1975, *Perceiving Women*, J.M. Dent & Sons, London.
— 1975, 'Sexual insult and female militancy', *Perceiving Women*, J.M. Dent & Sons, London.
Bachofen, J., 1861, *Das Mutterrecht*, Benno Schwabe Co. Verlag.

Berger, Iris, 1975, 'Rebels or status-seekers? Women as spirit mediums in East Africa', in Shirley Ardener (ed.), *Perceiving Women*, J.M. Dent & Sons, London.

Coote, Anna and Pattullo, Polly, 1990, *Power & Prejudice: Women and Politics*, Weidenfeld & Nicolson, London.

Diop, Cheikh Anta, 1978, *Black Africa: The Economic and Cultural Basis for a Federated State*, Lawrence Hill & Co, Westport, Conn.

— new edition, 1989, *The Cultural Unity of Black Africa: The Domains of Patriarchy and of Matriarchy in Classical Antiquity*, Karnak House, London.

Evans, Judith, Hills, Jill, Hunt, Karen, Meehan, Elizabith, ten Tusscher, Tessa, Vogel, Ursula and Waylen, Georgina, 1986, *Feminism and Political Theory*, Sage Publications, London.

Ifeka-Moller, C., 1975, 'Female militancy and colonial revolt: the women's war of 1929, Eastern Nigeria', in Shirley Ardener (ed.), *Perceiving Women*, J.M. Dent & Sons, London.

Lewis, I.M., 1971, *Ecstatic Religion*, Penguin Books, Harmondsworth.

Morgan, L.H., 1871, *Systems of Consanguinity and Affinity of the Human Family*, Smithsonian Institute, Washington.

Nwabara, S.N., 1977, *Iboland: A Century of Contact with Britain, 1860–1960*, Hodder and Stoughton, London, p. 188.

Onwuejeogwu, M., 1969, 'The cult of the Bori spirits among the Hausa', in M. Douglas and P. Kaberry (eds), *Man in Africa*, Tavistock Publications, London.

Ritzenthaler, R.E., 1960, 'Anlu: a woman's uprising in the British Cameroons', *African Studies*, 19(3): 151–6.

Strobel, M., 1976, 'From Lelemama to lobbying: women's associations in Mombasa, Kenya', in N.J. Hafkin and Edna Bay (eds), *Women in Africa*, Stanford: Stanford University Press.

Wipper, Audrey, 1982, 'Riot and rebellion among African women: three examples of women's political clout', in F. Jean O'Barr (ed.), *Perspectives on Power*, Duke University Press, Durham, N.C., pp. 50–72.

8 Cycles of Western imperialism: feminism, race, gender, class and power*

Agonizing about where to pitch this chapter and the perspective to adopt, there were several options open to me. One was an academic theoretical approach which would examine some of the studies on African women, relating them to some of the debates in Western feminist scholarship. But I decided against this, seeing it as a continuation in the cycle of Western imperialism through a hegemonic Eurocentrism – the history of one culture beaming down on others through its own distorted lens, for its own self-interest. It is a privilege which has led to gross abuse, appropriation and exploitation, both in a material and in a cultural sense. It is a very masculine structure of power. The alternative to this option, it seems to me, is to turn the lens inwards and observe women in Western structures of power in the West itself.

Looking at women's experiences and concrete situations in the West appears to me a more productive perspective, as it is not often that African women have the privilege of participating in social relations with European women on their Western home territory and observing them. This is what in social science research methodology is termed participant-observation or direct observation. Again, a mark of the unequal relations between the Third World and the West is the fact that even this so-called subjective direct observation is unconstrained and uncensored when used in Third World countries, and censored when applied in the West by Third World people. Historians, sociologists and anthropologists can, for example, mention names, incidents, and so on, and publishers would not raise the issue of possible libel, or seek the permission of African villagers to publish.

Having decided to approach this subject politically and concretely, I am going to use two case studies to raise general issues in Women's

Studies theoretics, debate, and politics. But, I will not name names, even though I am describing true situations. When necessary, however, I shall use fictitious names for more vivid characterization.

Case 1

The problem: racism   During a visit to Canada earlier this year, to deliver a lecture to a women's studies programme, I was invited to dinner by a women's studies committee. Little did I know that tensions were so high in this women's group that, even in front of a stranger, it was impossible to hide the conflict. Therefore at dinner, one of the women, an older White woman asked me – quite openly and in everyone's hearing – if I were asked to set up a women's studies course to resolve these problems (she spread out her arms without saying what the problems were) how would I handle it? I was agape, torn between embarrassment, anger and indignation. Why did I experience these emotions?

As a guest, I felt that my privilege of distance and neutrality had been abused. I had been taken for granted; I had not been informed that there was a conflict or a quarrel. As a scholar, I felt that I had been disrespected, since it was very clear that I was there to give a public lecture – I had not come as an education councillor. On what grounds then had I been taken for granted, or had I been approached? It could not have been as a friend, since I had not met any of the women previously, nor had I ever had any dealings with them. Neither could it have been as a possible member of staff, since I was not being offered a job – even though the women knew that I was unemployed. Could it then have been an appeal to sisterhood? Again, there was no basis for that, since it was never explained to me that there was a problem, and thus sensitizing me before appealing to my emotions, solidarity or intellect.

Given these facts, then, I had to reach the conclusion that it was purely on the basis of racist assumptions that I had been so abused. What was my reply? I said that I would work from the very concrete situation in the room; that the distribution of women around the huge dining table symbolized the conflict; that I had not met any of the Black women before, yet I knew exactly what their feelings were; that the problem seemed to be in the meeting of the two halves of the table. I said no more than that since no one else spoke up to add to what I had said – to oppose it, or support it – not even the woman who had put me in this fix. The Black women expressed their gratitude and solidarity later on and in private, telling me that I spoke for all of us. There was, however, one dissenting White woman who, a day or two later, expressed her support and solidarity – but again in private.

My reading of the situation   What did I mean by a table having two halves? The White women sat at one end of the table; the other women, consisting of a native Canadian, an African Canadian, two Afro-Caribbean Canadians and an African, sat at the other end of the table. These two halves, apart from their colour divide, also symbolized an unequal distribution of knowledge in the sense of degrees and qualifications, and unequal distribution of money – jobs, salaries, grants and management of the finances of the women's studies programme. The White women were lecturers; the Black women were students, but also being used as lecturers. Both groups formed a so-called collective in which power obviously belonged to the White group.

The conflict was about these White women's uses and abuses of their privilege – that is, power. Power in this case was quite concrete, and not illusive or metaphysical. The Black women recognized this very concrete reality of power and wanted to share in it. That was the conflict. Who is to decide what money should be spent? And on what? Who is to get the money? The unequal power status between the White women and the Black women left the latter silenced and unable to overturn that huge round table, as much as they wanted to. Their hands were tied, as the saying goes. Inherent in the conflict for the Black women was the risk of losing what little they had gained in terms of position.

But then, because of the elite nature of the conflict, there were two areas of contradiction. One was centred on the very objectives of the women's studies programme itself. Is it for the empowerment of already powerful women of the elite classes? Or is it for the challenging of the system in order to empower disadvantaged grassroots women? What is in it for Black women? Is it to fight to share class power? In the case of the latter, recent evidence shows how this quest for power-sharing at the centre has resulted in internal contradictions and conflict for Black women, in spite of our articulacy in claiming difference on the basis of race as opposed to class and culture. I shall return again to these issues after considering the second case study.

Case 2

Background   I want to cite another conflict experience, this time in Britain, in order further to illustrate these contradictions. By 1980, the class and gender conflict in the politics of the British Left and the Women's Movement, and the debate which this generated, had led to massive influx of activist women into the Labour Party. There they harped on the under-representation of women in the Party and its hierarchy. Seeking a place in the centre, they called for change from inside the Party – that is, change through internal legislation, or what in the African Left is called revolution from the top. One of the results of this was the creation of Women's Committees in local government councils. This was to result not in the empowerment of poor working-class women, but the co-option of middle-class women into power. The same system of co-option through tokenism, or representation, as opposed to participation is also true of state intervention and the destabilization of women's organizations in Africa.

In Britain, these Women's Committees were expected to promote women's interests, ensure that women's demands were met, and provide a stepping-stone for would-be female politicians at local government levels – from which they could then proceed to the national level. It was expected that through positive discrimination, women would be pushed into top positions in the power hierarchy of the establishment.

The bureaucratic arm which was devized to service the Women's Committees was the Women's Units. These units employed women's officers and dispensed the budgets of the Women's Committees through grants. The Greater London Women's Committee, for example, had an annual budget of as much as £8 million.

One of the main rhetorics for empowerment in the feminism of the 1970s was the promotion of sisterhood. This also led to speculations and theories on how, practically, to construct this sisterhood; giving rise to the theory of women empowerment through direct management of resources, businesses and cooperatives. The realization of a Women's Committee with its own budget seemed a golden achievement of British feminists in their quest for power.

It was, however, not long before differences on the basis of race, class and sexuality exposed the contradictions in the earlier assumptions in the feminist and Women's Movements both in the USA and in Britain. The bitter experiences and total disillusionment of many working-class women of various communities, and the effects of the bureaucratic co-option of its leadership in the Black movement, are yet to get past the censorship of White publishers – including the so-called women's and feminist presses – to reach public attention.

What I am going to do here is to fictionalize a true situation – or more accurately use fictitious names to describe what seems to be a general problem in all the so-called collectives, programmes, projects, and units of Black and White women. This is also a problem in publishing, the academia, the voluntary sector, or government departments and agencies. It is specifically about the concrete management of resources, knowledge, information and, therefore, power.

The characters

Tandie: An African woman with a very strong pan-African consciousness. She is also a committed trade unionist.

Joan: A White woman with a socialist and activist trade union background.

Vero: A White woman with a trade union background. She shares a job with Tandie.

Angela: A very ambitious Black woman, who, although conscious of being Black and knowledgeable on Black politics, does not necessarily see herself as an African Caribbean. Culturally, she is at ease in British middle-class traditions of the liberal intellectual Left.

Nora: A Black British woman who does not in any way see herself as Black. Culturally, she is simply middle-class British.

Candida: A highly political and class-conscious Black woman. She is an outsider – the victim.

Two unnamed White women: Very upper-middle class, very professional and very indifferent.

The issue: money and power   All these women, except Candida, comprised a collective working in a women's unit. The unit dispensed funds and gave grants to women's groups and women's projects. Ten thousand pounds had been allocated to be spent in Joan's specific job area; she had managed to spend only two thousand pounds. Since it was two weeks to the end of the financial year, the remainder had to be spent in the next couple of weeks, or the unit would lose the money.

As soon as Tandie knew of this available money, her mind went to disabled Black women in the street, women in mental hospitals, those in hostels for battered wives, those isolated and lonely in old people's homes. She thought of young Black women pining in White prisons, not to mention political and welfare groups which were desperate for funds. Tandie felt that the money could be put to a very useful purpose in a single day never mind two weeks.

The unit decided to work out how to spend the money at their next unit meeting. Somehow, Tandie ran into a group of Black women who belonged to an organization which was desperately in need of funds. They only needed a few hundred pounds for the purchase of a few pieces of equipment, such as a tape recorder, stationery, and some publicity material. Tandie promised the women she would put their case to the next unit meeting.

At this unit meeting, Tandie found herself shocked by the suggestions being put forward on how to spend the eight thousand pounds These included the purchase of flowers, houseplants, baskets, newspaper racks, wall decorations, tea pots, cups and saucers! Some wanted answer-phones and tape recorders, and so on. However, the items did not exhaust the money, so, Tandie mentioned the Black project which needed £200. It was agreed that they could be assisted and that they should get in touch with the unit as soon as possible.

That is how it came about that Candida, who represented the project, went to the unit to present a list of their needs and explain the work of the project. Tandie from her experience of racism knew that Candida's group had to be very desperate to consider and accept coming to the unit for such a small amount of grant. Long and repeated experiences of humiliation have come to make us very sensi-tive about approaching White people for money, even when that money belongs to us as of right – as, for example, with local government grants, which is revenue realized from public taxes and rates. It always seems to turn out to be White people dispensing these grants.

Tandie was, therefore, very consciously aware of the great effort which Candida was making by coming to the unit for money. She gave her support and encouragement as soon as Candida stepped into the office, introducing her to Vero, Tandie's job-sharer. But Vero ignored the equal status that she and Tandie were supposed to have as job-sharers and took on the superior role of sole interviewer, assessor and decision maker.

At first, Tandie controlled herself and was patient – providing Candida got the money for her project. Some of the questions that Vero was asking were not necessary; but, Candida, like Tandie, was patient, swallowing her pride. Each time Candida tried to describe what activities their project had undertaken, Vero interrupted her to make a patronizing assessment, like a school teacher, telling Candida what their group could be doing, trying to show how much she knew about Black people and their organizations.

In order not to be gagged and dumb-founded, Candida had to talk more than she should, repeating herself a lot – her anger and des-peration simmering under the surface. Vero was insensitive to these obvious emotions and went on regardless – without realizing the point at which she had grouped Tandie together with Candida. Tandie was answering her questions in order to support Candida and ease some of her anxieties, trying like mad to cover up, until she seemed like the one being interviewed. Vero did not notice, let alone be embarrassed by this fact, so that she would check herself.

Then Candida began to disintegrate, losing her dignity by explaining and talking too much. Vero, enjoying her power, ran through the list of items which the project was requesting money for. She questioned the justification for every penny entered. When she came to the cost entered for the purchase of a tape recorder, she challenged it. Right in the presence of Candida and Tandie, Vero picked up the phone. She rang the other unit office and asked the secretary the cost of the tape recorder which had been recently purchased by the unit. At this, Tandie's blood boiled. She said to Vero, 'Enough!' and told her to drop the phone.

Candida's eyes were dilating with anger. Tandie apologized to her and told her that the job she shared with Vero did not involve grant assessment and approval – that was Angela's job. Tandie then picked up the phone and called Angela down. When Angela came down, Tandie spoke gently to her, not counting on her support as a Black woman, but on her cool efficiency at her job. Tandie put the following questions to her: first, was the amount being demanded too much? Secondly, what was the fastest way of giving the money to Candida's group? Angela replied that given the amounts of money that were being approved for White women and their groups, the amount these Black women were requesting was chicken feed. Angela said her piece and left without getting involved with the situation at hand.

All the time, Vero said nothing, but got redder and redder with rage. Candida mumbled a few things half-heartedly and left. Tandie knew that Candida had sustained a very deep injury. As soon as Candida left the room, Vero got up like a mad woman and ran to Joan's desk, even though she knew that Joan was away on holiday. She picked up pen and paper from Joan's desk. Tandie wondered why this irrational action, since Vero had pen and paper right on top of her own desk. In her blinding rage, Vero obviously neither saw nor looked. She then scribbled something on the paper, turned menacingly to Tandie and asked her the spelling of Candida! Tandie wondered at this English woman asking an African woman how to spell Candida. Tandie ignored her.

What is racism? That same day, Tandie wrote a letter calling an emergency meeting of all members of the unit, even though she knew that some were away on holiday. At the meeting, she openly and squarely accused Vero of racism, describing the experiences to which Vero had subjected the two Black women – that is, both Candida and herself. Members of the unit were embarrassed by this open accusation. They did not really know what to say, as they had swept racism under the carpet in the unit. It was agreed to meet again with everyone present. Tandie had made this accusation spontaneously, without waiting to hear from or to liaise with Candida.

A few days after the incident, a letter addressed to the unit arrived from Candida. Candida's assessment of what had taken place between herself, Vero and Tandie corresponded to what Tandie had said to the unit meeting. Candida's expectations had been high. She had been reluctant to go to the unit, but had consoled and encouraged herself to do so by the thought that she would be dealing with convinced and committed feminists. Otherwise, what justification could they have for working in a women's unit which claimed to fight for women's interests? Even if they did not take cognizance of her Blackness, they would at least relate to her as a woman.

In her letter, Candida said that she was shocked by what she encountered. In Vero, she came face to face with a White woman who insisted on exercising her power to the fullest. At no point did Vero give her the slightest illusion that she was dealing with a sister. Vero had ripped her pride to shreds, treated her like a thief who was out to steal public money for herself. The incident of the tape recorder had left her shocked and speechless. She could no longer depend on the support which Tandie had tried to give her. When she left the unit, she was in such pain that she had to go and take a sauna bath. All that she could do there was think about the insult and humiliation which she had received from the unit – all for a couple of hundred pounds!

At the next unit meeting, with all members present, Tandie repeated her accusation of racism. Candida's letter was read out. Then Tandie began to recount step by step what had taken place. She made sure that at each point, she explained exactly how she had felt. She said that any Black woman put in her position, or in the situation that Candida had found herself, would feel the same way.

Vero was neither a fool, nor naive in the ways of politics. With the case presented so vividly, she could not wriggle out of what she had done. She just sat there, tears streaming down her face. But to everyone's surprise, it was not any of the White women who interrupted Tandie, but Nora, a Black British woman who said that she failed to see how Vero had acted in a racist manner! That if it had been a Black woman who was in Vero's position, would this Black woman have acted differently, and would she have been accused of racism! Had Joan, a White woman, not interrupted to answer Nora's question, if it were possible to do so, Tandie would have killed Nora with words.

During Tandie's account of what had taken place, Joan was biting her nails like mad, pressing them against her teeth, and fidgeting in her seat. She was generally uncomfortable and embarrassed, so much so that she could not hide it. To Tandie's surprise, Joan took on Nora and gently tried to explain to her how Vero had acted in a racist manner towards Tandie and Candida. She said that Vero's action apart, the system which put Vero and White people in general in an assymetrical power position in relation to Black people generated racism. Given the context of British racism, Candida, a Black woman, having to come to Vero, a White woman, for money, immediately put Candida in an inferior and disadvantaged position. She said that in that kind of situation, the White woman who was in the position of power could either exercise that power to the fullest, or act with utmost care, modesty and respect towards the Black woman.

Nora still said that she failed to see how Vero had been racist. Vero herself acknowledged her own racism and carrried out her own analysis, admitting how she could have acted in a racist manner. Nora still said that she did not see the racism. Joan therefore said that perhaps Tandie could explain more to Nora. Tandie replied that she could not educate, demystify or politicize Nora in an hour's meeting; that Nora should go to White women to teach her about racism; that surely Nora knew full well what racism is, but could not afford to recognize it due to her professional ambition.

Tandie was feeling really very sick by then. She had had to watch Vero cry and admit her guilt, but she still had to muster enough strength and courage to drive home the full implication of Vero's action, without being put off by the possibility of everyone thinking that she was unfeeling and hard on Vero. Tandie also felt particularly sad that Angela had decided to remain mute, giving her no support whatsoever – even though she knew that Angela, more than anyone else in the unit, had a complete analysis of the racist situation. Like Nora, Angela also had very high ambitions in the establishment.

Anyway, it was decided that a meeting should be arranged with Candida, in order to have a discussion with her; that the unit should look into the grant needs of Candida's project and help her get the grant. Tandie was given the responsibility of contacting Candida and arranging the meeting; she did not find it easy persuading Candida to attend.

When the group met, it was a different and determined Candida who spoke so confidently at this meeting. She took on the members of the unit one by one and told them off! She told them how unsisterly they were, given the fact that they worked for women. She told them how they were a pack of power-loving women. Didn't they see how the masculine and racist structures of government used them to oppress fellow women? She said that Tandie was, however, less guilty of these things than the others; but what was she doing working in such a place anyway? She said that they'd held a meeting at her project and decided that they would not accept the money.

Soon afterwards, Angela decided to call a meeting of the Black women in the unit. She gave the impression that she called the meeting to iron out the differences between Nora and Tandie, and also to organize a united Black front to face the White women in the unit. Tandie told Angela that the criteria on which she was calling and defining the meeting did not exist, as there was no basis for calling the three of them Black. Tandie said that she had operated on that assumption in the past and had not only been proven wrong, but had also received a terrible stab in the back from both Angela and Nora.

Tandie recalled the incident of a previous all-Black women meeting, where they had worked out a strategy for future action, and how Nora had dissociated herself from the decisions taken at that meeting. Silently, however, Tandie knew why Angela had called for a united Black front. When she first joined the unit, Joan and Angela shared a desk. They sat opposite each other, and shared a telephone extension. It did not take her long to notice that each time the phone rang, Angela and Joan went quickly for it. There was this terrible fight and competition to be the first to pick up the phone.

It seemed to Tandie that a lot was symbolized in the two women's fight for the phone. Sometimes, both hands actually met on the receiver; one woman's hand on top of the hand of the other woman who grabbed the phone. One hand was Black, the other White. It was as if control of that phone meant control of the unit, and the establishment of a central authority. Most of the phone calls were for Joan. It was then that Tandie realized that Joan and Angela were involved in some form of power struggle. She was therefore seeking Black support only for her selfish ambitions.

A comparative analysis of multiple identities and power

What are the similarities and differences between these two case studies? In both case studies, we see how class, race and gender are interrelated. In case 1, for example, class interest takes on a racially self-defined boundary in the form of White exclusiveness. This is also true of case 2, in spite of the possible presence of an odd dissenter. Again in both cases, the self-image in the wielding of class power is masculine, in the sense of exploitation and abuse of power in relation to the Black women.

The main difference between case 1 and case 2 is in the degree of co-optation of the Black women involved. In case 1, because the Black women 'have not arrived' (as we say in Black circles) – they are still to some extent on the periphery of power – they can present a united front in their critique of racism. This is not so in case 2, where, in spite of the racism of the White women, the Black women got their jobs on equal par with the White women. They were all employed at the same level and on the same salary, even though the White women formed a select inner core which actually ran the unit. Somehow, they behaved as if they owned the place, and treated the Black women like intruders or as guests. White women were employed first, and they had set up a routine before the decision to employ Black women was taken.

Since the Black women – on the surface – had equal status with the White women, it was therefore up to the individual or personal politics of the Black women whether to continue to struggle against racism on principle, or to see it as a hinderance to their ambitions. As we saw, they were very divided as a group, with individuals being very opportunistic in their maximization of their chances. Indeed, while Tandie resigned from her job, on the grounds that Joan was treating the unit as if it was her father's house, Angela went on to reach the very top in the executive of a government department, at a very young age, and on no Black community platform.

Paraded as a successful Black woman, Angela became a real token in a male establishment. She became a male-daughter in gender terms. She will be in a man's house, respond to masculine jokes, tolerate or even join in male hio hio laughter – as we can all see these days during the television screening of parliamentary performance – obey and execute male-decided policies. She will, in effect, be operating a male-generated and gendered power system.

The contradiction in the presence of women in power positions in this masculine system is the fact that this system is historically a violent and exploitative one, since it constructs a lesser 'other' which it seeks to control, and from which it appropriates. Historically too, the ruling class under capitalism has always been male gendered. I do not think that it would be unkind to argue that Western feminists, by defining their struggle as demanding a place in the centre – that is equal rights – have demanded to be males or to share masculine power. Yet that power entails massive abuse of human rights, given the facts of the global imperialism of the West.

African women and Western daughters of imperialism

As long as the power structures of capitalism remain intact, opposing individuals within that system are only dissenters. But even these dissenters seem to reproduce the same structures of inequality in their relations with Third World women. Their privileges seem to accompany them wherever they go. African women have not really felt the solidarity of the dissenters, but only the extension of their privileged position and continued imperialism, if not racism, as the history of this relationship indicates.

Concern with African women in feminist scholarship came via the debate on capitalism and the status of women in the West. Hence, the rush at that time to African data to look at the so-callled pre-capitalist societies and the status of women in them. Again, when the debate extended to strategies of protest and militancy, the forging of sisterhood, and means of women's empowerment, African women were the objects of debate and speculations. Our social systems provided the raw data for analysis. While Western imperialism, through imposed European education, was steadily undermining the self-worth of Africans, cutting them off from their historical memories, the histories of African women were co-opted by White feminists and academics of both the Left and Right. They were writing as if these African legacies belonged to them, when the data were positive. They were using generalized terms to co-opt achievements that were both culturally and historically specific, as for example, 'women did this ... ', and 'women did that'. While in actual fact, all women did not do it, but specific groups of women did specific things within specific cultures and histories.

Today, in the neo-missionary imperialism that parades itself in the name of development studies, African women are again objects of pity and charity. How the militant women and warrior queens have fallen. How the tables have turned, as Western women, who used to see themselves as oppressed, are now empowered to dispense funds to African women. They embrace token African scholars under their umbrella as research assistants. They form exclusive small cliques within which they circulate their papers, co-edit books – recycling the same ideas. Western women, supported by strong currency based on cheap petrol, are now telling African women what they must do economically, socially and politically.

The production–reproduction debate

With these preliminaries, I believe that I can now enter a current theoretical debate as an African woman, using findings from my own work which throw a totally different perspective on gender. This is the re-opened debate on class and gender as analytical concepts, and the long-standing production–reproduction debate, that is, the structural place of the household.

In recent concrete assessments of their experiences in the workplace and in the unions during the past thirty years, Western feminists have pointed out the sexual division of the workforce, and sexism in the workplace and in the unions. They all seem to have reached the conclusion that the 'sisterhood' formulation of the 1970s has been at the expense of the subjective woman. This sisterhood stressed an alliance with men, and consequently subsumed gender under class solidarity. It threw out patriarchy as an analytical concept in favour of Marxist materialism. Both the 1960s and the 1970s periods definitely concentrated on the possibilities of unity, contrary to recent criticisms. The current rethink is precisely as a result of a critique of that earlier strategy and an assessment of gains and losses. The point was that unity was assumed and not a reality, given the fundamental divides of class, race, gender and sexuality.

There is, however, a fundamental difference between the African condition and the industrialized West. Apart from the industrialized economies of South Africa and Zimbabwe, with their high migrant or urban workforce, most Africans are in rural subsistence economies which are based on agriculture, marketing, trade and commerce. Women are the backbone of this economy, which itself subsidizes African capitalism – and, by extension, Western capitalism proper.

In this rural economy, the economic sphere is also a social and cultural sphere, where people interact in multiplex relations, and in which African women participate in their varied identities. There is not therefore the housewife/home/unproductive/apolitical separation from public/production/politics, ideologized and gendered in the absolute patriarchal fabrications of European capitalism. This ideological fallacy has thrown Western feminists into a long-standing debate in the production–domestic scenario.

Western women have cited labour figures giving strong support to their importance in production, as for example, the growing economic activity rate of women, with women making up to fifty per cent of the workforce as we enter the next century. In the industrialized West, there will be a need for older women too in managerial and executive posts. Western women are, therefore, mostly in a world of paid work – that is, in contractual relationships determined by money.

In contrast to the situations of women in the West, in Africa it is through recent historical processes of Western colonialism and imperialism that European state systems were imposed on Africa. European structures are therefore juxtaposed with traditional African social systems and ideologies. The result of this is that these contradictions are our contemporary context of struggles and protests.

Given our history of the prominence of women in African social structures, such as women's institutions and organizations around the marketplace, it is not surprising that African women's struggles have historically centred on two issues. They are: autonomy, that is, women's self-government which has brought about the conflict between women's organizations and male control and co-optation of these organizations; and women's struggle to retain control over the marketplace, the spinal chord of the subsistence economy.

African women have, therefore, been concerned with the fundamental social issues of self-organization and the economy. The evidence points to a simple explanation for this perpetual concern. It is the fact that there was an alternative system: a matriarchal system which was in opposition to the patriarchal system, even though both systems were also in cooperation and shared social space. This matriarchy was both a social, economic and ideological system. It is not the direct opposite of patriarchy, or an equivalent to patriarchy, as it is not based on appropriation and violence.

The culture and rituals of matriarchy did not celebrate violence; rather, they had a lot to do with fecundity, exchange and redistribution. Matriarchy was not centralist either, but horizontally proliferationist and collective. Its fundamental base is the household as distinct from the family. These polities and societies were not static of course, since they disintegrated and reformed as people moved and formed new settlements, and as social forces disrupted existing forms. More radical and dramatic changes obviously occurred with the massive militarization, and the tilt towards more gradual masculinization of the African continent. The more radical transformations occurred as a result of the various processes of state formations, their material exploitative bases of power, which culminated in the one thousand years of commercial slave trade in which African labour and African economic resources built the economies of the Western and Arab worlds.

These are some of the fundamental differences between the very material and ideological worlds of African women and Western women. While the fundamental basis of the power of African women is the household organization, the power base of the oppression of Western women is the patriarchal family – in which there is no distinction between household and family. The exception to this is perhaps the recent development of female-headed households, such as one-parent families. But these households are, however, firmly grounded in the capitalist state structures and constitute the lowest poor class – for obvious reasons, such as lack of childcare and living on state benefits.

For the West, therefore, in spite of the women's and feminist movements, Engel's theory – expressed over a hundred years ago – of the privatized family as the seat of patriarchy and European women's oppression, has not altered. This is in spite of legislative reforms from the top and the so-called widening of personal choices. The basic patriarchal cultural values of European civilization have not altered, because European women have not produced an alternative or opposition culture as a social institution, with formal or structural recognition, as was the case with traditional African women's organizations.

I believe that this is precisely the point that their pioneer feminists such as Germaine Greer and Betty Friedan are making when they are talking about 'fulfilment of motherhood' and 'traditional women's values'. This is also what the new Western spiritualist feminists are seeking and constructing. However, since they have no history of matriarchy, they are again stealing a legacy from Africa, from the native Indians and from the Eastern cultures. Look at all their references and see whose communities they are visiting and whose histories they are citing.

The dilemma and anger for us African women is the contradiction implied in the actions of these Western women, whose cultural and historical legacies we know. Yet they leave their problems at home, and cross vast seas to go and dictate strategies of struggle and paths of development to Africans, as highly paid consultants and well-funded researchers. At the same time, their own imposed systems are eroding all the positive aspects of our historical gains, leaving us impoverished, naked to abuse, and objects of pity to Western aid rescue missions.

Yet in spite of our voiced anger, our criticisms do not seem to make any inroads at all. This expertise imperialism continues in new computer processing and reproduction of the same ideas, with one or two African women included or cited for credibility. This expertise consultancy also continues as these European women now administer and manage research funds about African women, or funds for projects by African women, or conferences on African women.

We are therefore back to that fundamental structure of inequality in the relations between women, and different groups of women, with which I started this chapter. In all of these situations, we see women grabbing opportunities in a man's world, managing and using power just like men. The difference of course is that we have women exploiting, oppressing and humiliating women in a masculine class gendered fashion. I have called these daughters of imperialism male-daughters in a capitalist exploitative system. The Western 'sisterhood' of the 1960s and 1970s was a false and baseless fabrication, with neither a material nor historical basis.

African women do not understand sisterhood individualistically, as do European women. Female solidarity in the African context is fundamentally associated with the culture of matriarchy and the ideology of motherhood, whereas motherhood has negative connotations in Western feminist concepts. In the current debate on the analytical status of gender and motherhood in Western scholarship, ethnocentrism and Eurocentrism are again the order of the day, as Western women transpose their values, prejudices and fears on to the realities and social values of Third World women.

For us African women, matriarchy – that is, African women's construct of motherhood – was a means of institutional and ideological empowerment. While for European women, the patriarchal construct of motherhood was an instrument of women's oppression, commoditization and self-alienation. Instead of dictating to African women on so-called conservation and development, Western women would do well to concentrate their efforts on deconstructing the history and dialectic of racism and imperialism, the very historical link and divide between themselves and us.

We cannot subsume everything under class, as class has masculine, racist and imperialist ideologies that are used for material exploitation and cultural imperialism. You have to construct the 'other' as lesser than self or non-self in order to abuse and exploit. Recent women's studies, I believe, will focus more and more, not so much on the question of empowerment, but on gender analysis of women wielding power in masculine systems, as working-class women gain confidence, enter and lead the debate. I for one, as an African woman, would like Women's Studies to theorize for me on how the Western system threw up Mrs Margaret Thatcher, who has been described as 'The best man in the job'.

Note

* Keynote lecture at the GLCA Women's Studies Conference on the theme, Feminism, Ethnocentrism, and the Production of Knowledge: Multicultural Perspectives on Women's Power, held at the Bergamo Centre, Dayton, Ohio, 2–4 November 1990. First published in *Women's Studies*, 1992, Vol. 4(1), published by the Department of Philosophy, University of Transkei in conjunction with the Transkei Association of University Women.

9 In the company of women: love, struggle, class and our feminisms*

I would like to recall a situation which took place four years ago in the United States. An event which in addition to two other experiences in the company of women, gave rise to the title of this chapter: 'In the company of women'. However, the juxtaposition of love, struggle, class and our feminisms would suggest conflictual situations and contrasting experiences in these various companies of women.

In November 1990, I flew into the United States from London and gave a keynote lecture in Dayton, Ohio, entitled, 'Cycles of Euro-Western imperialism: feminism, race, gender, class and power' at the GLCA Women's Studies conference on the theme, Feminism, ethno-centrism, and the production of knowledge: multicultural perspectives on women's power (see Chapter 8 in this volume). It was on that occasion that I met Sandra O'Neal, the host of this conference. The memory of that experience in that company of women remains as fresh and vivid as if it were only yesterday. Two words will suffice to describe that occasion – love and struggle! Struggle in the sense that all the women of colour at that conference unanimously voiced our tiredness at repeating the same things over and over again to White women. In that collective voice, White women were told to also refer to themselves as White women when talking about themselves, just as they find it easy to say Black women. Chandra Mohanti drove the message home by asking, 'Why can't White women say White women?' If I recall correctly, we – that is, the coloured women – named our-selves 'the tired women of colour'.

The second word – love – is in the sense of the support, solidarity and power that enabled us to form a solid voice of opposition in that company of women. I heard it said that for once they had strong Black women at their conference. Sandra O'Neal's account of her own experiences in another company of women, reported in order to sup-port mine, was for me the embodiment of the word 'love' demonstrated in total alliance and solidarity. And this is the origin of the present chapter, in these difficult and dangerous times when the voices of combative broad mass opposition and dissent appear to have died, and class seems a backward perspective in the face of opportunistic cele-bratory personal and body identity rhetoric.

In my lecture in Dayton, Ohio, I had pointed out the need for African Women to avoid the reproduction of cycles of Western im-perialism and hegemonic Eurocentrism, and to stop looking at ourselves through its distorted lens; pointing out the gross abuses, appropriations and exploitations – both material and cultural – as a result of this overwhelming power imbalance. Not only did I relate these experiences to oppressive masculinist male structures of power, I suggested an alternative approach, that of turning the lens inwards and observing women in Western structures of power in the West itself. This is where my third equation of 'class' and our feminisms comes in.

Appropriation

In May 1992, I again had the privilege of being in the company of women in the United States. I presented a paper entitled: 'Kinship ideology and socio-cultural systems in Africa and Europe: theorizing matriarchy in Africa' at the interdisciplinary conference on Matri-lineality and Patrilineality in Comparative and Historical Perspective, at the University of Minnesota (see Chapter 3).

The first session had been presented as the definitive or theoretical opening of the conference, and right from the start I found myself looking again at my programme for the topic of the conference, and the stated perspective, which was to be comparative and historical. I could not, therefore, fail to note the lack of balanced representative material for this comparison. This imbalance proved to be the case in all the sessions and throughout the entire conference. European materials were presented – from ancient history to the contemporary period – by world famous White women scholars.

Not only did European materials dominate the conference, Western Europeans were also the ones presenting their own researched materials about other cultures. It seemed to me that the European experience was insisting on its dominance, regardless of the voices of 'local scholar-ship'. I had thought the reflexive discourse and the production of knowledge was advanced, particularly in the USA, so I was dumb-founded at the lack of concern with these issues at that conference.

What is the possible explanation for the Eurocentrism of the con-ference? Could it be that the Europeans assumed their scholarship to be more 'advanced' than 'local scholarship'? Or was this an example of the euphoria of 'the victory of Western capitalism'; its claim of 'the end of history' and the assumption that there is no opposition or Left to be answerable to?

To expound on the problems of the dominance of European experience over local scholarship, I would like to draw my illustration from the more senior scholars at that Minnesota conference, hoping that their maturity will welcome and tolerate dialogue. Let us take for example the Chinese case, which was presented to us entirely by European women. Margery Wolf is a famous scholar on the Chinese. Her paper at that conference was entitled 'Beyond the patrilineal self: constructing gender in China'. Referring to gender in the first paragraph of her presentation she said:

> I admit that when I first began writing about Chinese society, I did not realize that these different perspectives had theoretical significance, but then few of us did. As a novice ethnographer, I was surprised when this gendered perception of the world became apparent, but I was far more interested in women's explanations of how they coped with a social system stacked against them.

I could not fail to wonder how a Chinese female scholar would feel in such a learned audience, where histories – that is, the achievements and failures of different societies and cultures – were meant to be compared. In this situation, a Chinese woman's access to her own history was subject to the level of perception of a White woman scholar. But, more fundamentally, I wondered why something so obvious even to an African child was not apparent to Margery Wolf. For example, African children experience the world differently through the type of stories told by women and from the type of daily chores and social activities done with women. They are quite different from stories told in the company of men.

Margery Wolf's textual revisitations of her varied interpretations of her field experiences in a Taiwanese village thirty years ago have been published in her book, *A thrice told tale: feminism, postmodernism and ethnographic responsibility* (Stanford, Calif.: Stanford University Press, 1992). Here she refers briefly to her own changes over this period: from the wife and assistant of an anthropologist, to coming into her own rights as an acknowledged anthropologist, informed by contemporary politics and feminism. While she goes into detail about her interpretations of the lives and activities of these Chinese villagers, she keeps the content of her own life – as entered in her personal journal – to herself.

Following Margery Wolf's presentation at the Minnesota conference,

I noted down three issues of concern to feminist scholarship. One was the problems resulting from ignorance and ethnocentrism. The second was to do with the choice of historical time-depth and, consequently, the order of knowledges – that is, the epistemological question. A Chinese woman scholar, for example, may want to know the character of gender before the Confucian construct as an archival source or a history indispensable to Chinese women for the project of political liberation and struggle.

The third issue was the total lack of enquiry into a women's organized political system, even though Margery Wolf's data indicated that there was a structural gendered opposition in the Taiwan kinship system in the mother-linked uterine family versus the men's family, each generating different loyalties and obligations, with the mother constructing ties of love and gratitude. How could one relate this unnamed, invisible but apparent system to a much deeper history of the link between mythology, the ideology of gender and socio-political formations (family and state formations), as presented to us by another White woman on the same China? This became particularly important as we learned of the existence of other texts which attested to claims that 'precivilized' peoples of antiquity only recognized their mothers and not their fathers. This was said to be considered a period of no rulers, no hierarchy and no gender distinctions. Political order therefore came with patrilineality, and this was the beginning of 'civilization' as patricentric lies would have us believe.

So again and again we meet this Eurocentric problem of the concept of hierarchy linked to social order and culture, and an assumption that the female gender is not self-structured. Yet we keep coming across the strong and positive structural significance of the female gendered principle in all the non-European cultures. However, it was not these cultures that provided a comparative framework for the Minnesota conference, but the invisible and negative female gender of the European construct. This obviously led to negativism. There was therefore no real comparison since the Europeans were in control of other materials from Asia, China, Native America, Latin America, the Caribbean, Africa, etc.

In the case of European societies themselves, including European Brazil, and so on, in spite of the various efforts to show instances or cases of women having access to material resources and custody of children, this did not somehow seem to have resulted in the wielding of structural power. The perspective of the conference theme – matrilineality and patrilineality as rules of inheritance and succession – did not succeed in providing evidence of European women having structural power. In cases where they seemed to have had a large material base for power, they did so as individuals in a male gendered system and not in an organized female collective as the historical evidence shows was the case with African women's organizations. In the European examples, therefore, individual wealthy women acted like men or became part of a male gendered upper class, elite class or ruling class, serving both class and White race interests, as in the case presented by Muriel Nazzari for Brazil.

It is significant that in spite of the appropriation and manipulation of the non-European concept of matrilineality by European women in order to indicate property ownership, custody of children or remembrance of more balanced kin networks, when these individual case histories are contextualized in the existing social structure – particularly in the link between social categories, the economy, ideology, symbolism, ritual and power in European social formations – the female gender is seen to be subordinate or invisible in very dominant patriarchal systems.

Consequently, at the session on the ideological or symbolic level, the matrilineality claimed for Europe could not produce evidence of structural representation. At the level of self-imaging or self-construct, European women had nothing to say about self. They reverted back to bemoaning patriarchal constructs of the female gender. It is interesting that it was White men in the audience who kept calling attention to the technical usage of lineality for describing descent-based societies of Africa, for example, and not European-type family systems. However, in spite of my criticism of the choice of the analytical concept of lineality, a top White woman scholar arrogantly reaffirmed the choice of lineality. I was firmly shut up!

Given the present political climate of almost total subjugation under the raw violence of European imperialism, it is now so difficult to sit through conferences in which one listens to White women talking nonsense about us when we know the reality to be different. As in the case of the experiences of voicelessness in another company of women, this time in Canada (see Chapter 8), when Black women chose to talk about their experiences of racism in private, away from the hearing of White women, in the Minnesota conference, other Black women said as much to me, and complained bitterly about White women and men 'talking for Black women'. Everywhere I go, I hear women of colour scholars saying that they are tired. By the third day of the Minnesota conference, this experience of solid attack had become overwhelming!

Multiple identities, politics and solidarity: coalition or alliance

In my Dayton, Ohio, lecture, I referred to contradictions in the objectives of Women's Studies programmes, particularly in the United States, raising the question: Empowerment for whom? Are the objectives of these programmes designed to empower already powerful women of the elite classes to challenge the system in order to empower disadvantaged grassroots women? And in the case of Black women, are they aimed at producing the sharing of class power? I also highlighted how the quest for power sharing at the centre has resulted in internal contradictions and conflict for Black women, in spite of our eloquence in claiming difference – as and when expedient in contrasting locations and spaces – on the basis of race, culture, ethnicity or sexuality as opposed to class and class-culture.

In the Dayton lecture, I had analysed the issue of political or career opportunism in the context of this multiple-identities politics. As far back as 1990, therefore, the lens was focused not just on White women, but also on our own internal contradictions. It is from this perspective that I wish to discuss briefly my recent experiences in February 1994 at the Massachusetts Institute of Technology in Boston, again in the company of women at The Black Women in the Academy: Defending our Name conference.

I saw Boston as the correct place for my first intellectual outing – this time during a more permanent stay in the United States. I felt that Boston would provide a good introduction into the heart of African-American women's scholarship, since the conference was advertised as the first such high powered gathering of the top African-American women scholars on such a large scale. Two thousand and ten women scholars attended, and emotions were raw, tender and running high. I confess to having wept; tears streamed down my face as I was overcome in the animated presence of two thousand and ten beautiful Black women of all ages and all colours too. The Massachusetts Institute of Technology College president described our realities as that of competence and expertise, but isolation and lack of recognition; we therefore had a 'need to talk'. And talk we all did – with a lot of crying too, particularly among the younger women when at the microphone addressing the famous 'Sister Comrades'. Crying is probably too weak a word to describe the mournful sobbing, revealing very deep wounds inside our young women and heartbreaking emotions symptomatic of the problems of isolation and the cancerous wounds of racism.

My reading of the class dynamic of the Boston conference was that the subject matter of the conference were not really the needy, 'orphaned' young Black women of the academy, weeping each time their voices were heard through a microphone, but the ones already at the top. The real subjects of concern were the examples given to us like Toni Morrison and an earned recognition, but negative public portrayal. Again negative portrayals in public following the humiliation of two Black women, namely, Anita Hill and Lani Guinier. Consequently, when the college president summarized the thrust of the conference as voice, identity, entitlement and recommitment, you kind of knew whose conference this was.

Now there was nothing wrong with being in the company of top Black women, since by any reasoning this ought to be empowering. Moreover, you generally expect you are going to go home with a clear agenda or a sense of an agenda of leadership and direction for the future. My focus was therefore on the Black feminist theory and agenda-proposing panels, and these were indeed where the top names were. What came out as a commitment to leadership? And what was proposed as an agenda for future direction?

The theorists seemed to have no answers when it came to the subject that, in my opinion, really matters – the African-American community and its chronic experiences of police and media harassment. The theorists wondered what terms and categories can be used to deal with the community in order to get away from dominant categories and their usage or appropriation at the margin. It soon became clear that this was an intellectual elite still caught up in its own self-assigned right to rule. Consequently, there was no opening for the consideration of emergent organic theories from the ground – from the community itself. If anything, individual women who have had historical involvement at the community level through activism in the Black Panther Movement, for example, now said that they did not remember a single thing that had worked or even what the aims of that movement were. That did incredible violence to my historical memory of the inspirations which the Black Panther Movement provided for the youth during that period, both in Africa and in the wider world. The negative side of an important historical experience had been used to cancel out the positive legacy necessary for the planning of the future.

I made sure that I kept alive my own positive recollections as I listened to current anti-establishment youth Rapp movements dismissed as a 'simplified essentialized' notion of Black nationalism as opposed to what these intellectual women described as the reality on the ground, which according to them was characterized by multiplicity and hybridity. Consequently when the top names began to propose coalition activities for the future direction, one could not help but wonder who would be in coalition with whom, and, more importantly, how did this word coalition begin to circulate among certain people? How did the notion of coalition come to displace the notion of alliance and unity? What are the differences between these forms of union in class context and in the context of unequal struggles?

Even as the commitment to a single national consciousness was dismissed as essentializing, so was the representation of self-privilege argued in terms of multiple consciousness and self-promotion through networking, friendship and bonding. These are obvious strategies of scratching each other's backs and professional climbing. We used to position now we have arrived! They, however, described it as reinforcing each other when others do not. They also called it collaboration.

It was of course Angela Davis who put her finger squarely on the class dynamic when she talked about middle-class neo-liberal hegemony in the Black community. In fact, it was she who said, 'These are Dangerous Times!' But then, she wondered how do we talk about feminism that rests on non-biologistic notions of race, as she found race restricting and imprisoning; so also did she find the politics of unity constraining. Angela Davis consequently demanded that Black women should step out and support Asian and Latino women. However, she also emphasized the linking of academic work and work in the community. Davis brought up that term 'coalition politics' again, describing it as a less rigid new political consciousness: 'It imposes on us the responsibility to be fluent in each other's knowledges'.

Here then is the problem of the neo-liberal elite eloquently articulated as anti-commitment and indeed anti-community in its unbounded self-identity politics, in zoning and re-zoning on the basis of self-interest. I must say that this is where I parted company with Angela Davis, even though I gave her my African drum to wear around her neck and wrote her a praise poem. Where Angela Davis found the platform of African-American women on which we met in Boston constraining, seeking a broader arena of Women of Colour, I want to say that I felt no such restriction. As an African woman in the United States in the company of African-American women in Boston via Nigeria and Britain, it never entered my head that I was not also African-American. All other identities dissolved into the electrifying and powerful one with which I was in communion at the time, and its needs became my needs. I was in total empathy as its pain also became mine; its achievements mine; its goals mine. I could only gain by listening and learning and enjoying all that was new to me. That to me did not mean that I would be incapable of solidarity with women of colour on another platform.

And in fact I have already referred to the experience in Dayton, Ohio, and our Tired Women of Colour bonding (see also Chapter 8), the memory of which compelled me to answer the call to attend the Sisters of Colour International conference.

In conclusion, I want to reaffirm my total commitment to feminism in the sense that I defined it nearly ten years ago in my book *Male Daughters, Female Husbands*. There I wrote:

> I must point out that I have retained the term feminist in spite of the controversy regarding to whom it refers and what is meant by it. The meaning of the word as I have used it is a political consciousness by women, which leads to a strong sense of self-awareness, self-esteem, female solidarity and, consequently, the questioning and challenging of gender inequalities in social systems and institutions. (1987: 10)

Note

* Keynote presentation at the Fourth Annual Conference of Sisters of Color International, 6–8 May 1994, University of Wisconsin, La Crosse.

Index

208